Primitive Revolution

Primitive Revolution

Restorationist Religion and the Idea of the Mexican Revolution, 1940–1968

❧

JASON DORMADY

University of New Mexico Press ❖ Albuquerque

LIBRARY OF CONGRESS CATALOGING-IN-PUBLICATION DATA

Dormady, Jason, 1975–
Primitive revolution : restorationist religion and the idea of the Mexican
Revolution, 1940–1968 / Jason Dormady.
p. cm.
Includes bibliographical references (p.) and index.
ISBN 978-0-8263-4951-4 (pbk. : alk. paper)
1. Church and state—Mexico—History—20th century. 2. Mexico—Church
history—20th century. 3. Luz del Mundo (Organization)—History—20th century.
4. Iglesia del Reino de Dios en Su Plenitud—History—20th century.
5. Unión Nacional Sinarquista (Mexico)—History—20th century.
6. Primitivism—Religious aspects—Christianity—History—20th century.
7. Primitivism—Mexico—History—20th century. I. Title.
BR610.D67 2011
261.7'2097209045—dc22
                                        2010034509

DESIGN: MELISSA TANDYSH

COMPOSITION: KAREN MAZUR

Composed in 10/13.5 Janson Text Lt Std

Display type is Bernhard Modern Std

For Carol

Contents

ACKNOWLEDGMENTS

I GRATEFULLY ACKNOWLEDGE THE RESEARCH FUNDING PROVIDED by the Department of History at the University of California at Santa Barbara (UCSB), as well as from the History Associates, who provided both encouragement and financial support while I was in Santa Barbara, where this project began. In addition, the guidance and suggestions made by Sarah L. Cline, for shaping the direction of the research, and the mechanical vigor of Francis Dutra—both of UCSB—were invaluable in moving this project forward from footnotes of cultural curiosity into a doctoral dissertation. Encouragement from Zaragosa Vargas helped me decide to transform the dissertation into a book.

I owe many thanks to those who made my visits to Mexico productive and informative, particularly: José Manuel Ramos López and Luis Gerardo Mercado Uribe of the Archivo Municipal de Guadalajara for their encyclopedic knowledge of not only the archives but also the neighborhoods of Guadalajara; Sergio Pagaza Castillo and Fernando Gómez of the Museo de Historia del Mormonismo en Mexico in Mexico City; Jakelíne Franco Olivares of the Archivo Municipal de Ozumba for her work to preserve and organize the municipal records; Martin Nesvig for his help in the Archivo General de la Nación (AGN); Erendira Gallo for her hospitality in San Pedro el Chico; Robert Curley of the Universidad de Guadalajara for suggestions and help in gaining access to records, as well as the librarians of the Universidad de Guadalajara for their patience; the helpful and friendly staff of the Biblioteca Francisco Xavier Clavigero; and the wonderful people of Barrio Providencia and the American Society of Jalisco that made the process of doing research with a family as comfortable as possible. Finally, this project would not be possible without the patient support of Carol, Isaac, Oliver, and Helen, who have expected much and endured more.

Introduction

❧

✦ THIS BOOK IS ABOUT REVOLUTION, RELIGION, AND COMMUNITY in
Mexico from 1940 to 1968. More specifically, it is about how some members of the urban and rural poor of Mexico used religion and community to
critique, adapt to, and interact with the concept of the Mexican Revolution
in the years following the armed conflict of 1910–20. This approach examines three intentional religious communities as case studies—Pentecostal,
Mormon, and Roman Catholic—that professed religious and revolutionary visions for a glorious, new Mexican society. Central to these communities were three issues that elucidate Mexico in the postrevolutionary
years: (1) the continued struggle to reconcile the informal religious corporate identity with formal secular identities; (2) local interpretations of
revolutionary laws and culture; and (3) the absence of the rule of law and
its relationship to religious human rights in Mexico. The nexus of these
issues of identity (corporate, local, and revolutionary) came together in
communities where believers used religion as a tool to choose among revolutionary programs, while the revolution, as practiced by authorities on
the federal, state, and municipal levels, reciprocally influenced the very
beliefs and religious practices of each group.

Intentional Religious Communities

Intentional community is the anthropological concept of physical communities (homes, churches, fields, businesses, etc.) organized around a shared religious ideology and dedicated to a unified purpose or purposes.[1] In the three cases considered in this book, one purpose sought by each group was the partial separation from outside society. But if these communities, most quite small in the period covered here, seek to "separate" only partially from Mexico, what then is the larger value of studying them in comparison? Are these three cases just narrow microhistories of marginal interest? Where are the grand politics or the battles between church and state that have so dominated the literature on religion in Latin America?

To answer those questions, I turned to scholars whose work on intentional religious communities demonstrates the importance of such groups to the study of societies in general. As anthropologist Susan Love Brown argues, in the Western nation-state, modern communities exist within layers of society, and there cannot be local entities completely divorced from the central state nor a central state divorced from the local: "Communities constitute viable units for the study of state societies and are also a powerful means of integrating the individual and society and providing a focus for the study of change."[2] In particular, scholars interested in the reaction of Mexico's citizens (especially the urban and rural poor) to the consolidation of the state and the rise of industrialization, as sponsored by that state, should take particular notice of intentional communities inspired by the armed period of the Mexican Revolution (1910–20) and the reconstruction era (1920–40) and then built during the cultural golden age and Mexican Economic Miracle of 1940–68. As Love Brown asserted regarding intentional communities, their formation is based "on a conscious critique" of the society as a whole.

In discussing revitalization movements, anthropologist Anthony Wallace addressed this concept of a social critique through community formation when he claimed that such communities centered on revitalization movements are "a deliberate, organized, conscious effort by members of a society to construct a more satisfying culture."[3] And why do they do this? asked Wallace. It is an attempt to "emphasize the institution of customs, values, and even aspects of nature which are thought to have been in the mazeway of previous generations but are not now present."[4] Unsatisfied with the glacial pace of cultural change, revitalization movements undertake to reshape the world around them in a generation.

According to Wallace, these movements "must innovate not merely discrete items, but a new cultural system, specifying new relationships as well as, in some cases, new traits."[5]

For this reason, I have titled this work *Primitive Revolution*. Each of the groups under examination was convinced that they were restoring both Christianity and the best practice of Mexican citizenship to more primitive and essential states. Both the Pentecostals and the Mormons firmly believed that they practiced pure Christianity from the time of Jesus Christ and his apostles. In terms of civic and Mexican identity, each felt that they participated in a restoration of their nation as defined by the liberal republic of Benito Juárez (1858–72). By contrast, the Catholic *sinarquistas* felt that religious restoration meant returning to their interpretation of the order offered by medieval Catholicism, while their vision for Mexico matched more closely that of Mexico's emperor, Agustín de Iturbide (1822–23)—as well as any number of later conservative opponents to Benito Juárez—for a state with a powerful ecclesiastical presence and the domination and division of society by corporate sectors. Each of these groups was convinced that they participated in a spiritual revolution of their own that ran, not coincidentally, in congruence (for good or bad) with the revolution of 1910.

But what can looking at these communities tell us? In analyzing the open display of conversion to and expulsion from the communities under study, I argue that we can "read" the lives of many poor and working-class people of Mexico who otherwise kept few first-person accounts for historians to consult. Where such rare gems exist, I have employed them. However, the number of participants who left known written records of their lives in these communities is low compared to the total number who participated. For example, of the over eighty founders of the community known as the Colonia Industrial de la Nueva Jerusalén (chapter 2), I was able to confirm the existence of only two written sources from direct participants. In addition, both of the non-Catholic groups under study here (the Iglesia Luz del Mundo and the Iglesia del Reino de Dios en su Plenitud) have passed through years of persecution from outsiders as well as anthropological investigations that these churches view with suspicion, making oral histories difficult.[6]

Therefore, in the absence of extensive written personal records, I argue that one can understand the desires and hopes of the members of these groups by analyzing the communities themselves as well as by assuming that their members left a critique of society by converting to these religions and communities. Choosing a particular religious denomination—and these organizations required conscious choice on the part of the participants—was a way for some Mexicans to express their opinion on the condition of Mexico in general. For the working poor of Mexico, perhaps one of the few records we can read is their association with particular institutions. This is a dangerous balancing act as the exact motivations of any individual—even with their own description of events—are difficult to ascertain without explicit written records. At times it requires what one scholar refers to as fleshing out "the documentable story with effective though arguable conjectures."[7] However, given the depth of dedication required of members by these communities in time, property, and labor, as well as the large number of members that dropped out, I assume a high level of determination and loyalty for those who remained faithful to their respective causes. From one perspective, then, this is a comparative history of what different movements hoped to "get" by building a closed community in a revolutionary age.[8] But participation in community, I argue, is not a paramount act of selfishness.

The decision participants make to build communities accompanies the idea of establishing a stewardship: They build not only to "get" something from the group but also with a fervent desire to "give" to the community, and to Mexico. As part of the new "conceptual, social, and philosophical" map for society as laid out by the community builders, responsibility to society as a whole is key to understanding why these groups build.[9] In all three cases, the desire to give back to their nation is seen as an expression of their service to God. A similar point of view marked the United States of America and its religious experimentation in the postrevolutionary era:

> At the heart of these ideals [the glorious destiny of the United States] was the deeply held belief that, like the ancient Israelites, God had given His people a land so that, for the glory of God, a people would grow and prosper and be a "light for all the nations." It was, therefore, up to the people to be about the business of building this great nation.[10]

As scholar Robert Bellah concluded about U.S. citizens thinking of their own society, Hobbesian power and accumulation are not always central to people building communities, but may proceed rather from "intrinsically rewarding" pursuits such as worship, work, friendship, and citizenship.[11]

To interpret the era following the military phase of the Mexican Revolution (1910–20), I have used something of the approach taken by historian Robert H. Wiebe in interpreting U.S. society between the Great Rail Strike of 1877 and the end of the Great War. Wiebe argues that faced with a depression, failed reconstruction, a paralyzed railroad economy, rising nationalism, and unemployment, many U.S. Americans wandered from place to place, seeking either to find or create order in a rapidly changing society. Prescient enough "to recognize that the old ways and old values would no longer suffice," these citizens sought movements that would reconcile past community life with a new urbanizing society.[12] Similarly, group members in this study chose to reconcile the past and present via religion, by forming intentional religious communities that mediated between the new consumer and urban society in Mexico and their former rural or village lives.[13]

This mediation with changing Mexican society and advocacy before federal, state, and local officials in combination with communal unity is what I have called a case of informal religious corporatism. And while these communities may not fit the model of formal exclusionary rights laid out by political scientists like Philippe Schmitter, or the "vast integration of labor and capital" of Howard Wiarda, they do fit into a more standard, lay definition of a group that creates a shared name and identity and acts as a single entity.[14] In effect, these intentional religious communities failed to find homes in the formal corporate sectors of Mexican society, as did laborers or agrarians, and simply created their own informal spaces.

Religious and Local Interpretation of the Mexican Revolution

In this work I do not presume to dislodge the foundations of the historiography of Mexico's twentieth century, but I do seek to fill important and previously unacknowledged gaps in the literature. As historian Matthew Butler wrote, religious interpretations of the revolution form an exciting new area of study where "revolutionary institutions could serve as laboratories of religious radicalism, promoting vernacular liturgies, the abolition of religious taxes, free-form devotionalism, and unfettered exegesis."[15] As such, we have another way to understand how everyday Mexicans experienced and lived the results of the Mexican Revolution and the attempt to define the idea of the revolution, both by the central state and by the people.

Influential in my conception of this idea are historians such as Ilene V. O'Malley and Thomas Benjamin, who both established solid examinations of the "use" and "idea" of the Mexican Revolution long after the cessation of the armed conflict.[16] National "reconstruction," progress, and unity became paramount issues for Mexicans seeking to harvest the fruits of the revolution, and explicit in the works of these scholars is the central state's effort to define and control the revolution and, subsequently, to define the correct civic engagement of all citizens.

Particularly during the period under study in this book (1940–68), the image of what was "really" Mexican was constantly on display for all Mexicans to see the "state's drive to construct a sense of nation."[17] Even foreign corporations understood the necessity of playing to the stylized Mexican identity, as companies like Sears and Coca Cola backed off from their strong U.S. American identities in favor of identities as companies seeking to work with Mexico and instill consumer identities. Even Palmolive soap got in on the act by using the Virgin of Guadalupe on soap wrappers to peddle their product.[18] With true revolutionary ideology in the back seat, the key to recognition from the central government was less about ideology and policy positions and more about the ability to perform Mexican authenticity. From the 1940s forward, "the wheel of power became a fiesta of disguises. Some dressed up through cynicism; others were not even aware that they were wearing costumes; some sincerely believed that they were not."[19] Icons of the radical Mexican Revolution— made safe from their original context by the institutionalized revolution— were tied by the president and his cabinet to the new consumer values. Through the post–World War II period, to consume *was* Mexican; it was "to belong."[20]

For this work, however, the important focus remains the local interpretation (via the lens of religion) of these efforts on the part of federal, state, and municipal officials to define the meaning of the revolution. Despite declarations of the death of the revolution by Mexican intellectuals such as Daniel Cosío Villegas, Jesús Silva Herzog, and José Iturriaga, the idea of the revolution still embodied the hopes of the citizenry. I argue this to be the case for several reasons: First, because the ruling Institutional Revolutionary Party (PRI; Partido Revolucionario Institucional) had, in fact, moved substantively away from the social agenda (such as land distribution, empowered unions, and education) of the 1920s and 1930s, while the ongoing discussion of the revolution kept hope alive in many;

and second, despite the best efforts of historian O'Malley's mythmakers and Benjamin's *voceros de la revolución* to monopolize the meaning of the revolution, the revolution continued to mean different things to different segments of Mexican society. As historian Mary Kay Vaughn has argued, "the real cultural revolution of the 1930s lay not in the state's project but in the dialogue between state and society that took place around that project." I have opted to move that argument ahead to 1940 and instead to look at a dialogue between religion and the state, rather than a formal wing of the ruling system (such as Vaughn's examination of education).[21] In fact, I argue that leaders and party functionaries had so many varying interpretations of their own programs, depending on region or level (federal, state, or local), that even what was once considered oppositional to the revolution—religion—found a home for its own interpretation of Mexico's greatest social movement.

Varying local interpretations of the programs of the revolution are not out of step with what some scholars have argued had been a conflict of multiple internal and popular causes of the Mexican Revolution. To do otherwise

> presupposes an idea of "the Revolution" as a clearly defined, consistent entity, as a kind of club, with approved, paid-up members inside, and blackballed cadres outside. Rather it was a complex collective experience, to which many groups contributed in different ways and for different reasons. It therefore deserves a catholic analysis, which neither prejudges the issues, nor privileges certain groups at the expense of others.[22]

What did the revolution mean, then, to segments of popular Mexican society after the armed stage and the populist fervor of the Lázaro Cárdenas years (1934–40), and how did it affect their behavior as a result? Intentional religious communities (founded by Mexicans for Mexicans) answered this question directly as they discovered reasons for both celebration and woe. For some, like the Mormons and Pentecostals, openly embracing the program and propaganda of the state while living lives of theological principles antithetical to the revolution and its mythmakers was the essence of the revolution lived. For others, such as the Catholic *sinarquista* community in Baja California (chapter 3), it meant vociferously decrying the results of the revolution while carrying out the programs and goals of the rulers they professed to detest. In the end, my aim in examining these communities is to investigate the "vast areas of the ocean where Leviathan did not swim," or at least where only the wake of its passing was felt and where some Mexicans maintained a reasonable distance.[23]

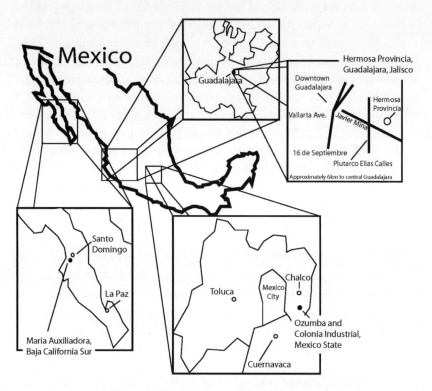

Hermosa Provincia, María Auxiliadora, and Colonia Industrial de la Nueva Jerusalén. MAP BY JASON DORMADY.

In particular, religion in the postrevolutionary era is one area that has received little attention by scholars of the period. In the definitive volume on cultural history for the period, *Fragments of a Golden Age*, historian Arthur Schmidt declares that

religion constitutes another neglected area in the history of contemporary Mexico where popular cultural creativity intertwines complex domestic and global networks of unequal power. University-based intellectuals, especially North Americans, do not always find themselves as inherently familiar with matters of religiosity as they might be with issues involving television or tourism. Contextual blinders should not lead students of contemporary Mexican history to neglect the vital wellspring of religious belief and practice in looking at popular cultural creativity in Mexico.[24]

As historian Brad Gregory has pointed out, it can be difficult for modern scholars to spend significant time with people whose sincere core principles are so entirely foreign to their own, and who hold beliefs not only to be theorized about in conferences and journals but are "beliefs boldly enacted."[25] Religion is an aspect of the cultural life of Mexicans that, in English, has been little explored for the "golden age" of Mexican culture beyond Catholic Action or folk Catholicism.

Law, Rights, and Religion

Just as this work enters into new ground regarding religion and local communities, it both identifies and aims to fill a void regarding the exercise of rights, law, and justice. In particular, I am influenced in the exploration of law in Latin America by the work of historians Carlos A. Aguirre, Ricardo D. Salvatorre, and Robert Buffington on concepts of social deviance. While religion in Mexico and the relationship with the state has been well explored by scholars of religion in Mexico, scholars of law and deviance have not yet applied their observations of law to religions that deviate from mainstream Mexican culture and law. In addition, I have utilized observations on English law by Douglas Hay and E. P. Thompson to explore how local justice worked in revolutionary Mexico. I should also point out that when I argue that there is an absence of the rule of law, I am not arguing that Mexico is a lawless society, but rather that the law is applied unevenly and conditionally, especially in religious matters. To define the rule of law, I am relying on the definition advanced by political scientist Guillermo O'Donnell.

Whatever law there is, this law is fairly applied by the relevant state institutions, including, but not limited to the judiciary. By "fairly" applied I mean that the administrative application or judicial adjudication of legal rules is consistent across equivalent cases, is made without taking into consideration the class, status, or power differentials of the participants in such processes, and applies procedures that are pre-established and knowable.[26]

I have been guided in this course of research by historian Douglas Hay's call for more attention to "popular justice," and especially, as historian Ricardo Salvatorre put it, the "adaptation of state law by popular or subaltern agents."[27] This study answers that call by approaching an important paradox in the law: If law and criminalization is designed to regulate and exclude deviant members of society, how do deviants who still conceive of themselves as ideal citizens maintain the rights they are convinced belong to them? This study addresses how members of Mexican society with criminalized beliefs (in this case religious beliefs) negotiated the system of law locally.

In his *Whigs and Hunters*, British historian E. P. Thompson addresses an important aspect about the service of law. He argues that law does not easily or comfortably equal class power because as much as rulers use law to dominate property, the rule of law imposes, "again and again, inhibitions upon the actions of the rulers."[28] Thompson points out that on occasion even the government itself is defeated in court, paradoxically serving "to consolidate power, to enhance its legitimacy, and to inhibit revolutionary movements. But to turn the paradox around, these same occasions [serve] to bring power even further within constitutional controls."[29]

While Thompson turned that paradox around, I want to turn it inside out for a moment. If the rule of law strikes an imperfect balance between the rulers and the ruled, what happens in societies where the rule of law is absent? As Thompson points out, it is often in the best interest of judges and landed elite to espouse the rule of law and then use that same law as a shield. In a society of arbitrary state power at varied levels, then, is there no recourse for the poor? Is there no defense other than the "weapons of the weak" and "everyday forms of resistance" for the ruled? This study of three religious groups finds that in a society lacking the norms and protections of the rules of law there are also benefits apportioned to them as a result. When little power exists to centralize legal authority, the local rulers, themselves the ruled, are in these cases willing to negotiate and redefine the law. In the end, if there are no rules for the rulers, then the ruled can play the game of self-defining law as well. Their position at all times is tentative and dangerous, but far more acceptable than the restitution, fines, jail, or exile that otherwise might exist under the rule of law.

With this flexibility in mind, I would like to put forward the position of historian Felipe Fernández-Armesto. He argues that, while the United States exists almost entirely outside of comparative analysis with Latin America, "many of the good things about U.S. exceptionalism, such as dynamic wealth creation, the democracy, the accessibility of opportunity, the cult of civil liberty, the tradition of tolerance . . . are common virtues . . . of many modern societies, throughout and indeed beyond the Americas."[30] I would include in his categorization of "civil liberty" and "tradition of tolerance" an interesting flexibility in Mexico for non-Catholic religion in a land supposedly solidly anchored in the faith of Rome. As Harry Leonard Sawatzky points out for Mennonites persecuted in Canada, and F. Lamond Tullis demonstrates of Mormons from the United States, whose religious beliefs were criminalized, each had significant numbers of participants who fled to Mexico in order to retain their religious rights.[31] In each case, significant constitutional and legal restrictions were set aside to allow massive colonization of northern Mexico to suit the economic needs of the government while simultaneously giving refuge to persecuted groups.

But what about Mexican citizens? How did the state deal with them on the question of exceptions for religious deviance? And how could the state find a way to overcome the long-standing conflict between Catholicism and Protestantism when Protestant churches could (on occasion) still expect to be dynamited, their pastors shot, their chapels sacked, and their congregations harassed?[32] Indeed, Protestants could expect to find their own churches targets of expropriation by unions or assaults by government soldiers for distributing anti-Catholic literature.[33] Even the controversial Summer Language Institute, a fundamentalist Protestant organization dedicated to the translation of the Bible into indigenous languages, received "fierce resistance" on the local level despite much support from the federal government.[34] In addition, by 1944, Catholic bishops in central and northern Mexico were leading a successful boycott of the YMCA and Protestant businesses before pressure from the ruling party—who dubbed the campaign unpatriotic during war time—forced the church to call off the campaign.[35] This did not mean state support of Protestants, however. As sociologist Kurt Bowen points out, hundreds of evangelical church permits were denied during this period (though many applications in the Archivo General de la Nación were denied simply for not meeting basic registration requirements in the paperwork).[36]

The antagonism in the Catholic-Protestant-state triangle left a lasting impression on religious Mexicans, particularly those not involved in the hierarchy of their respective churches. When the state made peace with the Catholic Church and signaled a definitive respect for Catholicism with President Manuel Ávila Camacho (1940–46), many Protestants clung to the notion of the "state-as-ally" for the next five decades, just as many conservative Catholics continued to view the state as a mortal enemy. Consequently, both groups would look back to previous golden ages of history in their interpretation of the meaning of the Mexican Revolution. Conservative Catholics desired a return to the age of Iturbide, Catholic generals, or even the Hapsburg Empire, while Protestants clung to the memory of Benito Juárez and other liberal champions—and both groups would find their worlds turned upside down by the course and consequences of the Mexican Revolution.

On the other hand, as each case study will demonstrate, the central state was ever pragmatic and more than willing to be flexible in certain cases depending on the size or influence of the "offending" group or the convergence of the group's interests with those of the official revolution. For smaller and less influential groups, exemptions and flexibility could be worked out at the state and local levels—at times to achieve simply an economic benefit like settling underutilized areas of the nation, and at other times to maintain community harmony or preserve rights not enshrined in the Mexican constitution. In fact, the construction of communities undertaken by each of the groups examined in this book fits nicely with the program of the revolution as defined by the state between 1940 and 1964.

Everywhere, new communities sprang up around Mexico, but nowhere more than in Mexico City to which all the massive new infrastructure led—roads, railways, water systems, and airports—and from which flowed the presidential power of progress, serving as the "axis of national development."[37] Salvador Novo would call it all the "New Grandeur of Mexico" and signs appeared across the nation declaring "We Are Building the *Patria*."[38] And not just building for building's sake, but a sustained effort that served to "not only fortify social legitimacy, but also [make] evident the strategy."[39] In other words, construction made more than buildings; it provided continued evidence of the revolution.

New construction also diverged from the past decade by moving away from ejidal (communal) development and into a preference for colonization and private property. Rodolfo Sánchez Taboada, president of the PRI under President Miguel Alemán, even declared that

> in consensus with the governors and the governing secretaries of the Agricultural Commission Leagues, the resolution of the economic problems of Mexico rested on the security of private property, and the communal system of property was not beneficial for the development of agriculture in Mexico.[40]

By 1952, 8,272 families from populated central states like Tlaxcala, Michoacán, Guanajuato, Nuevo León, Puebla, Oaxaca, and Mexico were shifted to states on the coasts such as Tamaulipas, Veracruz, Sinaloa, and Colima. The central government parceled out 100,033 hectares to colonists as they settled these areas with adverse agricultural conditions and as the northern border economy in general was developed. In the northwest, Baja California Norte shot up from just under 80,000 inhabitants in 1940 to 250,000 in 1950.[41] In the end, however, corruption, poor planning, insufficient infrastructure, and low market demand contributed to the near failure of almost all of these attempts.[42] In addition, many communities of indigenous groups that still spoke no Spanish and "made a point to mock or even commit hostile acts" toward those who failed to speak or dress according to village traditions resisted internal colonization as well.[43] Even foreign colonization was declared a dismal economic failure in 1950 by government agronomists. After reflecting on French, Italian, Mormon, and Mennonite colonization from the nineteenth century through 1950, Mexican agronomist Moises T. de La Peña observed that it is "easy to point out that" that colonization "has failed in Mexico, both the artificial and the spontaneous." He goes on to say that "the only colonias that have properly prospered economically are the Mennonites; but for Mexico that has been the most glaring failure for their failure to assimilate."[44] Colonization in Mexico required more than economic contribution; it required the ability to become "Mexican." Thus, as scholars of religion John K. Simmons and Brian Wilson put it, religious groups found the right "place" to bring about their "new order of things."[45] It is no surprise that each group associates itself heavily with the Israel of the Old Testament and their obsession with the promised "land of milk and honey," with Mexico being that Promised Land and themselves being God's chosen people to carry out a special task. For each group, that task was to restore "Christianity" and consequently bring about a "new order" for the present and future in the newly established revolutionary society of Mexico.

Of course, Mexican history is full of similar examples of movements uniting place and religion at times of revolutionary tumult. Eric Van Young's *The Other Rebellion* provides a masterful example of how local piety combined with village-level concerns during a time of upheaval.[46] For the late nineteenth and early twentieth centuries, Paul Vanderwood's exploration of the Tomochic rebellion (1891–92) shows a combination of local concern and religion during a time of stress that resulted in a movement to create the kind of "new order of things" mentioned by Simmons and Wilson.[47] This book seeks to demonstrate that after the revolution and during Mexico's cultural golden age, this combination of local concerns and piety still resulted in people seeking the redemption of place. For each of three groups presented here, their rhetoric is not only about the salvation of their own *pueblo*, but about their divine mission regarding Mexico as a whole. The Mexican Revolution and the centralizing state moved Mexicans to consider themselves part of a larger political entity. One piece of evidence for that is the religious and political language of all three groups in this study, which demonstrates that while they had local concerns, they were anxious about the salvation of Mexico as a whole.

An Introduction to the Chapters

The leaders of the organizations examined for this study were shaped by the tumult of the 1920s and 1930s, and their critique of the 1940s and 1950s is based on their experience with religion and power in that earlier period of turbulent church-state interaction. While the idea of economic progress was an important facet of the church-state debate in Mexico from the beginning, I assert that the important discussion of modernization continued in Mexico after the revolution, permeating all levels of society and appearing in almost every corner of the nation. For religious groups seeking a "new order of things," a similar push by the state to reconstruct Mexico powerfully resonated with them, but also moved them to criticize that progress by forming intentional communities. Religious communities that sprouted in the midst of what scholar Claudio Lomnitz refers to as a "cultural revolution" could not help but serve as critiques of that movement.[48]

For the members of the Evangelical Pentecostal movement known as La Luz del Mundo, or LDM (see chapter 1), their move to form a community provides several critiques of revolutionary Mexico. First, it serves as the group's response to the militarism of the 1920s as well as to the political and religious strife that tore Mexico into various warring camps under the final gasp of the regional caciques (local political bosses often at war with one another until 1923). Second, LDM also serves as a response to the growing urbanization of Mexico. Most early LDM members were rural immigrants from western Mexico forced to move to Guadalajara (Mexico's second largest city) by the failure of state agricultural policies and the growing industrialization of Guadalajara that destroyed the small economies surrounding it. Once concentrated in Guadalajara, political and economic survival—so much intertwined as the national state centralized—became a viable part of the religious mission for spiritual salvation. In the shelter of LDM's Hermosa Provincia community, members could enjoy a level of protection from the vagaries of the market they were tied to, as well as reenact the small-town life they had been forced to leave.

I explore these actions by focusing on the group's founder, Eusebio "Aarón" Joaquín González, and the crucial period of development that occurred after his arrival in Guadalajara in 1929. These early years are key to understanding the establishment of LDM's first two community experiments as well as LDM's most famous project, the Hermosa Provincia in eastern Guadalajara. This is a little-studied period of Luz del Mundo history, earning only passing comments and a paragraph or two in most of the literature on this important transnational group.[49]

The LDM is situated in my theoretical framework as a critique of Catholic persecution of Protestants in Mexican society and of the central state's inability to provide protections for those Protestants. However, due to the absence of the rule of law, LDM was able to adapt itself to the situation and carve out an exclusive community that proved to be a boon to the efforts of the central state to promote colonization, urban development, literacy, and economic upward mobility. As such, LDM chose the goals of the state that best matched their theology while rejecting other state projects, such as a growing reconciliation with the Catholic Church.

In chapter 2, I will discuss another group that supported the official project of the central state while simultaneously separating itself to form a protective buffer from the market and the lack of legal protection for religious liberties. The Iglesia del Reino de Dios en su Plenitud (IRDP— Church of the Kingdom of God in its Fullness), a Mormon-based organization, combined political and Christian principles to establish its own religious community in southeastern Mexico State. This case study marks a departure from the LDM in that while the group was vocal in their support of the ruling party, religious beliefs and limited numbers kept them from the same open political participation with the ruling party. These beliefs included wealth redistribution and plural marriage (polygyny), which put them more egregiously outside of the law than Luz del Mundo. However, the IRDP demonstrates, to a greater degree than the LDM case, to what extent the absence of the rule of law in Mexico allowed protections of religious liberties in Mexico: In the case of the IRDP, had the rule of law been adhered to by the state, the polygamous group would simply have been crushed. The group also provides a critique of the growing pull of Mexico City's economic influence in the surrounding rural area. The group's founder, Margarito Bautista Valencia, will serve as the foundation for the study of this group, displaying a distinctly rural cast that glorifies the hard work of agricultural cooperation. While Luz del Mundo hovered on the outskirts of Guadalajara, the IRDP remained firmly entrenched in one of Mexico State's small market towns, though just as tied to the economic pull of Mexico City as the LDM was to Guadalajara.

By extension, the IRDP, more than the Luz del Mundo, serves as a response to the growing presence of market forces in Mexico and the desire of some rural Mexicans to protect themselves from its fluctuations. Bautista's largest theological influence is Mormonism, for whom capitalism is simply the lesser of all human economic evils to choose from and needs heavy tempering by moderation in consumption and profuse redistribution of goods and services under private initiative.[50] The IRDP, while participating in the market, sought to temper it through their redistribution of property and goods to the community. Even the health code that Bautista and his followers adhere to (abstaining from coffee, tea, alcohol, and tobacco) is based more on the fear that the addictive qualities of those items put consumers at the mercy of corporate forces than appreciation of the health benefits involved.[51] As consumerism came to define what it meant to be Mexican during the postrevolutionary golden age, the attitude of the IRDP stands as a sharp critique of the Mexican state's choices and of its ability to provide a social safety net for Mexico's rural inhabitants.

Chapter 3 introduces a group that readers might at first consider out of place among my selection of case studies. However, once more, I will use the life and mission of a central patriarchal figure to explore the foundation and life of a community built as a criticism of Mexican society as a result of the Mexican Revolution. The community is the María Auxiliadora of Baja California, and the man is Salvador Abascal Infante, leader of the conservative Mexican and Catholic organization known as the *sinarquistas*. Fiercely nationalist and traditional, the Unión Nacional Sinarquista (UNS) hardly seems the "anti-Mexican" movement that its critics in the 1940s painted it. Placed within context, as well as in a comparative lens, the actions of this group (though not the rhetoric) seem less anomalous and certainly less counterrevolutionary than either they or the ruling party at the time would have been comfortable admitting.

The UNS also resisted the forces of cultural change and urban modernization afoot in Mexico, though they developed a far sharper portrait of what a "true Mexican" ought to be and how they should be engaged civically. Socially conservative in nature, the group relied on Catholic social doctrine to criticize the failure of the state's social safety net, agricultural policies, and its growing friendship with the United States (and other capitalist powers) as well as the Soviet Union. This UNS critique argued that the economic morality of liberalism and socialism denies "the naturalness of human solidarity" as opposed to the Christian order of Catholicism.[52] In this fervor to unite Mexico and preserve human integrity, the UNS set out to colonize some of the least settled areas of Mexico, such as Baja California, Sonora, Durango, and Tamaulipas, in order to make them into Christian societies and economic engines for Mexico while at the same time aiming to stop possible U.S. invasions and annexation.

The UNS, however, suffered from its own success, drawing the wrath of the state for its ability to challenge the power centered in Mexico City with nearly six hundred thousand members nationwide. In addition, when the movement abandoned its more radical principles, it abandoned its membership—which was soon co-opted into party politics by either the Partido Acción Nacional (PAN, or National Action Party), or by the increasingly conservative PRI of 1940s and 1950s Mexico. Far more than did the other intentional religious communities, the UNS represented a movement with numbers large enough to change the direction of Mexico in the 1940s, but (like the other groups studied) because their perception of the church-state relationship was based in the 1920s and '30s, it failed to gauge the changing scene in Mexico until it was far too late to reverse its decline.

In chapter 4, I make final comparisons of the three groups and discuss some implications of the comparative local approach taken in this work. In addition, I reflect on the efforts by the state to create a rule of law and regulate the relationship between churches and the state. As Mexico experiments with liberal traditions such as party politics, representative democracy, and the rule of law, this work draws attention to the role that corporate religious bodies have played in even the late twentieth century and early twenty-first. In addition, as the nation seeks to deal with the legacy of the Mexican Revolution, assessing how it unintentionally served multiple interests with different meanings can encourage a more intentional respect for divergent beliefs as Mexico steps into the future.

CHAPTER ONE

La Luz del Mundo and Hermosa Provincia

❧

⸙ OF THE THREE COMMUNITIES whose case studies I present, the Iglesia
del Dios Vivo Columna y Apoyo de la Verdad, La Luz del Mundo (typically shortened to Luz del Mundo, or LDM) is the most successful religious community in terms of scale and longevity. Luz del Mundo is also
the largest non-Catholic religious association in Mexico with (as of 2005)
1.5 million members domestically, and 3.5 million in thirty-four nations.[1]
With its headquarters in Guadalajara, a bastion of Mexican Catholicism,
this Christian organization firmly eschews the label of Protestant, instead
seeing itself as a restoration of the primitive church of Jesus Christ in the
last days of the world. Such restoration includes a belief in spiritual manifestations such as tongues and healing, an emphasis on individual salvation
but in a close-knit community setting, and a firm conviction that God
has called a "living apostle" on the earth to head their church. Its unique
beliefs and explosive growth has garnered LDM and its religious colonies
attention from Mexican journalists and scholars for over forty years.[2] This
chapter explores the foundation of LDM, the formation of their little-
known first colony in the poor neighborhoods of eastern Guadalajara, and

the establishment in 1954 of the community and church headquarters of
Hermosa Provincia. While anthropologists and sociologists have studied
LDM, no historian has yet examined the organization in historical context
nor made a significant comparison to other similar intentional community
projects outside of the state of Jalisco.[3]

In addition, this chapter will look at the LDM quest for authenticity in
both citizenship and religion on the local level. As a restorationist religion,
LDM saw itself as the only pure and true form of primitive Christianity
available to Mexicans—the authentic Christianity of Jesus Christ himself divinely returned to the earth to stamp out the error and corruption of other so-called Christian sects like Catholicism and Protestantism.
The formation of LDM coincided with the consolidation of the Mexican
Revolution under the leadership of presidents Álvaro Obregón (1920–24)
and Plutarco Elías Calles (1924–28; *maximato*, 1928–34) and their drive
to define and monopolize the definition of a "good" Mexican after the
revolution at the national level. And while I do not argue direct causation (such as direction or intervention by the central state), I do argue
that one of the survival tactics of the newly formed and oft persecuted
Pentecostal church was to adopt the definition of model citizenship set
forth by the rulers of the nation and make it part of their religious mission.
However, despite this adoption of *lo Mexicano* and civic participation as
laid out by the ruling party, it is important to remember that LDM success
comes as a consequence of the failure of their political *patrón* to provide
a safe and integrated society for all sectors, belief systems, or informal
religious corporate bodies that appeared after the revolution. In this case,
as LDM gained first informal and then formal legal recognition of local
and state authorities, they were able to parley their vocal adherence to
PRI (Institutional Revolutionary Party) policy into favors and protection
in a system absent the rule of law for religious rights and freedoms. Such
negotiation helped the group reconcile its outsider position with its role as
a positive contributor to Mexican society.

Eusebio Joaquín González

The foundation of LDM begins with Eusebio "Aarón" Joaquín González,
the son of Roman Catholic peasants from the town of Colotlán, Jalisco,
Mexico. As with many religious movements, the early life of the founder
is taught to every LDM child and convert, and in Mexico it has even been

turned into a *corrido* (ballad) focusing on Eusebio's humble birth and indigenous roots.[4] This mythologizing is part of the difficulty of elaborating on the early years of Joaquín González's life, as the history of LDM has become akin to a recited catechism. In addition, the official biographical narrative by LDM member René Rentería Solís reflects the LDM perception of Eusebio Joaquín González rather than the actual occurrences of his life. The official church archive is off-limits at this writing, open only to the highest levels of LDM leadership.[5] This explicit process of memory formation through oral tradition and text creation is in itself important, making clear the points that Eusebio Joaquín González felt important enough to stress to his followers in creating and marketing the image of his movement.

Born in 1896, on the day of San Eusebio (August 14), in the village of Colotlán, Jalisco, Eusebio was the oldest of four children in a traditional Roman Catholic family. As members of LDM are quick to point out, he was indigenous in appearance (*tez moreno*), a trait equated with humility by LDM.[6] In fact, in a 1987 decree on government and religion, LDM used the indigenous appearance of Eusebio to distinguish their movement from Catholicism as an authentically Mexican religion and a more logical choice for Mexicans seeking God. Said the press release:

> The founder of our Church, didn't have green eyes and was no blue-blood with a strange name like Wogtila and Priggioni [a reference to Pope John Paul II (Karol Józef Wojtyła) and Gerolimo Prigione, Apostolic Delegate (and later Papal Nuncio) to Mexico].

> He was an Indian *de tez moreno* named Eusebio Joaquín González, with a great similarity in physical appearance and ideology to the Indian of Guelatao, Don Benito Juárez, the Great Reformer.[7]

And like the great Juárez idolized by LDM, when the family relocated to Tlaltenango, Zacatecas, after "armed uprisings" in Jalisco "altered the quiet and calm" of the area, Eusebio pursued a path of education. In Zacatecas, Eusebio received a scholarship to attend a state school and later returned to this same school as a teenager to teach first-grade students.[8]

The official biography says that, while teaching, Eusebio felt compelled "to participate fully in the social movement of the age [the Mexican Revolution], with the necessary determination to fight for just causes, and thus, not to teach letters but defend ideas, not to teach reading but to fight for a world that requires peace and justice as bases of human development."[9] Whether this reflects Eusebio's true motivation for joining the revolution is unclear, but it does display the level of devotion to the revolution instilled in the official chronicle of his life by the organization he founded. This devotion comes, however, despite the official LDM position that dismisses war (including the Mexican Revolution) as an aberrant act of humankind.[10]

Eusebio joined Francisco "Pancho" Villa's División del Norte where, says his biography, he was offended by the "injustices" caused by the *villista* "bandits."[11] He later deserted the *villistas* and joined the constitutionalist (*constitucionalista*) forces under Venustiano Carranza. Indeed, the biography mirrors Mexican state "myth" formation, or "official history," with the vilification of *villistas* and the sanctification of *constitucionalistas*. Eusebio's biographer says that the *constitucionalistas* taught him "character, obedience, and discipline" that educated and "prepared him for a destiny of greater proportions he could then not imagine."[12]

While on leave from the army in the early 1920s, Eusebio visited Guadalajara and his parents, who had relocated to that city. While there, he met and married Elisa Flores González, eight years his junior and an indigenous woman from a family with ties to his home village in Colotlán. He soon returned to military service and was transferred to customs duty in Ciudad Juárez, Chihuahua. He relocated again in 1925 to the military station in San Pedro de las Colonias, Coahuila, and shortly thereafter Eusebio and Elisa came in contact with some of the evangelical Pentecostals who had been making in-roads in northern Mexico for a decade.

Conversion and Early Ministry

Like many family conversions to Protestantism, Elisa began the conversion process to Pentecostal Christianity before her husband. While attending the market in 1925, Elisa befriended a merchant and member of the Iglesia Cristiana Espiritual, a Pentecostal Apostolic church.[13] The church itself was a direct descendant of the Azusa Street revivals that had taken place in Los Angeles in 1906, where African American, Mexican, and Euro-American Californians had all gathered together and claimed an ecstatic "manifestation" of the spirit—just as on the New Testament day of Pentecost. As the *Los Angeles Daily Times* described it, the revival was a "Weird Babel of Tongues," a "wild scene," and a "state of mad excitement."[14]

When participant and Mexican citizen Romanita de Valenzuela returned to her home in Villa Aldama, Chihuahua, she started her own Pentecostal movement that resulted in several breakaway groups, including the Iglesia Cristiana Espiritual, one of whose members approached Elisa.[15] After his wife's contact with the Pentecostals, Eusebio agreed to meet with representatives of the congregation in his barracks, but the captain of the detachment chased the Protestant missionaries from the military base with insults. When the Pentecostals responded that such suffering was "for Christ," Eusebio sympathized with the movement and continued to meet with them.[16] Nevertheless, his captain concurred with the antireligious, anticlerical atmosphere of the times, warning Eusebio and his wife that religion only "contaminated" military men. The next day Eusebio was transferred to Torreón.

Biographer Rentería stresses that the couple immediately sought a "community" in Torreón, and upon meeting an evangelical and vendor in the market, the couple attended the Iglesia Cristiana Espiritual in Torreón. However, unity and community eluded Eusebio and Elisa as the congregation was divided between two factions, a condition Rentería refers to as "anarchy." The dissension was precipitated by the presence of two figures in long tunics, sandals, and long beards and hair. Calling themselves Saulo and Silas, they introduced asceticism and promoted spiritual learning over reading the Bible.[17] Eusebio sided with Silas who later baptized the soldier into Pentecostalism.

Eusebio faced persecution in his own military garrison as well. His new lifestyle of "clean living" (no drinking, smoking, carousing, swearing, etc.) set him apart from his fellow soldiers, and when he convinced several colleagues to attend services, they were horrified that they had to remove their boots, and thereby be out of uniform, before entering the Pentecostal chapel (a custom taught by Silas and practiced for a short time in the Torreón congregation). Eusebio also refused to attend a firing squad where he was responsible for giving the *tiro de gracia*, or killing shot to the head. The refusal to obey, in deference to the commandment "Thou shalt not kill," cost him three days in prison, though he avoided a full military tribunal because of his previous record of perfect obedience, according to his biographer.[18] His biographer claimed that Eusebio came to see the military as a place of "vandalism, delinquency, vice, and crime

that [did] not correspond with the Christian faith," and that "it was difficult to reconcile military life with Christian life." Eusebio found that
"the problems of the military were each day more difficult and complex,
his superiors looked down on him, [while] his companions mocked his
religious practices and made them the object of humor."[19] LDM painted
the resignation of Eusebio from the army as similar to Moses's separation
from the Egyptians.[20] Later in life, however, Eusebio would use his military connections to save his life and to establish a personal rapport with
the political leadership of Guadalajara.[21]

Perhaps the trauma of these conflicts formed the foundation of
Eusebio's later dual approach to religion and country—in which his religious identity as a pacifist and his civic identity as a citizen called upon
to defend the patria were not experienced as contradictory—a position
setting the tone for LDM policy in general. Following his resignation
from the military, Eusebio preached submission to the laws of the state,
even if they contradicted the commandments he agonized over, such as
"Thou shalt not kill." When the assistant director of international affairs
was asked about military service for LDM members serving in the armed
forces of Colombia, who might have to kill as part of their service, she
responded that, since governments are instituted by God, each member
of LDM had a responsibility to maintain their "civic duties."[22] For the
developed church with evangelizing projects in dozens of nations and an
expanding base, the concept of civic duty that includes full military service reigns supreme. The present-day LDM often calls on historic clashes
between the Catholic Church and the Mexican state and contrasts those
conflicts with the position of their own church:

> We do not bless firearms with "holy water" nor commission
> "religious women" (madre Conchita) to assassinate presidents
> of our republic, as was in the case of General Alvaro Obregón.
> By contrast, we dedicate time weekly to pray for our rulers,
> from the President of the Republic to the lowest public servant
> as Biblically ordered (1 Timothy 2:1–3) so that our nation will
> continue on in peace, without provoking fanatic religious move-
> ments like the Antigovernment and Cristero movements of sad
> memory.[23]

However, for the young Eusebio at that time, the contradiction of the commandments of the state and commandments of God required the state to take a back seat. After sending three requests for his resignation to the Department of War, Eusebio abandoned the military to "seek asylum" in one of the evangelical Protestant churches in Monterrey. Eusebio immediately sought out the congregation of Silas and his companion, Saulo. Upon arrival, the former military man and his wife were told to "clean up and wash their rags [clothes]," and instead of a private room, they were given a pantry off the kitchen in exchange for working in the house of the two self-proclaimed prophets and their multiple wives. With few other options for income, and trusting in the man who baptized them, Eusebio and his wife stayed.[24]

In April 1926, the opportunity to leave Saulo and Silas presented itself, and as with Eusebio's flight from the military, it came with divine permission. According to Eusebio, as told by Rentería, the call came as he and his wife slept: "Here is a man whose name will be Aarón." Eusebio woke his wife who said she had not heard the voice. He returned to bed only to hear the voice once more, this time accompanied by a vision that appeared on the adobe wall. Eusebio saw an enormous hand that pointed at him and announced, "Your name is Aarón." This was followed by a hole that formed in the ceiling of the pantry, through which Eusebio could see stars and galaxies that gradually moved to spell out the words, "Your name is Aarón, and I will make you known to all the world and you will be a blessing." This, claims Rentería, was followed by a "pact with God for humanity, established by means of a new dispensation in a man whose calling was confirmed that night."[25] Thus, the revolution and the promise of a brighter future for Mexico neatly coincided with a new theological dispensation for humanity taught by LDM.

The power of symbolism cannot be underestimated with Pentecostal biblical literalists. The vision of Eusebio/Aarón mirrors the calling of the Old Testament's Samuel, a young boy in the care of Israel's prophet Eli, who received a nocturnal calling that no one else could hear.[26] This calling came at a time when Eli's sons (the spiritual and authoritative superiors of Samuel) abused their powers as priests in Israel, especially with sexual impropriety. Eli and his sons are subsequently removed from the high priesthood of Israel, and the righteous Samuel is put in their place. According to the official story, Eusebio was also young in the faith and in the care of men who had abused their authority, and, like Samuel, was called to replace the corrupt authority of the self-proclaimed prophets Saulo and Silas.[27]

The choice of the name Aarón also carries significant power. As the brother of Moses, Aarón was called as the high priest to preside over Israel, and consequently had the responsibility and authority to enter into the holy of holies of the tabernacle as well as carry out the intercessory rituals to atone for the sins of the Israelites. The biblical Aarón's sons were called to continue on in the function of high priest. Also, as members of the tribe of Levi, they held exclusive priestly function in Israel. Using the name of Aarón establishes a definitive dynastic stamp on priestly authority.[28] The military man who was on the fast track to leadership before his encounter with evangelical Christianity discovered a new path to authority. Indeed, Rentería says that Aarón was part of a "new dispensation" for humanity—a telling phrase. The term *dispensation* is a key millenarian phrase, most prominently featured in the New Testament, particularly in Ephesians 1:10, where the Apostle Paul refers to the last days of the earth when a gospel restoration would occur—or at least that is how it is read by many believing they are involved in restoring "true Christianity" to the earth. In other words, just as Adam, Moses, or Jesus Christ marked a segment of earthly time by the importance of their mission, so important was the mission of the newly called Aarón that he himself marked a new dispensation of time.

After the vision, Aarón began to gather followers to his own cause in the congregation of Saulo and Silas. At this point, Aarón claims a second revelation from God, during a manifestation of glossolalia (speaking in tongues), directing him to leave Monterrey the following Thursday. In the spring of 1926, Aarón and Elisa departed on foot southward into the interior of Mexico on a journey much like a combination of the Apostle Paul's evangelizing mission and Muhammad's Hegira to Medina. LDM compares the journey to the flight of Abraham from Ur.

Leaving Monterrey on foot with a small group of followers, they followed railroad tracks to Ciudad Victoria, then south to Tampico. Rentería writes that along the way the trip was filled with persecution by Cristeros (Catholic rebels fighting against the anticlerical measures of the Mexican government), occasional jail time, and constant privation of shelter and food. The official LDM narrative takes special care to point out the "fanatic" nature of the Catholics they met on their journey and the attempt of "ecclesiastical hierarchies from the priestly pulpit" to "challenge the institutions legally constituted by the government of the republic."[29] The narrative of the text also celebrates the physical suffering of the journey—mostly self-imposed rejections of food, clothing, shelter, and money—and reads like a text on Catholic asceticism.

Like the Hegira of Muhammad, Aarón's travels concluded in his own "holy city" of Guadalajara, Mexico. LDM teaches that upon Aarón's arrival within view of Guadalajara, that city of "indifference [and] profound paganism," God ordered Eusebio to "preach the gospel in this city, because here I have a great people that will serve me and be an example for many nations that will know me, and this will be the proof that I have sent you. I will be with you."[30] December 12, the day of Aarón's arrival in Guadalajara, is an LDM religious holiday and a celebratory challenge (of divine origin for LDM) to one of the strongest religious symbols in Mexico—the Virgin of Guadalupe. The LDM official narrative contrasts Eusebio's appearance in Guadalajara and his dedicatory prayer to God with the celebration of the Virgin:

> In all parts they celebrated the appearance of the Virgin of Guadalupe with idolatrous practices, pagan actions, ringing bells, fairs, bazaars, and the pretext of alcoholism, excessive violence, thievery, pillaging, and the lack of respect—practices understood as an obligatory and un-thinking tradition.[31]

Aarón's arrival in Guadalajara also coincided with the armed struggle of the Cristero War and the administration of Governor José Guadalupe Zuno, appointed to the position to crush the public expression of Catholicism in the Mexican state of Jalisco.[32] Anticlerical intentions notwithstanding, Catholicism was far from disappearing in the state capital of Guadalajara. In addition to the continued public celebration of Catholic feast days, labor unions were also disturbed to find their ranks honeycombed with believing Catholics, as an inspection of a Guadalajara factory revealed that workers of El Sindicato Obrera de la Experiencia still had images posted in the work place of the Virgen de Guadalupe and the Virgen del Refugio.[33] Historian Luis Rodolfo Morán Quiroz claims that evangelical preachers themselves noted an increase in persecution from Catholics in 1926 as tensions between the central state and Catholics also increased.[34] Attacks came in the form of verbal abuse, resistance to missionary work, and, at times, physical abuse.

"Pagan" celebrations aside, the couple crossed the city to visit their families, only to be received by them as nothing short of social outcasts themselves. Elisa's parents reacted in horror to their daughter's emaciation and unwashed appearance, while Eusebio's family wished them dead rather than abandon Catholicism for heretical beliefs, poverty, and filth. The pair lived on the streets for several days before finding shelter with the pastor of the Baptist church who fed them and let them live— for forty days—in the baptismal font.[35] Finally, they found space in the home of an aged widow and midwife on the east side of Guadalajara in a *barrio popular* that they used as a base for their missionary work in that city.

The story of the biblical Samuel reappears in Aarón's life as God promises him and Elisa a son—one that would be born despite the apparent sterility of Elisa, just as the biblical Samuel was born to Hannah despite her sterility. The narrative does not explain how we know Aarón was not the one "afflicted" with sterility. Apparently such intimation would vary both from a biblical parallel as well as impugn the masculinity of the leader. At any rate, according to the official narrative, God would take away a son from Aarón after fourteen years of life as a test of faith.[36] Samuel, as well, was offered to the service of the high priest of Israel, Eli, as a test of faith for the promise of overcoming Hannah's sterility. In a new ceremony that became a common practice for the whole congregation, called a "presentation," Aarón offered the newborn baby to God and promised him (as Hannah did Samuel) to the service of God.

Not long after Elisa's first pregnancy began, Aarón started selling shoes to provide for his growing family. In fact, anthropologist Renée de la Torre reports that many of Aarón's converts were street vendors like himself, allowing for both the itinerant sale of goods in Guadalajara as well as the mobile preaching of evangelical Christianity.[37] Considering the group's need for donations from congregants to sustain the movement, the fact that the early members of the church had any work at all helped keep the church afloat.

What these early converts found was a congregation of around ten people that met in Aarón and Elisa's apartment near Guadalajara's Degollado Theater. In 1930 the group moved to the *barrio popular* of San Juan de Dios to use different members' homes for meetings, including the home of a couple recently converted from the Congregational Church. As of yet, Aarón still had not registered with the state as a preacher, nor his congregation as a legal neighborhood association, as required by Article 130 of the Mexican Constitution of 1917.

The lack of Aarón's registration raises the subject of his legality as well as advances a popular and erroneous assertion that LDM was a project perpetuated by anticlerical president Plutarco Elías Calles to combat the Catholic Church. This allegation comes mostly because of the historical coincidence of Aarón's arrival in Guadalajara in 1926 with the start of the Cristero War (1926–29)—an assertion made to me by Guadalajarans of both Catholic and non-Catholic persuasions during my stay in that city. While documentation overflows for Calles's project to establish a Mexican Catholic Church with a state-employed patriarch, the same cannot be said for Aarón's evangelical project—there is simply no evidence.[38] More likely it belies the intense competition among Catholics, LDM, and other evangelizing sects in Mexico: If, as detractors of the faith claim, the church was "founded" by the state, then surely its claims to be the only authentic Christian organization on the earth are also clearly false.

Assistant Director of International Affairs for Luz del Mundo Sara Susana Pozos Bravo listed several reasons why—from her point of view as a member of LDM—the official state encouragement of LDM seemed unlikely. And while Pozos Bravo's duties demanded she put the best face on the history of LDM, her research makes important points about the possibility of a presidential conspiracy to overthrow Catholicism using an itinerant Pentecostal preacher. First, she pointed out the personal poverty of Aarón and the death of two of his children due to malnutrition as a lack of state support. Why, if he had state funds and support at his disposal, did he not at least buy food for his children? She went on to observe that Aarón's constant movement during the *maximato* (the period in Mexican history between 1928 and 1935, in which the former president, Plutarco Elías Calles, maintained control of the country as *Jefe Máximo*) hurt his chances of establishing a fixed and thriving congregation to challenge Catholicism. Why didn't any of the many Catholic churches taken by the government arrive in his possession during or after the Cristero War? Indeed, an examination in the national and municipal archives reveals numerous requests by mainline Protestant churches, such as Congregationalists, Methodists, and Baptists, for Catholic properties, but none by Aarón.[39] In addition, through oral interviews, Pozos Bravo demonstrated that conversion to LDM, like other evangelical groups, came from individual relationships, often at great personal risk, and not

from some state incentive.⁴⁰ While so many of the party functionaries
and hangers-on of the *maximato* grew wealthy and led comfortable lives,
Aarón and his followers seemed to have carried on with lives of poverty—
a living that I argue helped drive them to desire to establish an exclusive
community and to work in a cooperative manner. It is this poverty that
makes another important point about the apocryphal government origins
of LDM: The hypothesis that Calles would back Aarón is essentially teleo-
logical, looking at the success of LDM in the mid-twentieth century and
projecting that success back onto the impoverished and miniscule congregation of 1927. And beyond the teleology, if there was any direct benefit
offered the members of LDM by the state, evidence is not forthcoming
either in the documents or the lives of the members of the tiny sect during
the Calles administration.

On the other hand, personal relationships with local leaders are easy
to find, and are exactly the reason why corporate groups such as LDM
were so important to the success of the ruling PRI party across Mexico.
Despite the rhetoric of individual rights and citizenship, the PRI was
intent on forming corporate bodies bound by either formal or informal
personal relationships. For example, while no Calles proclamation excused
Aarón for running a clandestine church, it did not stop the police chief
from tipping off Aarón that his meetings would be raided, allowing the
LDM members to disperse, and the police to appear to be enforcing the
law. Anticlericals, Catholics, and Protestants could all be satisfied with
such a strategy. On another occasion, members of the group were arrested
under suspicion of being a subversive body on the way to Lake Chapala,
Jalisco to celebrate meetings (apparently suspect for traveling as a large
group). When Aarón discovered what had happened, he obtained a lawyer "from the municipal presidency" to get his congregation released.⁴¹
Personal relationships worked directly to benefit his congregation.

While one might assume that bribery (*la mordida*) played a role in the
releases, personal sympathy and different conceptions of extraconstitutional
justice seem likely as well. For example, in the case of the warning from the
jefe de policía to escape before he arrived at their clandestine meeting location,
the message was passed to LDM via another Protestant pastor who claimed
the police chief had said, "Advise brother Aarón that I have an order to detain
him and his group. I'll try to delay while they escape because I'm sympathetic
to their group and I would rather not detain them for preaching the gospel."⁴² Indeed, aid offered to LDM tended to come from higher members in

the city government of Guadalajara instead of the more easily bribed members of the police or building and health inspectors that spent their time censuring or harassing LDM, forcing the group continually to move their meetings as well as seek locations outside the city of Guadalajara.

The group also benefited from other connected members of LDM. J. Jesús Nuñez, the municipal president of Tala, Jalisco, and a convert to LDM, wrote a letter using official municipal letterhead on behalf of LDM preacher Julián Zamora to the municipal president of Guadalajara. The letter stated that Zamora was a bread baker and pastor of a "*culto evangélico*" and requested that the municipal president of Guadalajara "help the aforementioned Zamora with the end that he obtains the most success possible."[43] In a world of uncertain political boundaries and immigrant poverty, LDM served as an intercessor with military, police, and politicians at the local level through the auspices of their pastor, Aarón Joaquín. And while some may argue that such relationships do not explain the success of LDM, it does mean that instead of crushing the nascent illegal movement, the local community allowed it to firmly take root. In addition, this acquiescence is portrayed in the narrative as a miracle of God and part of his plan to let LDM succeed. In short, the church itself contains a dual identity whereby they, as Mexican citizens, deny the extent of the aid received from the state, yet among themselves refer to such aid as divine.

This relationship seems, at first glance, contradictory to the image of the sharp lines between the *callista* and early *cardenista* administrations on one hand and religious organizations on the other. On the part of the state, place names such as San Francisco de Asis, San Gabriel, or San Andrés continued to be targeted for name changes to patriotic figures such as Francisco Javier Mina, Mariano Escobedo, or Ciudad Venustiano Carranza. Committees formed to unite "anticlerical and antireligious" groups such as the Anticlerical Front of Jalisco Teachers, the Public Health League (whose network of informants worked to root out and close "clandestine" schools and churches), the Antireligion Action Group, and the Cultural Anticlerical Block. The united organizations held a massive rally and conference in July 1933, complete with anticlerical dramas, classes on how to "defanaticize" Jalisco, and talks condemning the state employ of religious believers. The rally was topped off with a banquet, hosted in conjunction with "the respectable Masonic lodges of this city." The flyer inviting members of the city of Guadalajara to participate in the gathering bears the seal of the National Revolutionary Party (Partido

Nacional Revolucionario, or PNR)—the ruling party—and the closing lines, "God is a myth; Religion is a fable; Clerics are bureaucrats of a theological farce." The meeting was directed by none other than "General de División, Lázaro Cárdenas," shortly to be named president of the republic. Such a rally, dedicated to "do away with all superstitions in general," hardly appears friendly to religion of any stripe, Protestant or Catholic.[44] Other rallies in support of the leftist Chinese and Russian revolutions as well as the anticlerical Spanish republic also appeared in public spaces during the same period.[45]

Religionists in Guadalajara also contributed to the continued tensions. Catholic priests in Tonalá, just east of Guadalajara, excommunicated parents sending their children to public schools, saying it was better to "enter into heaven stupid then learned into hell."[46] Teachers as well continued to be special targets of assault and even murder through the 1930s.[47] Protestants, for their part, continued to agitate the Catholic majority with petitions to the government for the gift of seized Catholic property.[48]

Such a climate, however, belies the amount of innovation and toleration that could be created in a society experimenting with ideas of freedom, worship, and the relationship between the secular and the sacred found in recent scholarship.[49] For example, Episcopalians requested a Catholic chapel from the state not only to carry out religious services but also for "anti-alcoholic conferences, hygienic conferences [personal and building cleanliness], and cultural gatherings lacking any religious content."[50] Though they were not granted the chapel of Santa María de Gracia, allowing Episcopalians to continue their services invited criticism from both Catholics and leftists—each using the same key language of condemnation. While Catholics condemned the "schismatics" for using property in an "unhygienic manner" [the building was left in a dirty condition] that should better go to the use of the *patria*, leftist neighbors made the same complaints; only instead of "schismatic," the Episcopalians were "bourgeois" and "capitalist."[51] A spiritualist Marian church that formed in 1932 also tapped into the preoccupation with cleanliness, organizing their society around a leader (whom they called the *director no guía*— "administrator not spiritual guide") "whose only duty it is to maintain the cleanliness of each meeting house."[52] Such language appears to mirror the growing trend through the 1930s to cease shutting down churches and instead focus on shutting down unhygienic operations, such as hundreds of "covert" bakeries, *tortillerías*, dairy vendors, charcoal sellers, and sellers of other mobile foodstuffs. Order and hygiene surpassed the question of God as a preoccupation of the state.

During this period of religious ambivalence, LDM found a place in society and experienced moderate growth, introducing several new customs to challenge or replace Catholicism in the hearts and minds of converts. For example, after visiting with a new member whose husband had remained Catholic and was openly unfaithful to his wife, Elisa proposed to Aarón that prayer meetings for women be held to deal with the problems of life they faced. They held the meetings at 9:00 a.m., by which time husbands were at work. Elisa is said to have told the women to pretend they were taking children to school or going to the market, but instead to come for prayers.[53] This action is similar to the programs of other evangelical movements in Latin America. Anthropologist Elizabeth Brusco reports that in Colombia, Lutherans and others used house meetings and prayer groups to provide vital psychological support for the difficulties perpetuated by machismo in society. They contrasted their own Protestant cultural underpinnings with Catholicism, where men dominated the visible aspects of Catholic leadership and worship.[54] Rentería says of the prayer meeting that the women "recovered all their confidence with more vigor than ever."[55]

Another custom the group began was the *velada de oración* (prayer watch) to replace the customary Catholic *velorio* over the dead. With the death of Aarón's Catholic mother, the preacher took the opportunity to introduce a practice that further differentiated his group from Catholicism while still maintaining a sense of ritual. The Catholic watch over the dead with candles and silent prayers was replaced with all-night public prayer, hymns, sermons about death, and establishing that the "death of believers is only an intermediary step before being present at the coming of Christ."[56] Once more, Aarón replaces Catholic rituals with practices of an evangelical flavor, thus retaining the sense of ceremony that was important to the members of his flock, so recently drawn from the ranks of the Roman Catholic Church.

This penchant for replacing Catholicism prompted anthropologist Patricia Fortuny to describe LDM as not only a syncretic manifestation of Mexican nationalism and Judaism (for their use of Old Testament symbols and obsession with being thought of as the "children of Israel"), but also a syncretic blend of Catholicism and Protestantism. Among the elements of Catholicism she mentions are:

1. A hierarchical organization
2. A temple of cathedral proportions [Fortuny writes of the later LDM church]
3. Mass ceremony in a "Vatican City"–like setting[57]

I would add to that list the physical use of relics and their mystic power to heal, as well as a vow of celibacy. In an interview, elderly guardians of the LDM temple charged with interacting with visitors from the public recounted stories of items touched by Aarón having healing powers. For example, servants working in Aarón's house in the late 1950s and early 1960s would remove napkins used at dinner by the apostle and pass them to ill members of the community. One of the interviewees himself had done so when asked to dine at the home of Aarón. Another told me that socks given to him by Elisa Flores cured him of an illness. His family kept the socks and used them on any member of the family that might have taken ill. Such incidents, when recounted to the official representative of the church, caused her to reflect that converts to the church brought in many of their Catholic traditions, and in this sense, anthropologist Fortuny has reason to consider the first years of LDM syncretic.[58] Unofficial beliefs aside, LDM even had a celibate priestly class known as men *de pacto*, or under oath. These preachers had "vowed not to marry," and, considering the prohibition of extramarital sexual relations, they had in effect taken a vow of celibacy.[59] This does not mean to say that they perfectly adhered to such celibacy, but the creation of a celibate class of men under vow not to marry—whether they strictly adhered to it or not—is certainly a practice with which converts from Catholicism would be comfortable. Indeed, considering the sexual exploits of some Catholic priests, it is possible that converts to LDM undertook a celibacy pact to demonstrate their own moral superiority over Catholicism. In fact, during the revolution in Guadalajara, revolutionaries had publicized the "clerical sexual peccadilloes, which they found recorded in secret Cathedral archives."[60]

By 1931, Aarón also instituted a new ceremony within the congregation known as the Santa Cena. For the first time Aarón and twenty-three of his followers met to commemorate the crucifixion of Christ with unleavened bread and wine in a former granary annexed to a house in the San Juan de Dios neighborhood of Guadalajara. Here they would "symbolically" take of the "body and blood of Christ" in, once more, a challenge to Catholic sacraments. In my assessment, it seems no coincidence that as the number of converts to the church from Catholicism grew, the number of ceremonial celebrations increased. Rentería does not give a date for the first celebration, but today it is held on August 14, the birthday of founder Aarón, and has become the most important religious holiday of LDM's calendar. Rentería mentions celebrations of the meal at various times of the year. In frequency, method, and style, it appears the Santa Cena has been—according to one member—a process of "evolution."[61]

Luz del Mundo offered a little bit of everything for varied religious tastes. For those disgruntled with Catholicism but still attracted to ritual and hierarchy, it sated those predilections with ceremonies of a holy supper, baptism, childhood blessing, and celebrations of miraculous moments in the church. However, for those attracted by the anticlericalism of Protestantism or moved by the emotional spiritualism and expression of spiritual gifts found in Pentecostalism specifically, LDM covered those bases as well. In an era of secular revolutionary experimentation and consolidation, those seeking access to sources of sacred guidance also dallied with new forms of what for them were truly revolutionary spiritual innovations.

Hierarchy, Consolidation, and the First Community Projects

The year 1930 marked the introduction of the first levels of an official church hierarchy into the small organization. Surprising the congregation one Sunday morning, Aarón announced that "with the authority God had given him," he was instituting the offices of deacon into the congregation. For those familiar with the fairly patriarchal modern LDM, they might be surprised that the church was expanding its leadership in the early years via the women of the church. The first deacons of LDM were in fact deaconesses: Elisa Flores and her friend Francisca Cuevas.[62] Rentería fails to mention what responsibilities such a calling included in 1930, other than more "dedication to the things of God." An emphasis on women's leadership in such small movements is not unheard of, however. For example, the Iglesia Pentecostes Independiente was a small Pentecostal group whose head, Elisa F. Flores (not to be confused with Aarón's wife), directed a Mexico-wide church from her offices in Mexico City.[63] The Asociación Cristiana Femenina (YWCA) was also active in Mexico and led by women.[64]

For the modern LDM church, however, deaconesses (*diaconisas*) are generally the wives of the most important members of LDM hierarchy, and no woman presides over or even preaches to congregations other than those designated specifically for the presence of married women (though

Men and women sit separately during worship services in the Luz del Mundo church. These women are experiencing "manifestations of the spirit" at the group's 2007 Santa Cena celebrations in the LDM community of Hermosa Provincia in Guadalajara, Mexico. August 14, 2007. PHOTO COURTESY OF DAVID AGREN.

men may attend).[65] The growing firmness of patriarchy in LDM, in the years following the calling of Aarón's wife, to their complete exclusion from the hierarchy is, says LDM, based on the New Testament sanction of Paul in 1 Corinthians 14:34–35 that "it is not permitted unto them to speak." This apparently included transferring the 9:00 a.m. worship service designed for women into the hands of male pastoral authorities.

Creating a loyal hierarchy topped by a single leader, however, requires a legitimizing recourse to authority. The official church narrative is careful to point out that Aarón carried out all his actions with the "authority God had given him." His permission to preach and call people to the service of Christ did not come from an ecclesiastical body or a divinity school but from a direct calling from God. Not much later, Aarón called his first minister to watch over thirteen members of the congregation in

Ameca, Jalisco.[66] While God may have called Aarón directly, Aarón now did the calling and assigning of ministries that reported to him, and those with contradictory manifestations not only contradicted Aarón but God himself. When a member of the community challenged Aarón as the only prophet of God, inspired dreams came to Aarón's wife uncovering the challenger's "lies." Shortly after the expulsion of the man and his wife, the official church narrative says the expelled woman was paralyzed as a "punishment of God."[67] Indeed, older members of the modern congregation related with much levity and humor stories of men who contradicted Aarón's position and ended up with leprosy or in accidents resulting in the severing of limbs and tongues.[68]

In late 1931 or early 1932, the church suffered its first schism. Jesús Cuevas, owner of one of the homes in which the congregation met, argued that the congregation should call itself the Iglesia Espiritualista, only to be rebuffed by Aarón for the name's proximity to *espiritista* (spiritualism)— an association Aarón did not want to form in the minds of his followers. Enraged, Cuevas ordered the congregation from his home, retaining several members of the group to form his own church. As for Aarón and the congregation, they moved to Calle 32, near Calle Pablo Valdez, where Aarón began more lucrative work as a bread salesman.[69] However, trouble brewed not only within LDM but externally as well. But, like the move that resulted in greater income for the group, tension with their neighbors turned out to serve as a benefit for LDM in the end.

Due to their location in some of the most crowded *barrios populares* of Guadalajara, many neighbors of LDM complained about the constant singing and noise caused by "manifestations" of the spirit. Therefore, the congregation developed the custom of retiring to the edge of the city to hold meetings in isolated *barrancas* (canyons), groves, fields, or other secluded rural places to avoid harassment from their Catholic neighbors. Rentería quotes his oral interview sources as considering such meetings restful and tranquil experiences away from the crowded noise of the city and the complaints of strangers.[70]

Guadalajara during the 1920s and 1930s was a city flooded with immigrants from the rural Altos region of Jalisco and surrounding states for several reasons. First, as a powerful economic and political force in the region, Guadalajara drained the surrounding countryside via rail and highway traffic, drawing in resources from surrounding Jalisco *pueblos* and other states. In addition, first the revolution and then the Cristero War

drove thousands of peasants to the city, only to be followed by the crushing effects of the worldwide depression that moved many rural Mexicans
to abandon their fields for the city. Though many of the immigrants originally had desires to return to their *pueblos*, it became economically impossible to do so.[71] Although Jalisco had one of the lowest cost-of-living indices
in Mexico, this was coupled consistently with some of the lowest average
wages in Mexico—though often higher than those found in the neighboring states of Aguascalientes, Nayarit, or Zacatecas.[72] Guadalajara also
showed a lower rate of unemployment.[73] It was exactly these sorts of job-
seeking, rural-to-urban migrants that became members of LDM.[74] For the
converts of LDM, rural religious meetings gave them an opportunity to
escape, if only for a moment, the city that bound them economically.

The establishment of a community became a key component of LDM
membership beginning in 1934. This was not just the psychological or
spiritual sense of shared membership, but actual physical community. In
early 1934 or late 1933, the congregation purchased a plot of land in Calle
46—still in Guadalajara's urban zone. José María Gómez, in charge of the
construction of this first chapel, is said to have commented that it was a
"humble place but it would be the property of the *hermanos*." At Aarón's
suggestion, members of the congregation purchased plots in the area "with
the end of surrounding the new temple, and living as a community."[75]
Dislocated from family and home and tied to the city economically, these
immigrants began to create their own village within the city—providing
both an oasis of faith and a sense of place.[76]

The year 1934 also marked the submission of paperwork for official
recognition of the organization as a *culto*, or "neighborhood organization,"
as the Iglesia Cristiana Espiritual—the same name as the congregation
Aarón and his wife had joined in Coahuila.[77] In addition, Aarón does not
appear as the head of the congregation; instead Julián Zamora, the bread
baker and convert from Ocotlán, Jalisco, was its leader, a move that probably reflects Aarón's early desires to head a religious movement and not
simply a single congregation.[78] In the dedication of the Calle 46 chapel,
Aarón claims to have heard the voice of God telling him that his church
was the "light of the world" (*luz del mundo*) and that the followers were
the Iglesia del Dios Vivo Columna y Apoyo de la Verdad. However, in the
official registration with the state it would remain the Iglesia Cristiana
Espiritual for decades to come, with an annexed notation that they met in
the "templo denominado La Luz del Mundo."[79]

The church was not the only entity using multiple identities. Despite his name change by God eight years earlier, Aarón continued to register with the state under his birth name of Eusebio Joaquín González. On several occasions he signed letters as Aarón Joaquín, when it was to just one of the members of the "neighborhood association," and in 1954 the municipal approval for his Hermosa Provincia colony was addressed to Aarón.[80] However, when it came to the legal use of his name, he remained Eusebio and preserved the dual nature of his patriotic and sacred identities.

The growth of LDM continued gradually and perceptibly through the 1930s. In 1938, Aarón returned to Monterrey, intent on converting his former associates of the Iglesia Cristiana Espiritual in that northern city. Upon arriving in the city he went to the home of a former associate to communicate his new gospel message only to find her now a Baptist and stridently opposed to Aarón's Pentecostal theology. In a doctrinal showdown, the former *hermana* in the gospel confounded Aarón by pointing out that he had no right to condemn her since he was nothing but a Trinitarian—baptized in the name of the Father, Son, and Holy Ghost. For one who preached baptism for the remission of sins in the sole name of Jesus Christ, such an allegation struck at the pastor's core. He immediately sought out his former teacher, Silas, who confirmed that Aarón had indeed been baptized in the name of the Father, Son, and Holy Ghost.

At this point in the narrative there seems to be some confusion and contradiction. Anthropologist Renée de la Torre maintains that Aarón's discovery of his "invalid" baptism did not occur until 1943, after the loss of hundreds of members in a near-violent schism. She argues that he used the moment to perform an auto-baptism in front of the congregation, communicate a new revelation, and consolidate his position as the sole charismatic leader of LDM. Rentería's account has the rebaptism occurring in 1938, and claims it was performed by LDM pastor Lino Figueroa. Considering Rentería's sources, I am inclined toward his version, and argue that de la Torre has confused a different 1943 baptism (discussed shortly) with the 1938 baptism. Either way, this period marks Aarón's firm break from the rest of the evangelical and Pentecostal community. With his former associates turning to heresies and even his initial baptism invalidated, Aarón further assured the authenticity of his own divine calling over those of his former friends for his followers.

By the end of 1939, LDM described their old meeting house as being in "very bad condition in both security and hygiene," causing them to seek a gathering space in a new, spacious temple in the street 12 de Octubre and the corner of Calle 68 within the urban division known as Sector Reforma.[81] By 1939, Guadalajara was a city divided into four divisions known as sectors: Hidalgo (northwest), Juárez (southwest), Libertad (northeast), and Reforma (southeast). Poorer members of society lived in sectors Libertad, Reforma, and eastern Hidalgo. Sector Juárez boasted of middle-class and wealthy homes in broad avenues, including grand Porfirian-era homes, and later the U.S. American–style Chapalita area.[82]

The movement of LDM to northern Sector Reforma in 1939 marked an increased retreat from the city as the members grew both more prosperous and numerous. In fact, the area to which the group retreated was the complete opposite of central Guadalajara, receiving little attention from developers or municipal authorities until the mid-1950s. For example, as late as 1952, neighbors in nearby Calle 46 complained of an arroyo one and a half meters deep (about four and a half feet—the full width of the street) that filled with water and became a source of disease for the neighbors.[83] This small arroyo, however, and any associated potential disease pale in comparison to the 1937 influenza epidemic that ravaged urban Guadalajara—perhaps another reason to move to the fringes of the city despite poor conditions and price gouging for basic services like water.[84]

However, Calle 46 could almost be called a full development in comparison with the area east at 12 de Octubre and Calle 68. Aerial photographs from 1948 reveal an area with no paving or even the occasionally approved graveling common in other developing neighborhoods. Most lots along 12 de Octubre sported crumbling walls around uncultivated fields, adobe yards, or several houses with large shared orchards or shaded areas of indiscernible use. Almost every *manzana* (block) in the neighborhood has an area of apparent agricultural production—until we arrive at *manzanas* 237, 242, 320, and 345—the location of the new Luz del Mundo chapel and the second physical community project of Aarón Joaquín.[85]

The move reflects the vastly improved economic condition of the church since it first registered with the state in 1935. The required inventory of the chapel shows a congregation that progressed from ten backless benches and a few used wicker chairs to twenty new pews, fifteen electric lamps, a new pine pulpit, and three chairs to sit in front of the congregation on the stand. By 1951, the inventory grew to include clocks on the wall, thirty-four pews, fifty chairs, and much more.[86] Photographs in the municipal archive of Guadalajara show a well-decorated church with stylish external brickwork, and the leadership displays suit jackets, ties, and wingtip shoes. Compared to registration photos from the 1930s, the economic status of the pastors appears to have improved markedly.[87]

The growing church moved to this sparsely populated fringe of Guadalajara "far from intolerant people to the extent that they enjoyed more liberty, spontaneity in meeting when they wanted . . . for singing and praying with all their strength, as a right . . . to believe and worship God."[88] The fact that Catholic neighbors were greatly annoyed by the singing, praying, and shouting of spiritual "manifestations" can be seen in a letter to the municipal president concerning a Protestant group meeting in Neptuno Street in Sector Reforma. The noise of their meetings, said the neighbors, disturbed families, the nearby school, and workers coming home to rest. Such "scandalous" behavior surely must be a cover for some other activity, they argued, for so much noise was "too loud and raucous to belong to a religion."[89]

The LDM exclusive community project is also revealed by mapping membership lists (names and addresses) submitted to the city of Guadalajara against aerial photographs from the Jalisco State Historic Archive.[90] The list shows a large concentration of members living in a ten-block by four-block section running west from the 12 de Octubre chapel. The greatest concentration, however, comes in the four blocks bounded by Gómez Farías Street on the south, Gigantes on the north, Calle 66 on the west, and Calle 70 on the east. By comparing the addresses and the aerial photographs, we can even ascertain a general sense of living conditions in the area.

As mentioned above, the aerial photographs of empty lots and enclosed fields suddenly give way in a four-block area located at 12 de Octubre and Calle 68 to a concentration of houses with very little agricultural space. Only the lots bordering Gigantes show single houses with "yards" and trees, but these do not show signs of cultivation. However, in blocks 320 and 325 the lots bordering on 12 de Octubre show signs of mass construction, with equal sizes in house and patio (about four and a half meters wide by sixteen meters long). Of the 158 numbered addresses, 92 (about 58 percent of households) are listed as inhabited by single adults (fifteen and older). The other 66 addresses (42 percent of living space) contain 71 percent of the population. If we subtract only two adult households, the number becomes 50 percent of the community living in households with three adults or more. The largest household consisted of ten adults (at number 75 Calle 64) in a space eleven and a half by thirteen meters.

These numbers exclude children under fifteen, who were not considered "members" of the congregation. Nevertheless, we see the ability of many members to procure their own living space and a need for only half of the community to live in multifamily dwellings. Of these dwellings with several adults, it is difficult to tell familial relationships, though many of the occupants appear to display concurrences in *patrinomos* and *matrinomos*. We can assume that only a minority of the community actually lived in multifamily dwellings with people to whom they were not related.

The LDM is not an attempt to create a utopian society of egalitarian communalism, but a retreat from the city to which they were economically bound in exchange for lives in less crowded and more sanitary conditions than those found in the *barrios populares*. They show no romantic desires to live in common, but they do display a tendency to create a village atmosphere with the church at the center and close friends and relations surrounding them.

By 1942, though firmly established as a community, dark times came to LDM. The Department of Public Works, after a tip by an urbanization inspector from the department, launched an investigation and discovered that a second temple at 1680 Gigantes was occupied by people "that for the moment are completely unknown to us" and was in violation of health and safety regulations as well as being built "without the corresponding permission" and "outside the zone of urbanization." By January 6, the temple was closed by order of the Department of Public Works. Following four months of activity, including registering the church once again with the federal government, the chief of police ordered the building reopened in April 1942, though the federal Gobernación (Department of the Interior) continued to inquire as to the church's status until August.[91]

Later in 1942 and into 1943, LDM passed through its largest internal schism yet. The group had experienced schisms before, losing a quarter of their congregation in 1931 and again in 1932 (approximately twenty members of ninety total members). However, the 1942–43 division proved a definitive watershed for the church and culminated in the consolidation of Aarón Joaquín's power. The roots of the schism are somewhat debated, as many in LDM chalk the loss up to jealousy and ambition on the part of the schismatics.[92] While the ambitions of Aarón are interpreted by the modern group as the humble calling of God, the aspirations to leadership by members under Aarón are seen as little more than grasps at power.[93]

The tale of the schism begins on Aarón's August 14, 1942, birthday celebration. Beginning with hymns at 4:00 a.m., the congregation continued with a breakfast, including gifts of flowers and a children's chorus that celebrated the birthday of "God's missionary." This celebration, however, became a point of contention between members in Guadalajara and members in Mexico City. If the preacher was a human being, some dissidents asked, why had he accepted hymns sung to him as well as gifts of flowers? As the debate over the celebration heated up, LDM lost several congregations and some of Aarón's key pastors. The official church narrative claims, however, that this was only a pretext used by several power-hungry pastors to "seduce" members of the congregation and instill doubts about Aarón's intentions. Indeed, the narrative by Rentería is filled more with vitriolic polemics than information. He does briefly mention accusations of adultery, rape, and theft, while Ibarra and Lancyner assert that allegations of sexual impropriety made by a Teresa Larios were part of the charges.[94] Among those lost were almost five hundred members and some of Aarón's closest pastors, including Lino Figuero, who had rebaptized him in 1938.[95]

Central Mexico was not the only site of the schism; the Guadalajara congregations experienced a split as well. The drama, according to *El Occidental* (a mainstream Guadalajara newspaper) of November 30, 1942, began when sympathizers of the schism in central Mexico challenged the authority of LDM in the Gigantes Street congregation. By October 3, 1942, the municipal authorities became involved when twenty-seven members of LDM wrote the city of Guadalajara, denouncing alleged "anomalies, injustices, and abuses" by members that "fanatically follow Mr. Eusebio Joaquín (his real name)," an "evangelical bishop." They also attempted to sway authorities by saying that the chapel at 1680 Gigantes Street still failed to meet "the requisites of security and hygiene," though as mentioned above, the chapel had been inspected and approved for reopening earlier that year.[96] The group appears not to have been successful in shutting down the chapel.

Among those who had signed the petition requesting the LDM ouster from the 1680 Gigantes chapel was J. Jesús Núñez, former municipal president of Tala, Jalisco, and patron of Aarón's right-hand man, Julián Zamora. With the loss of Núñez, along with former close confidants such as Pablo Olguín and Lino Figueroa, there remained few in LDM leadership with more than a basic education or leadership experience to stand in the way of his total control of the congregation. Dissension had not weakened Aarón, but instead allowed him to consolidate his own control of the church.

The turmoil of 1942 gave way to the final consolidation of Aarón's power in July of 1943. In another timely vision of the "glory of God" and scenes from his life, Aarón saw not only his baptism by the "false prophet" Silas, but also his baptism by the "traitor" Lino Figueroa. Following these two scenes, the voice of God told Aarón that "the time has come. Arise and baptize yourself, invoking my name." As the dust of Saulo and Silas had been brushed from his feet by the baptism conducted by Lino Figueroa, so too would Figueroa's baptism (and hence his authority) be cast aside by an order from the very creator of the universe for Aarón to baptize himself. Finally, the prophet was the ultimate source of baptismal legitimacy and "the beginning and foundation of a new generation of believers."[97] Using the biblical order issued to Paul of the New Testament to arise and *bautízate* (Acts 22:16), Aarón literally baptized himself and sealed what he saw as his calling as Christ's "new apostle." The authority of both the Old Testament (Aarón) and the New Testament (Paul) was made complete in him. Who could challenge such a genealogy of divine authenticity and authority?[98] In addition, what had been a passive challenge to Roman Catholic apostolic succession became a direct challenge with the renewal of authority in the person of Aarón. Indeed, the Luz del Mundo church was now the sole true "catholic" or universal church on the face of the earth.[99] Every member of the church was then rebaptized.

LDM strongly focuses on the authenticity and authority claimed by the Church. Just as Mexico passed from a stage of general political diversity to an obsession with centrality, Aarón passed from an ecumenical view of evangelicals to a period of complete and total authority for access to the sacred. LDM maintains that Aarón was called to "undertake the restoration of the primitive church" and to form "the chosen people" of God. By adopting this identification as the original people of God, LDM thereby takes on a direct lineage as the inheritors of the biblical legacy, from the original promises of God with Israel to the coming of Jesus Christ. However, through the corruption of the Catholic Church, the true gospel of God (and the authority to preach it) was lost on the earth; but the restoration of authority was returned to the earth in the form of Aarón and LDM. Not only do they claim, then, the connections of New Testament gospel authority, but the Old Testament authority of

God's covenants with Israel—made available only to themselves through the person of Aarón.[100]

Such rhetoric of authenticity based in "restoration" is, of course, predicated upon the premise of Catholic corruption. As noted above, while Catholicism is characterized as "pagan" and "idolatrous," LDM claims authority by being biblical, spiritual, and directed by God himself. LDM also emphasizes that Aarón spent much of his teaching on the very steps of Catholic churches to win converts. Needless to say, relations between LDM and the Roman Catholic Church are hostile at best. Rumors among Catholics that LDM abuses its young women sexually have abounded for decades. Ibarra and Lancyner found no incidence of such in their 1972 research, though the church narrative does carry a story of abuse carried out by one of its followers.[101] Catholics even claim that Aarón called a priest to hear his dying confession of guilt and abnegation of his ministry on his deathbed, a story often mentioned by Catholics.[102]

Consider now the similarity between LDM and the state. While LDM inherits the authority of the Old and New Testaments, as well as the restored apostle of Christ (Aarón), the Institutional Revolutionary Party (PRI) inherits its legitimization not only from the pre-Porfirian republic of Benito Juárez, but from such "new" prophets of the revolution as Francisco Madero, Álvaro Obregón, and Venustiano Carranza.[103] It is little wonder that while no official relationship existed between LDM and the state in the early years, they still had an affinity for each other, most likely based in Aarón's years as a constitutionalist soldier and expanded upon by a mutual dislike for the Catholic Church. In particular, the Catholic Church posed a threat to the singular legitimacy that each group sought. While salvation in LDM was an individual decision, it was only possible as part of the true and restored church of Jesus Christ (the LDM church); while liberty was an individual right within the new Mexican state, true revolutionary behavior and correct civic engagement occurred only within the limits and definitions set by the ruling party.

Ironically, the very formation of LDM as a religious community occurred because of the failure of the Mexican state to preserve individual liberties, such as political representation or freedom from religious persecution. The arrangements between the Catholic Church and the state made during the late Cárdenas administration and early Ávila Camacho years assured a situation whereby the state took a hands-off position in relation to Catholicism.[104] By 1943, the extent of the interest in Jalisco for moderating the hierarchy of the Catholic Church was a distribution of flyers to all *ayuntamientos* (municipal governments) instructing them to observe the laws of Mexico but not to "offend society" by enforcing laws (i.e., anticlerical) on religious regulation.[105] Over the course of the 1940s, churches went from being denied registration for using the term *iglesia* (church) in their applications to accepting and registering neighborhood associations under the listing of *church*.[106] In addition, the language of liberal president Benito Juárez urging respect for the religious rights of others, which had been so skillfully employed by the state to attack Catholicism, now became used as a reason not to offend Catholics. Where Juárez had said that the "respect of other's rights brings peace" (*el respecto al derecho ajeno es la paz*), which had been used to force Catholics to respect others, the flier mentioned above takes that idea, turns it on its head, and alerts Catholics that their beliefs are now to be respected. With the Catholic Church entering into a less openly violent and competitive relationship with the state, non-Catholic entities such as LDM found themselves more openly subject to the persecutions of Catholics—an important factor in their next decision to move.

The Hermosa Provincia of Guadalajara

By the late 1940s and early 1950s, the LDM community on 12 de Octubre was no longer isolated as population growth overtaxed the infrastructure of Sector Libertad and the city developed a massive urbanization plan for Sector Reforma.[107] Such growth had brought in many non-LDM residents and the secular pleasures of dance halls, cantinas, and continual annoyance at the presence of the non-Catholic group—the chapel was even robbed as well.[108] The members and leadership concluded that despite their work in building a community, it was time to relocate. Said Aarón of the move: "I want an exclusive space for the *hermanos*, as it was with the people of Israel with a 'promised land' where the formula of life will be 'better Christians are better citizens,' because to be a Christian does not mean to be a social outcast."[109] Aarón's language here is clear: By providing the LDM with an exclusive space for their worship, they can be the best Christians possible and, as a result, the best citizens for Mexico. Rentería describes Aarón's dream of constructing a place to escape the abuse of their neighbors for "not being Roman Catholic" as one where this citizenship and Christianity would manifest itself as "a territory for an enterprising population, hard working, honorable and generous, simple and hospitable, with the possibility to drive themselves to develop their social and spiritual potential."[110] The community Aarón planned represented not only an attempt to restore true Christianity but also to establish the place of the non-Catholic Christian within Mexican society—the ideal citizen. Nevertheless, LDM's Catholic neighbors seem to have felt otherwise and found the group more an annoyance than a set of model citizens.

The apprehension that LDM and their Catholic neighbors felt about one another simply reflects the state of affairs between Catholics and non-Catholics generally in Guadalajara—a relationship that appears to have improved little since Aarón's arrival in Guadalajara in 1926. While the Mexican state and the Catholic Church had entered into a détente, the same cannot be said for Catholics and Protestants. With only twelve small registered *evangelico* congregations in Guadalajara as compared to fifty-four Catholic buildings, the sheer numerical difference remained overwhelming.[111] Assaults on Protestants—though not common—still occurred, including the murder of an Apostolic Fe en Cristo preacher, Benito Peña Cortes. In addition, Protestants themselves were in constant division, with LDM shunning other Protestant churches as untrue faiths, and other congregations continuing the pattern of splitting and dividing, some even using government connections to try to gain an upper hand in the religious conflicts.[112]

Out of this conflict, LDM began the process of locating a new community for their congregation. The fiftieth anniversary celebratory pamphlet of Hermosa Provincia—the community they would eventually found—lists potential building sites south of Guadalajara on the road to Tepic or in the municipality of Tapalpa, "but this was too far from Guadalajara."[113] Bound to the city as merchants and vendors, Aarón could not conceive of the community abandoning the economic power of Guadalajara. In addition, though LDM sent missionaries all over the region by 1954, to move the center of the community far outside the ability to attract new converts to the group (who themselves would be bound by work to Guadalajara) might be detrimental to the growth of the organization.

This search for land and a new community came during an urbanization boom of divisions know as *fraccionamientos*. Land purchased by a private developer—with plans that met the basic requisites of Guadalajara and Jalisco state laws—was transformed into new urban communities. Requirements included wide streets, sidewalks, drainage and water systems, and electricity; in exchange, the city allowed construction to go forward and then installed schools, parks, markets, and police *puestos* (substations).[114] In a city where federal housing was poorly constructed and frequently lacked repairs and debt reduction, *fraccionamientos* served as practical and attractive alternatives.[115]

Originally, LDM selected a *fraccionamiento* in the southwest of the city. However, when Aarón understood the size of the development, its form of organization, and its proximity to other people, he undertook negotiations with developer and member of Guadalajara high society J. Jesús Rodríguez Barba for his hacienda, Rancho Blanco, east of Guadalajara. Thus, in 1952, Aarón Joaquín came into the possession of fourteen hectares of land for his community on the east side of Guadalajara—well outside the urbanization zone set at Calle Felipe Angeles.[116] The area Aarón settled on was outside of the urbanization zone, it turns out, because construction of *fracciones* in this area of Guadalajara was prohibited. Because of the massive growth that had stretched into the west and east of the city, *fracciones* were limited to the north and south of Guadalajara.[117] Thus, two years after acquiring the land (while Rodríguez Barba continued to plant and harvest) the potential colonists approached Municipal President Jorge Matute Remus about their situation. The colonists argued that as a persecuted religious minority their safety and liberty hinged on settling on the land they had purchased.[118] Then, against all state and local laws of *fraccionamientos*, Matute Remus and the director of public works, Héctor Bracamontes, authorized the settlement of the area without the required accompanying *acta de cabildo* (pronouncement or approval of the municipal council). The agreement was directed to Aarón Joaquín and the Organization of the Hermanos de la Luz del Mundo and reads in part:

> [W]e concede permission . . . taking into account that:

> First: The need you have in resolving the problems of a social character created by problems in your neighborhood born of ideological conflicts of a Religious character that you say have caused you innumerable vexations;

> Second: That with the houses you propose to construct that you will solely resolve the problems of your associates and not attempt any profit-making endeavor;

Third: That you yourselves are obligated to pay for all urbanization improvements required in the material laws; and

Fourth: That you strictly confirm that you do not attempt to execute a *fraccionamiento* by converting undeveloped land into urban property with the end of offering it to the public, but that you build homes for each one of your members.

It then goes on to lay out certain conditions of the deal:

First: Each member of the Organization called the "Hermanos de la Luz del Mundo" must certify before this department your position as owner or legal proprietor of the lot over which you propose to build.

Second: Urbanization improvements will be carried out at the expense of the owner as cited in point three.

Third: You must carry out the following basic urban improvements:
1. Survey and leveling of streets
2. Sewage and electrification
3. Potable water network, pavement, and sidewalks

The aforementioned improvements can be constructed in steps and in the above order and must be finished within five years from this date.

Construction of homes may be carried out simultaneously with those of urbanization. . . .

In order to complete the public works mentioned in point three, this Organization agrees to present before this Department, in each case the plans, estimates, proposals, etc., corresponding.

When the members of said Organization, owners of the property mentioned in point three, fail to complete the improvements in the fixed time, the *Ayuntamiento* [municipal government] can carry them out according to the cooperative program established

by the law or at the exclusive expense of the remiss property owners and extract payment as indicated by the cooperative laws of
the Ley de Hacienda Municipal.

All contracts of buying-selling must contain the aspects of the
present authorization.

Any breach of the aforementioned agreement will result in the
declaration of null and void the present agreement.[119]

The letter is signed by Héctor Bracamontes, director of public works,
and dated November 12, 1954. The first colonists, two families, had already
taken up residence in the new community the previous month.

This agreement initiated a period of semi-covert existence for the *colonia* (neighborhood) that lasted until at least December of 1958. Contracts
of land deals with the city, such as the Cinco de Mayo market in the *colonia*,
even reveal that the original land purchase was not registered with civil
authorities until 1961.[120] Furthermore, the original agreement conceding
authority to LDM was not, as required by law, approved by the *cabildo*
or entered into the published *actas de cabildo*. A March 1954 list of *fraccionamientos* forwarded to the federal Department of Finance and Credit
(Hacienda y Crédito) carry no mention of the Hermosa Provincia proposal.[121] While this could have been a simple case of the approval date
coming after the request made by the federal government, similar lists from
1957 also fail to mention Hermosa Provincia.[122] Later publications by the
city on the creation of Hermosa Provincia do not acknowledge its existence
until after 1960.[123] Even public celebrations of patriotism and basic street
maps rarely mention the existence of the colony.[124] Either LDM failed to
live up to its end of the bargain to provide accurate plans or the city and
private parties involved in the urbanization of Guadalajara were only partially aware—and in some cases not at all aware—of the work going on in
Hermosa Provincia. Considering the state of Guadalajara urbanization in
the 1950s and the lack of filed plans of Hermosa Provincia in the municipal archive, it could be a case of both. In fact, Municipal President Matute
Remus declared in 1954 that no "exact plans" exist for the entire eastern
portion of the city contained in sectors Reforma and Libertad.[125]

The arrival of public services is another questionable area of Hermosa
Provincia's fulfillment of their agreement with the city. Contrary to the
assertion made by anthropologist Renée de la Torre that "in very little

time after the foundation of the colonia it had all public services," it took over six years to complete public services, though not without help.[126] The municipal president, Juan Gil Preciado, provided the *colonia* with the tubing needed for drainage, though the colonists themselves dug the system.[127] The ability of the colonists to complete the works on time also seems to be in question. While plans in the municipal archive record the intention of installing electricity in 1959, electricity did not arrive until January of 1960, three months after the deadline set by the agreement.[128] The colonists, however, did pay for the services at the cost of 142,816 pesos.

While de la Torre alleges that such cooperative actions were a product of an explicit and unusual pact between the state and the colonists to trade building permission for political favors, joint development projects between private parties and the city seem to be very common for the era—without the quid pro quo demands.[129] For example, de la Torre's coauthor, anthropologist Guillermo de la Peña, demonstrates that the group Catholic Action and the priest known as Padre Romo arranged for cooperative works to take place in the exclusive Catholic neighborhood of Santa Teresita.[130] Evidence in the *actas de cabildo* shows that through the 1950s, cooperative agreements between the city and neighborhood associations were common, including paving projects, drainage, and water.[131] And, unlike those of Hermosa Provincia, those projects were legally approved in the published *actas de cabildo*.

Help did not come from municipal authorities alone. Hermosa Provincia appears to have solicited outside aid when problems with different municipal departments did not seem to go their way. In June of 1957, a state legislator named Enrique Chavero Ocampo intervened on the part of the colonists regarding roads. Chavero Ocampo was an up-and-coming member of the state government, a permanent fixture in PRI power in Jalisco, and the future president of the state PRI apparatus. The request prompted a response from the public works department that the "colonos de Hermosa Provincia" make themselves present at the *ayuntamiento* "so as to resolve satisfactorily the road problems that affect the colony." No correspondence or *actas de cabildo* exist regarding the resolution of the request.[132] The need for intercession apparently decreased, for by August of 1959 the Association of Colonists of Hermosa Provincia started sending their inquiries and complaints directly to the public works department.[133]

Through such efforts as those elaborated above, the Hermosa Provincia grew into one of Guadalajara's most famous—and for those opposed to

LDM, infamous—neighborhoods. A cooperative exercise in both religion and citizenship, life in the Provincia became a model for dozens more such colonies around Mexico and in Central America.

LDM and Hermosa Provincia

After the efforts of the colonists to obtain a place to live out their religious and civic dreams, what was the resultant lifestyle? To understand what the community was like during Aarón's time merits examining the very choice of the name for its revelation of the hopes and desires of the colonists for their city.

The name is found in the reflection of King David and his psalms, specifically 48:2. Psalm 48 is part of a series of compositions for performance that starts in Psalm 42 and runs until Psalm 49, reflecting that the righteous are persecuted, while the wicked mock them. This mockery by evil quickly gives way in Psalm 45 to the glorious arrival of God—a chapter seen by Christians as a messianic psalm. In Psalms 46 and 47 God overwhelms the wicked, becomes king over the earth, and by the opening verses of Psalm 48 establishes the City of Zion. Due to translation differences, the name chosen for Hermosa Provincia makes more sense in the Spanish Bible used by LDM, specifically the Casiodoro de Reina translation (revised by Cipriano de Valera).[134] Psalm 48:2, as cited by LDM, reads as follows:

> Hermosa provincia, el gozo de toda / la tierra, / Es el Monte de Sion, a los lados / del norte / La Ciudad del gran Rey.[135]

The verse refers to Mount Zion—the Mountain of Light and the location of the City of David (Jerusalem) and the temple of Solomon.[136] Like all things scriptural, it also carries multilayered meanings, referring to actual, multiple temporal locations (past, present, and future) as well as to multiple symbolic meanings (past, present, and future). Thus, while the community of Hermosa Provincia is not actually referred to as the City of Zion, it is couched in verses that, for evangelical Christians, hold deep symbolism. For LDM, Hermosa Provincia is the location of their central temple with a status similar to Jerusalem. Indeed, as a simple illustrative device (to which members of LDM would probably object) I would draw a parallel with Mecca for Muslims. Hermosa Provincia is where members make a pilgrimage to participate in the annual Santa Cena celebration on August 14, and LDM itself makes the comparison to Guadalajara as a Vatican City for their organization.[137]

The position of this city, thus, has its feet in a world where the religious life has overcome the political and aspires to exist under the single kingship of the divine—the messianic city. As Psalm 48 continues in verses four and five, it declares:

Porque he aquí los reyes de la tierra se reunieron; / Pasaron todos. / Y viendo ellos así, se maravillaron / Se turbarón, se apresuraron a huir.[138]

The Hermosa Provincia is deeply associated with a messianic hope for the future when secular kings will marvel at what is accomplished in that community and even see the end of the worldly order of politics.

However, as the original registered name of the church (Iglesia Cristiana Espiritual) reflects, such cities and aspirations for the believers of LDM can only come to pass in a spiritual sense.[139] What believers can do in the physical sense, then, is to create a reflection or similarity in this life that will allow them to participate in the Kingdom of God in heaven after the Last Judgment and the destruction of the earth. But just getting to heaven was not enough of an end game. The gospel that LDM preached had to drastically alter and improve the society in which they existed.

With the construction of Hermosa Provincia, LDM specifically rejected vice, smoking, alcohol, drugs, cantinas, prostitutes, gangs, brothels, robbery, rape, street fights, laziness, vagrancy, unemployment, mendicancy, and illiteracy. Says Rentería, "Aarón showed that mysticism does not only consist in qualifying for the spiritual world of the gospel, but to insert into the personal life a touch of Christian action." This was to be accomplished in a "society free and egalitarian, but still exclusive."[140] While egalitarian is probably not the most exact depiction of life in the *colonia*, Hermosa Provincia did prove beneficial to the economic, physical, and social welfare of its inhabitants.

Hermosa Provincia and LDM provided affordable housing in the *colonia* for all of its members in Guadalajara.[141] Like the 12 de Octubre community, the living structures varied from modest houses to large single-family dwellings and multifamily apartments with shared patios.[142] From the construction of the homes to the streets that divided them, the members of LDM and Aarón worked side-by-side during construction, perhaps giving the group a sense of ownership that contributed to the colony's continuing cleanliness and order. For some members of the community, the participation in the construction of the *colonia* provided practical experience that they used to take them out of their lives as low-level workers to skilled workers.[143]

Indeed, the ability to improve employment skills and abilities is a constant theme with the *colonia*. Just as a cacique (village strongman) provides references and work for members of his village, Aarón (also a former school teacher) provided informal training, formal schooling, and connections that allowed an improved economic status for members of his group. One member recalls how, for those members too old or unable to take advantage of the opportunities provided by the colony, jobs were found in gathering cardboard to recycle or collecting dog feces for the tanning factories.[144] Businesses even developed within the community such as bakeries, stores, food stands, and a small packing company of salsa. The prosperity of the community hinged not upon a socialist experiment, but on small-scale capitalism and Christian charity; congregation members sold goods to nonmembers outside of the community, but did most of their own buying and selling among themselves. Thus, profits remained within the community and surpluses or profits could be used for the informal charity networks that existed among neighbors and families to help the poor and elderly.[145] Profits also returned to the body of the church as donations, further increasing the power and reach of the organization as a whole.

Gradual improvement in the quality of life also manifested itself in the falling stillborn-infant rate reflected in the civil registry statistics begun in 1959. According to the records, while the birthrate in the community increased by 307 percent over five years (1959 to 1964), the stillborn rate dropped from just over 10 percent to zero. This shows a marked improvement, as the 1959 figure shows a stillborn rate five times that of the rest of Guadalajara, though the colony had yet to construct its own hospital until after 1964.[146] Several factors could account for the improvement. Increased income and the attendant improved nutrition, improved living conditions, the lower presence of alcohol or narcotics that increase risk factors for newborn infants, or even a decrease in domestic abuse as part of a newfound moral code all could have played a role in improving birth statistics.

The colony also devoted itself to education. Through the efforts of Bible study and the arrival of state schools in Hermosa Provincia, the colony claims to be the first in Mexico certified as entirely free of illiteracy—a crusade of the revolutionary state from the beginning and a long-standing crusade for Mexican liberals.[147] LDM mirrors perfectly the image of the modernizing and progressive character that Mexico tried to develop both internally and as a demonstration to the world in the decade of the 1950s. The governor of Jalisco (1943–47), Marcelino García Barragán, cited *colonia* construction as a parallel alternative to distributing ejidal lands, and a way to carry out the *conquista economica* of outlying areas. Uncultivated land and *latifundios* (large estates) needed colonization, not ejidal division.[148] A colony like Hermosa Provincia, which backed those colonization ideals while eliminating illiteracy, must have served as a feather in the cap of Barragán.

In this era of development of Hermosa Provincia, the participation of LDM with the goals of the Jalisco Institutional Revolutionary Party (PRI) appears to go beyond the informal relations found in the earlier period of the church. Anthropologist Renée de la Torre claims that in the files of the *ramo de fraccionamientos* (the branch of Public Works concerned with private housing) in the municipal archive of Guadalajara, letters exist between Aarón and the municipal government that construct an explicit relationship of support between the PRI and LDM.[149] This correspondence reportedly lays out a clear quid pro quo exchange of LDM support for the ruling party in exchange for favors for the Christian church. However, subsequent investigations reveal no such letters.[150] The inability to locate the letters does not mean that they never existed. However, as Pozos Bravo discovered with her oral interviews, more often than not PRI voter fraud created the illusion of total LDM support for the party, just as it had done with all of Mexico.[151] For example, one of Pozos Bravo's informants recounts that after working the voting booth all day and seeing three voters, published results claimed 100 percent turnout for the PRI. Such actions on the part of city, state, or federal officials that benefit government agendas without the full understanding or even knowledge of those actions on the part of involved religious communities is not impossible. Consider the Brazilian case of Santa Brígida in Brazil where the elevation of that community to municipal status was hailed as the fulfillment of prophecy while behind it was a move by the congress to limit the powers of a populist president.[152] Despite it being their community, few in Santa Brígida seemed to understand the role their community played in local and national politics. In the case of LDM, while it is entirely *possible* that

the head of the patriarchal pyramid of LDM requested that his parish-
ioners vote for the PRI,[153] there may have been an even more important
conduit of relationship between LDM and the PRI: the Federación de
Organizaciones Populares de Jalisco, or FOPJ.

As part of the attempt to make the party of the revolution an all-
encompassing force that embraced all sectors of society, President
Manuel Ávila Camacho (1940–46) included a Confederación Nacional de
Organizaciones Populares (CNOP) in the new PRI. This organization
was to share power with the farmers, laborers, and politicians of the nation
as a representative of all groups that did not fall easily under the former
categories.[154] In other words, if any person sought to belong to a group of
people outside of the party, the CNOP existed to bring them back in.

Below the CNOP existed state organizations, and for the state of
Jalisco that was the FOPJ. Immediately following the state level, the
FOPJ contained various organizations of united business people, small
vendors, or poor urban residents.[155] These groups, known as *ligas* or
leagues, could provide contacts for jobs, support for candidates, resolve
property disputes, or provide access to important members of society.[156]
In Guadalajara, among these various *ligas*, existed the Liga Municipal de
Diversos 4 del Sector Libertad—the political arm of the PRI in Hermosa
Provincia. While Pozos Bravo argues that such organizations are part of
the dual nature of LDM membership and Mexican citizenship, it is difficult to see where LDM ends and the FOPJ begins. As anthropologist
Guillermo de La Peña observes, joining a group like LDM created "spaces
of intermediation in front of civil society and the government," and LDM
did this by infiltrating the party structure and keeping its feet both in
Caesar's and Jesus' domains.[157]

For example, the August 1959 Santa Cena celebration required a large
amount of provisions for the "various thousands of people" attending.
Thus, the FOPJ Liga 4 requested exceptions to urban sanitation regulations to butcher "four pigs daily" and the municipal presidency approved it
that same day.[158] Is it a request from the church requesting help organizing
Santa Cena celebrations? Or is it a request from a political arm of the PRI
on behalf of members that just happen to need to kill four pigs a day?

The August 1959 letter is informative for other reasons, as well. The
officers of the FOPJ Liga 4 reveal a veritable who's who of LDM leadership, as well as Aarón's relatives. The person in control of the financial
resources of the organization is Samuel Joaquín, Aarón's son and later

the head of LDM after Aarón's death. The secretary general of the Liga 4 is Ignacio Castañeda, the educated ex-seminarian turned LDM member, later to become secretary of LDM under Samuel.[159] Cornelio Mozqueda Melgoza, Aarón's son-in-law, took charge of the secretariat of Social Action, while Aarón's daughter, Ana María, took charge of the women's organization. While it was an absolute right for members of LDM to belong to the FOPJ, it also formalized the relationships proportioned by Aarón's connections. For example, the former advocate of the community, Enrique Chavero Ocampo, was listed as the organizational secretary for the FOPJ of all Jalisco by 1960.[160]

In consequence, the combined efforts of the church and *liga* concentrated in one neighborhood the power and influence that other neighborhoods did not have, inasmuch as their memberships in sectoral and not spatial organizations diffused their power. The correspondence of the municipal archive of Guadalajara shows no direct correspondence between citizens residing in Hermosa Provincia and the municipal government, while it does show petitions delivered to the city via the party organ of the FOPJ. LDM citizens could essentially "bulk" their complaints via a single representative (with party connections) that clearly represented the whole community of Hermosa Provincia while citizens in other neighborhoods could shower the municipal palace with correspondence and petitions from different groups with a multitude of complaints for decades and still receive no response.

For example, while the Colonia Ferrocarril, a workers' community near the rail yard of southern Guadalajara, was founded in the 1930s, it failed to receive the most basic of services until the mid- or late 1950s. As a matter of fact, after five years without services, a 1935 commission of neighbors sent a letter to the city of Guadalajara requesting to be annexed as part of that municipality, assuming that their poor treatment had been because they belonged to one of the outlying areas. The reply from Guadalajara? They already were part of Guadalajara. Colonia Ferrocarril also lacked the clout to get cantinas removed, as LDM had done near its own colony, even after reporting constant public urination by male customers, excessive noise, fighting, and the frequent discharge of firearms.[161] The police, they said, had refused to do anything. This is not surprising when those same police—a service the Colonia Ferrocarril had waited over a decade to receive—were clients of the cantina where they would get drunk, then leave to shake down or assault passing residents.[162] Members

of Ferrocarril, though mostly members of various unions, did not have
the added layers of an FOPJ *liga* and the informal relationships needed to
thrive in the world of mid-century Mexican politics.

The Death of a Prophet and the Birth of a Basketball Court

Probably the most controversial interaction between the Hermosa
Provincia and the local government was the burial of Aarón within the
colonia. In the winter of 1964, while in Mexico City en route to Central
America, the self-proclaimed apostle of God suffered a severe heart
attack and his health deteriorated until his death on June 9, 1964. While
the funeral was attended by thousands of members of LDM, as well as
"public and military functionaries," the pomp and circumstance of the
day was interrupted, according to the official narrative, by something of
a crisis.

Rentería claims that no cemetery in the city of Guadalajara would
receive the body: "Those in charge of the civil cemeteries refused to appor-
tion an adequate area for the remains of Hermano Aarón and other *hermanos*, arguing that there was 'no space.'" Rentería acknowledges that there
was a failed attempt before Aarón's death to acquire their own LDM cemetery because of restrictions on explicitly religious sections of cemeteries.
Was this a further request denied for a group cemetery? Or, considering
the massive monument the group's apostle did receive, was it a rejection
of a grand mausoleum? Or, like past incidences of discrimination, had
unspoken Catholic biases worked to exclude the "apostle of God" from a
burial? LDM certainly favors the latter reason, and they appealed this lat-
est round of what they felt was discrimination against their patron to the
state governor's office.[163] And what was the result of this conference with
the governor? "A miracle!"[164] The miracle came in the form of a phone
call from the governor to the municipal authorities demanding a special
provision allowing Aarón's burial in Hermosa Provincia—a *colonia* that
had no cemetery. This exception, a seeming violation of Mexican health
and sanitation laws, has been at the center of a much-heated debate for
decades. Rentería claims that the oral agreement was for a municipal cemetery within the Hermosa Provincia. Then, when the body of the apostle
had been interred, the cemetery was to be declared closed. Aarón Joaquín
received his own exclusive cemetery, complete with a massive Carrara-
marble headstone with gold letters.

A reading of the concessionary contract reveals something of a different story. The contract with the municipality states that on June 11 (a day before Rentería says the request was made), Rebeca Joaquín de Mozqueda (Aarón's daughter) and her husband, Cornelio Mozqueda Melgoza, were donating four lots of land (2,500 square meters) to the city in order to build a municipal cemetery. They argue that this was necessary because there were no cemeteries on their side of Guadalajara and it was a hardship for the people of Hermosa Provincia to carry their dead to other cemeteries. They offered land, however, only if the city would allow exclusive burial rights to all residents of Hermosa Provincia.[165] That a municipal cemetery would be provided for an exclusive religious or cultural group when state regulations controlled all burial grounds is not entirely without precedence. Guadalajara does have an exclusive Jewish cemetery, and the "Japanese Colony" of the city was allowed a sizable portion of the Panteón Nuevo for the exclusive burial of those of Japanese descent.[166] The land, however, is owned by the municipality, though apportioned exclusively to the aforementioned groups; and those cemeteries house more than one person. If the burial ground had gone on to become an LDM burial plot for all members, little controversy might have ensued. However, no one else was ever buried in the expansive area.

At this point, the tale of Aarón's burial takes a twist into the complicated relationships of a *telenovela*. According to contracts from the municipal archive, after Aarón's death LDM informed Guadalajara that the city's failure to develop the land into a full cemetery had voided the contract and that the land now devolved back to the Mozqueda family, who would offer to preserve it in its state as a memorial garden. In a turn of munificence, however, LDM would offer to pay for the land that was now being returned to the church—with the caveat that the money be used to build a sports center on the edge of the colony.[167]

In essence, LDM arranged for a private resting place for Aarón by using loopholes in the law. Then, by coupling those loopholes with a demand that the city abide strictly by laws, they arranged for a sports center complete with a full basketball court to be constructed on the edge of the community. Open to surrounding neighbors, it provided not only a place for LDM youth and adults to solidify their own community experience but it could also be used to make contacts for proselytizing nonmembers.

In a final twist, the money for the sports center purchased land from José Guadalupe Zuno, former governor of Jalisco, who had just purchased the land one year before (from the prominent Barba family) and had sold a portion of it to his son, Rubén Zuno Arce, just months before the LDM offer to buy the land from the city.[168] Consequently, the land deal profited both the powerful Zuno and his extended family. Did Zuno know about the impending deal? If Rentería is correct, and LDM had no intention of using the area as a community cemetery, the most cynical point of view could see it as a simple land scheme. LDM got both the private cemetery for their founder and a sports center, while several ruling PRI families made a tidy profit on a land purchase from the city. Thinking of this as a questionable land deal is not an unthinkable proposition, considering that Rubén Zuno Arce was also brother-in-law to the secretario de gobernación (secretary of the interior), in 1968, and future president of Mexico, Luís Echeverría. The character of the deal falls further into question when one considers the extensive criminal ties of Zuno Arce. In 1990, he was charged in the United States for "racketeering, kidnapping conspiracy, and aiding and abetting the 1985 kidnap-murder of US Drug Enforcement Administration agent Enrique Camarena."[169] Zuno Arce was convicted in 1992. LDM's business associates had come a long way from the sympathetic tip-offs from local police officers to this land swap involving PRI power brokers with connections at the highest levels of Mexican society, marking the beginning of the rise of a Luz del Mundo presence on a national level.[170]

Conclusion

LDM claims that the reason its founder sought to build the exclusive community at Calle 12 de Octubre, and then later in the Hermosa Provincia, was to protect the congregation from religious persecution. Ironically, the very state he supported was failing to provide those basic protections, driving LDM out of greater Mexican society. However, due to the bitter divisions existing between Catholics and Protestants in Mexico, exacerbated by the violence of the armed 1920s and 1930s, the former *constitucionalista* soldier Aarón had already cast his lot with the newly founded ruling party—in his mind the great counterbalance to Catholic power. Instead of protesting the failure of the state to protect his congregation as citizens, he burrowed deeper into the party structure for protection by joining the FOPJ, a beneficial move that extended the apostle's own connections to his congregations in over one hundred Mexican cities and in twenty-three Mexican states at his death in 1964.

There simply existed no other method of protection than to join the party and then use the organization of the church as a mediating power with a state that professed secular goals and had long ago come to a pragmatic détente with conservative Catholicism—two points LDM chose to ignore because of the long-standing mindset and revolutionary claims of the state to stand above Catholic interference in society. This mediating power with the state and the intentional communities formed by the state's failure to protect, however, helps explain the success of LDM. With so many poor and weak immigrants attracted to the movement, they could find a patron that could navigate a confusing political situation, preserve their religious beliefs, and provide a shelter for the vagaries of modern urban life.

The ambivalence and selective application of the Mexican rule of law allowed all three groups—Catholics, Pentecostals, and politicians—to share the same strange bed. Indeed, even had LDM sought to oppose the state for its lack of protections, they would have found their only allies in two groups their theology rejected even more bitterly: left-wing Catholics and the weak socialist and communist opposition.[171] Instead, LDM continued to utilize the moments of historic tension between the Catholic Church and the state as foils for their own argument that they were the most authentic Mexicans, as defined by the PRI.

For example, in 1987 the convergence of two events provided the LDM with an opening on the national stage to voice their claim to being ideal citizens for the republic. The most important at the time was a debate on the national stage in which the National Action Party (PAN)—generally associated with a history of strong support from conservative Catholics— charged the PRI with fraud in several 1986 gubernatorial elections. Furthermore, a movement within the PRI itself, known as the Democratic Current, questioned the methods and policies of the ruling party as the nation prepared for what would be a hotly contested 1988 presidential election. The second occurrence was the visit of Pope John Paul II to San Francisco, California, in which the pope called for religious tolerance. The LDM responded to the criticism of their patron, the PRI, as well the pope's speech with a biting letter to the Mexico City daily *Excélsior.* In what de la Torre calls an "appropriation of national values," LDM lays out why they are true Christians and good Mexicans, as opposed to Mexican Catholics (and perhaps even Protestants).[172]

In the letter, LDM argues their place as the nation's most authentically Mexican religion by pointing to the indigenous roots of the group's founder, the LDM total respect for national symbols and holidays, as well as the similarities between Aarón and liberal reformer Benito Juárez. LDM pointedly contrasts what they see as their own respect for Mexican culture and freedom of worship with that of the Catholic Church, whom they attack for not only the Inquisition and the religious wars of Europe but also for the "Spanish" and "Roman" racist attempt to defile the "true architectural jewels" of Mexico's pyramids by building on top of them a "rubbish heap of foreign architecture" (*bodrio de arquitectura extranjera*). Most pertinent for the period of the late 1980s and the increasing challenges to PRI power, LDM maintained that while Catholic churches were simple fronts for political meetings where priests "inflamed the masses with haranguing speeches of a political nature," LDM churches "serve exclusively for the exposition of religious positions."[173] Over sixty years after the founding of LDM by a former constitutionalist soldier, who himself had suffered persecution from both state representatives and the citizenry of Mexico, LDM employed their founder's tactic of drawing attention to the faults of greater enemies of the state (Catholicism, opposition parties) while pointing out the benefits LDM had to offer *la patria*— loyal followers of the revolution (as defined by the PRI), made that way by the legitimizing hand of God himself. As the storms of political challenge raged about the PRI, the LDM clung to an increasingly less protective harbor in the shelter of the ruling party in 1988.

Not all intentional religious communities, however, would seek to burrow so deeply into the structure of the state. As we will see in chapter 2, with the community of Colonia Industrial de la Nueva Jerusalén, existing on the periphery of the state could provide as much or more shelter than crowding into the center.

CHAPTER TWO

The Fullness of the Kingdom of God and the New Jerusalem

✛ IN THE SUMMER OF 1901, Margarito Bautista Valencia lay dying in his father's house in Atlautla, Mexico, a small village in southeast Mexico State. Unable to work or leave his bed for six months, the unidentified illness troubled Bautista's family, and relative Juana Páez called for a member of her church to minister to Margarito. Ammon M. Tenney, a gringo missionary for the Church of Jesus Christ of Latter-day Saints (LDS, or Mormons) came to the home of the twenty-three-year-old and "administered" to him. Bautista's health quickly improved, and by November, he abandoned his brief dalliance with Methodism and other unspecified denominations, permanently left behind Catholicism, and walked eighty miles to Cuernavaca, Morelos, where he requested baptism at an LDS conference.[1]

While Margarito Bautista's story appears to be a standard story of a Latin American peasant on the "straight path to Americanization" through conversion to Mormonism (as sociologist of religion David Martin argues), Bautista's experience does not bear that out.[2] As his exposure to Mormonism broadened and his participation deepened, so too did Bautista's devotion to the nationalism of reconstruction and consolidation

63

during the presidencies of Sonorans Álvaro Obregón and Plutarco Elías Calles. As a result, Bautista ended both his conversion to Mormonism and the Sonoran revolution by arguing that while Mormonism made him a better Mexican, the revolution as well as his indigenous heritage made him a far better Mormon than even the gringo missionaries that converted him. In the shadow of revolutionary reconstruction, the absence of the rule of law, and the struggle for modernization, Bautista eventually carved out his own Mormon community in Mexico State, independent of the mainline LDS Church in the United States, but also free of tight supervision by state and local authorities, where adherents successfully reconciled their religion, indigenous identity, and nationalism with their revolutionary fervor.

Missionaries: Mormons in Mexico and Mexicans in Utah

Margarito Bautista Valencia was born to a bilingual (Nahua and Spanish) peasant family in San Miguel de Atlautla, Mexico State, on June 10, 1878.[3] Though raised Catholic, he met frequently with a local Mexican Methodist minister. Said Bautista of Methodism, "I soon found the confusion of the sectarian world in their ideas and creeds. I did enjoy their education, their beautiful language, their polished manners, but when they left I was just as empty in principles as I was before."[4] Then Bautista met Ammon Tenney.

Almost fourteen years earlier, a delegation of seven missionaries from the Church of Jesus Christ of Latter-day Saints entered Mexico at El Paso, Texas, in January of 1876.[5] Securing permission to proselytize, the LDS Church set to work as missionaries in central Mexico and later established colonies of Anglo Mormons in the northern states of Chihuahua and Sonora. Among those seven missionaries was a young man named Ammon M. Tenney, who, by the time he met Margarito Bautista in 1901, had grown into a prominent member of the Mexican LDS community.[6] His efforts brought Bautista into the LDS Church at a time when it had grown to over a dozen congregations throughout central Mexico.

Immediately after Bautista's baptism, Tenney reports that the new convert was functioning in various positions, such as secretary to Tenney, and even—just ten days after baptism—as a missionary in the area. By December 1901, he was listed as an "elder" and was delivering sermons at meetings.[7] Consider for a moment the new position of Margarito Bautista. In just a matter of weeks he went from an ill, nominally Catholic peasant living in the home of his parents (along with his wife) to preaching a new gospel that empowered him to wield the same power with which Tenney had healed him that summer.

Although Protestantism offers individuals direct access to the sacred, Mormonism believes it takes divine access beyond that offered by Protestantism, pointing to the story of the group's founder, Joseph Smith Jr., and other members who claimed that one could not only receive answers to prayers without clerical intercession but could also commune directly, face-to-face, with Jesus Christ.[8] As for the authority offered Bautista, it was conferred as part of Mormonism's claimed genealogy of priesthood directly from the hands of Jesus' twelve apostles.[9] For Bautista, these Mormon promises may have been both enticing and empowering.

By 1903 Bautista and his wife, Juana, participated in the marriage ceremony the LDS Church denotes as the highest ordinance necessary for "eternal progression," an act in LDS belief that can qualify men and women as couples (and only as couples) to become like God.[10] Again, the direct contact with divinity that Mormonism promises the faithful takes access to the sacred far beyond the other groups with which Bautista had contact. From peasant to a god in embryo in two years—quite a leap for any person, let alone a peasant subject to the positivist ideas of turn-of-the-century Porfirian Mexico that judged religious belief and indigenous status as both obsolete and backward.

In 1903, the loss of part of his family's land to the local *hacendado* (landowner) dimmed Bautista's economic prospects, and he moved with his wife to the largely Anglo LDS community of Colonia Dublán in Chihuahua, Mexico. While there, he farmed successfully and mastered English.[11] Living in Colonia Dublán in 1903, however, educated Bautista not only in language and agriculture but in plural marriage and cooperative community as well.

At the turn of the century, the Anglo Mormon colonies in Mexico were transitioning from polygyny—a practice banned by the church in 1890.[12] This ban did not dissolve existing marriages, as the United States government demanded, but simply attempted (with varying levels of success) to halt new plural marriages. As historian Jan Shipps observes, the U.S. government confiscation of LDS property between 1887 and

1890—both corporate and private—and the ultimatum that the Mormons
comply with the government or be erased from existence sent ripples of
fear through the Mormon U.S. West.[13] Consequently, polygynous families residing in the United States fled to colonies in Alberta, Canada, and
northern Mexico, or they kept their plural-wife families in the foreign
colonies while maintaining a single-wife family in the Rocky Mountain
West.[14] The community bond and sense of identity from plural marriage
made many Mormons loath to abandon the practice, and the LDS Church
was not able to control the marriages until the early 1920s.[15] Bautista's
exposure to the colony's polygyny came at a time when the practice was
not a thing of the past for members of the LDS Church in Mexico, but part
of a lively debate, as much able to be practiced as rejected—a major plank
in his later platform for reviving plural marriage.

Bautista also came to the colonies when the financial mission of the
LDS Church still influenced the lives of members. LDS Church business
ownership supported the organization and allowed it to remain a volun-
tary structure while stimulating member-owned enterprises—a practice
that stretched back to the 1830s.[16] This focus on the total community of
spirituality and economics was still an important, if toned down, tenet of
the faith during Margarito Bautista's time in the Mormon colonies. Said
Joseph F. Smith, president of the LDS Church at the time Bautista first
joined, "A religion which has not the power to save people temporally
and make them prosperous and happy here, cannot be depended upon to
save them spiritually, to exalt them in the life to come."[17] The economic
aid of the community also bound Mormons together. As Smith said, in
1893, communities prepare for both natural and manmade disasters "by
studying and carrying out the principles of true economy in our lives,
and by a system of fraternity and love by which each one will help his
brother, and all stand united, so that none suffer from want when it is
within the power of others to alleviate it."[18] Bautista experienced only the
end of Mormonism's total economic influence, however, as pressure from
the U.S. Congress on the LDS Church to withdraw from Utah economics
rippled through the church in general.[19]

Speaking of these practices, and of early Mormonism in general,
anthropologist Lawrence Foster writes that there was a

sense of passionate involvement, camaraderie, and enthusiasm of
selfless Mormon dedication to achieving the supremely important

goal of realizing the Kingdom of Heaven on Earth, and a willingness, as in the ritual process, to follow trusted leaders implicitly in
doing whatever they might demand.[20]

For Bautista, entering into the LDS faith at this time when the church
was integrating rather than withdrawing from society must have been jar-
ring. Having lost his own worldly kingdom in Atlautla, Bautista was seeking a protective spiritual home, not a mechanism to catapult him back into
the world. His later withdrawal from the church makes sense when one
considers the context of this transitional period, Bautista's own personal
trials, and the hope provided by the great upheaval of revolution.

By 1912, the Mormon colonies could not hold back the tide of the
Mexican Revolution that until that point had passed them by. The U.S.
American presence in Chihuahua and Sonora dismayed anti-U.S. Mexican
factions, but, according to historian F. LaMond Tullis, their propensity
to supply followers of Pancho Villa led to more persecution from federal
forces than rebels. However, by 1912, the Mormons fell under the threats
of General Pascual Orozco, an evangelical Protestant and anti-*villista*, and
his subordinate José Inéz Salazar. Faced with Salazar's cannons, the Anglo
colonists surrendered their weapons, dissolved their militia, and retreated
to Arizona.[21] Given the choice to remain in Mexico or flee north, Margarito
Bautista moved to Arizona in 1913 and then to Utah soon after.

While in Utah, Bautista threw himself into ecclesiastical service,
though his employment during the time is unknown. Much of his church
work included an intense investigation of his and other Mexicans' gene-
alogies as part of a key LDS doctrine that allows living members to perform essential ordinances, such as baptism, for deceased family members.
In addition, he aided in the founding of the first Spanish-language congregation in Salt Lake City.[22] Bautista also attained a measure of ecclesiastical fame, publishing his biography in the LDS Church magazine
Improvement Era under the title "A Faith Promoting Experience, by
M. Bautista, a Descendant of Father Lehi." The story recounted how
Bautista had chosen Mormonism over Protestantism through spiritual
experiences and reasserted his personal convictions of the benefit of LDS
doctrine to him as a "Descendant of Father Lehi."[3] Lehi is a figure in the
Book of Mormon (an LDS book of scripture) who, according to the book,
led a band of Israelites to the Americas, and it is from him that Bautista
claimed descent. The LDS Church displayed Bautista's experience as an

exemplar of Mormonism's success and a model for other Mormons. Such was Bautista's charisma and leadership that members of the Spanish-speaking congregation in Salt Lake City even rejected other leadership when Bautista returned to Mexico.[24]

In November of 1922, Bautista traveled to Mexico as a full-time missionary, leaving his wife and children in Utah. He returned to central Mexico during President Álvaro Obregón's (1920–24) consolidation of power, becoming an adherent of Obregón and his vision for a modern Mexico based on agricultural efficiency. Ever the pragmatist—with a résumé that included undefeated general, small landowner, and inventor—Obregón's rhetoric could match many of the varied currents that emerged from the armed struggle of the revolution. Bautista, however, focused on his discussions of the rise of an industrious, if not entirely industrial, state geared to benefit both the working class and those with entrepreneurial spirit, supposedly free from the corruption of the Porfirio Díaz regime. A perfect example is Obregón's speech before Mexican leaders of banking, commerce, industry, and agriculture at the beginning of his presidency on December 5, 1920, in Mexico City:

> We believe that the most effective manner to carry out national reconstruction is by providing all manner of aid and security to men of capital and action so that they will develop our natural resources, without, of course, abusing the just desires for financial betterment of all the working classes who have rights as well.[25]

In a 1920 booklet, President Obregón (*ciudadano*, or Citizen Obregón, as he is called) even promotes "evolved" modern farming backed by capital investment to "make the earth produce maximum returns with minimum investment and permit farmers to pay very high wages and sell grains at very low prices. The direct consequence of this is to favor the welfare of the workers."[26]

Obregón's ability to deliver on those promises of development is of little consequence to this study, but the influence of such rhetoric on Margarito Bautista most certainly is. Of the president, Bautista would later write, "President Obregón was an idol of the nation. His effort and force to pull Mexico from chaos and put it on the road to progress was felt around the world. Even from the grave he cries, 'Follow me.'"[27] In other words, Bautista's politics were explicitly nationalist and sympathetic to the Sonoran constitutionalist cause of agricultural and industrial capitalist modernization, as well as sympathetic to their anti-Catholic ideals.

Indeed, Bautista was present in Mexico during the 1923 Obregón expulsion of the papal legate, Ernesto Filippi, for violating Mexican restrictions on religion by serving in a clerical position without holding Mexican citizenship. To the objections of the Roman Catholic Church, Obregón pragmatically replied that any friction between church and state could be eliminated with "a little effort" from the Catholic Church.[28] In fact, according to Obregón, the effort of the state to address social problems

> affects in no way the fundamental program of the Catholic Church, and though they are not entirely parallel, they complement each other in essence; and if we conclude that the social program of the Government, born of the Revolution, is essentially Christian and is complementary to the fundamentals of the Catholic Church, it is surely not necessary for more than a little sincerity and good faith in men . . . [engaged] in a work that is entirely pious.[29]

The president went on to state that any problem that the Catholic Church had with the programs of the revolution were only due to the difference between Catholic "theory and practice." Obregón presents a strategic marriage between Christianity and the revolution, with the only apparent divide coming from the ill will of foreigners and those in positions of power— positions that certainly influenced Bautista's views, as we shall see.

In 1924, Bautista completed his missionary assignment and returned to the United States carrying with him his new boosterism for the consolidating revolution. His political stand for the Mexican project of modernization and reconstruction came into play in, of all places, Salt Lake City in 1926. Bautista witnessed the debate between Roman Catholic priest Reverend Duane G. Hunt and LDS apostle and long-time Mexican resident, Anthony W. Ivins, over the role of the Mexican state and the Catholic Church. Ivins incited the wrath of Hunt and the *Salt Lake Tribune* by stating in public (at a community service organization luncheon) that the Catholic Church needed to remove itself from the internal politics of Mexico. Calling upon Fray Pedro de Gante, conquistador Bernal Díaz, nineteenth-century Catholic missionary Abbe Emanuel Domenech,[30] and others on the theme of Roman Catholic influence in Mexico, Ivins argued that the revolution lessened the influence of Catholicism in Mexico.

According to Ivins, the state had the ultimate right to defend its sovereignty, even against competing powers like the Catholic Church.[31]

Hunt responded via the *Salt Lake Tribune* that the LDS Church would never abide similar treatment and that should such a thing happen to "the saints" (Mormons), the Catholic Church and the LDS Church should stand together to oppose such persecution.[32] For Hunt, the Mexican Revolution was a step back for Mexico and society in general. After hearing these arguments, the returned missionary Bautista embarked on a new mission—to win converts to *obregonismo* and *callismo* in Utah. Contrary to Hunt's beliefs, Margarito saw the revolution as an "evolution," and any opposition to the central state was pushing against the "evolutionary wheel."[33] He submitted his reply to Hunt to the *Salt Lake Tribune*, which the paper refused to publish. Bautista then approached the LDS Church–owned *Deseret News*, a rival of the *Tribune*, which published his rebuke of Father Hunt. Thereafter, he toured Utah speaking against Hunt and for anticlerical president Plutarco Elías Calles, whom he called a "guide and sentinel."[34] This placed Bautista's politics squarely in the nationalist, modernizing camp of the regime ruling Mexico at the time. For Bautista, Calles's anticlerical moves were not "anti-religious" but a means to break the Catholic Church in Mexico and create the freedom of religion found in a liberal republic. According to Bautista, Calles and the revolution "made our hearts as free as the flowers of the field."[35]

By the end of the 1920s, Bautista considered himself as part of what he called the "great army" of "External Mexico," engaged in a battle to thwart betrayers of the revolution—defined as those who disagreed with Obregón or Calles. In other words, Bautista saw all Mexicans residing outside of Mexico in solidarity as long as they supported the cause of the Calles government. Said Bautista of himself and other "exiled" Mexicans (Bautista did not differentiate between the self-exiled and political exiles): "Perhaps all of us that for so long have formed External Mexico understand, appreciate, and truly love our nation." This solidarity did not include exiles who rejected the Sonoran generals, such as intellectual José Vasconcelos, whom Bautista considered bitter and "satanic" for his opposition to President Calles.[36]

So the stage was set. Bautista solidly supported Mexico under the guidance of the northern generals-turned-politicians, like Álvaro Obregón and Plutarco Elías Calles, and their policies of modernization. He combined that notion with Mormonism's intense focus on the divine position of the

Americas as the site of Christianity's "restoration" and the future site of the New Jerusalem, or capital of Christ's millennial reign. In addition, he also steeped himself in the doctrines of genealogy, cooperative communities, and open revelation from the heavens, setting the foundation for his later activities in central Mexico. For Bautista, the ideal community would be an agricultural colony, bound together by religion, reciprocal economic cooperation, polygyny, ancestry, and the glorious future of both Mormonism and Mexico.

The Evolution of Mexico and the Destiny of America

While in Utah, Bautista busied himself with activities other than speaking tours and thwarting the enemies of the revolution. Beginning some time in the "late twenties" and concluding in early 1935, Bautista penned a nearly six-hundred-page book—*La evolución de México, sus verdaderos progenitores y su origen: El destino de América y Europa.*[37]

An eclectic mix of nineteenth-century religious and secular sources, the book is not only a defense of the Mexican Revolution and the ensuing reconstruction, but it also claims that those events are all just a manifestation of Mexico's greater role in God's plan to restore true Christianity to the world. Using nineteenth-century Porfirian Mexican scholars Gregorio Torres Quintero and Luis Pérez Verdía, known for their nationalist views of Mexican education and history, Bautista paints the conquest of the Americas as a base exercise in the "right of force" that brought little benefit to the Americas.[38] For Bautista, even principles such as democracy were not imported from Europe but sprang from an indigenous tradition, as was evidenced in the rise of the indigenous president and restorer of democracy Benito Juárez, whom he refers to as "inspired by God" and "a great Law giver."[39]

Interestingly, Bautista does not comment on the indigenous ancestry of the dictator Porfirio Díaz, who ruled without effective democracy for thirty-four years before the Mexican Revolution of 1910. This diversion, as he refers to the reign of Díaz, was not only a slap in the face of Mexico, but in the face of God as well. He refers to it as the "national mockery," and not only for the lack of democracy but also for the lack of benefits to Mexicans, as opposed to foreign capitalists.[40] As a result of this deviation from democracy and material benefits for the population, Bautista argues that a time of "regeneration and renovation" was necessary, and this was

brought about by the Mexican Revolution—restoring Mexico to democracy. This, of course, was all part of God's grand plan where "America
and not Europe is predestined to bring forth from its bowels the light of
eternal life, and immaculately go forth to all the nations of the earth."[41] As
he says of the combined religio-political message of Mexico, "Let us make
an effort that we can call totally NATIONAL, first to redeem our nation
from its condition, and then to enlarge our sweet and beloved *patria*."[42]

Now, consider this nationalist and religious proclamation in the light
of the secularizing state as discussed in chapter 1. Such rhetoric of secular nationalism placed more than Mexican Catholics in a quandary. How
could Mormons like Bautista maintain devotion to the state and still be
associated with a foreign church whose headquarters rested on confiscated Mexican soil and whose highest ecclesiastical figures were Anglos?
Mexican Mormon Margarito Bautista had such questions in mind when
he penned his reflections in *El destino de América y Europa*. Bautista did not
seek to live comfortably with multiple conflicting identities, but to reconcile them, and in order to do so, he found a middle ground from which he
could be both Mexican and Mormon. The answer for him lay in history,
prophecy, race, and the language of restoration as used by Mormonism.

Bautista sought guidance from the LDS text called the Book of
Mormon. Believers see the book as a record kept by ancient inhabitants
of the Americas that LDS prophet Joseph Smith Jr. translated. The
Book of Mormon states that around 600 BC, several families fleeing the
destruction of Jerusalem landed in an unspecified location in the Americas.
These families soon divided into two, called Nephites and Lamanites, that
alternately mixed and fought for centuries until, after his resurrection and
ascension to heaven, Jesus Christ descended to teach because they were
a "remnant of Israel."[43] Eventually, both abandoned their "Christian"
practices for idolatry, with the Lamanites finally destroying the Nephites.
According to LDS belief, these Lamanites are the ancestors, either in whole
or in part, of Native Americans.[44] Said Bautista of the Book of Mormon:

> I feel that the Book of Mormon is one of the most glorious books
> on earth, because from that holy book I have become acquainted
> with my ancestry, the dealings of the Lord with them, and the
> glorious promises to them in the near future, although because

of transgression we have suffered the wrath of the Almighty for centuries until the present day. The nations of the world should profit by our experience.[45]

Relevant to his own indigenous heritage, Bautista saw the Lamanites as his direct ancestors.

Margarito seized on this story and took it several steps beyond the official LDS position, saying, "The victorious Lamanites, who with the passage of time were known as Chichimecs or Aztecs . . . arrived in the Valley of Mexico and majestically constructed the great city of Tenochtitlan."[46] Bautista, then, tapped into Mexican nationalist notions of Aztec glorification that focused on the past in order to predict a glorious future. Bautista even reported these beliefs in a 1935 secular Conference on Pre-Hispanic History, held in Yucatan.[47] But what of Bautista's Christian identity, would that not suffer with his Lamanite ancestors as rejecters of his beliefs?

According to the Book of Mormon, the Lamanite rejection of Christianity was not a permanent state of apostasy, for Book of Mormon prophecy stated: "Then shall the remnant of our seed know concerning us, how that we came out from Jerusalem . . . and the gospel of Jesus Christ shall be declared among them; wherefore they shall be restored unto the knowledge of their fathers, and also unto the knowledge of Jesus Christ, which was had among their fathers."[48] For Bautista, the arrival of Ammon Tenney and the other LDS missionaries fulfilled that prophecy, restoring the lost knowledge of pure Christianity. But wasn't the arrival of the Spanish with their Roman Catholicism a possible fulfillment of that prophecy? Again, Bautista turned to the Book of Mormon.

For Mormons, after the death of the original twelve apostles of Christ, Christianity entered a state of corruption.[49] Consequently, according to Bautista, the Catholic Church had only a portion of truth but not the entire "fullness of truth." In his view Protestantism, whose roots lay in the reformation of Roman Catholicism, had even fewer claims to "truth" than Catholicism—being nothing more than branches off an already rotted tree of religious practice. With this in mind, the Book of Mormon states that "gentiles" (pre-Mormon European Christians) would arrive in the Americas and that the Lamanites they found there would be "driven before the Gentiles and . . . smitten."[50] According to Bautista, the fall of the Americas to Spain is a fulfillment of that Book of Mormon prophecy and came not as a product of Spanish valor, but by the Indians' failure to remember their ancestry as children of the House of Israel.⁵¹ However, eventually the descendants of this branch of Israel would return to a preferential position after there was a restoration of the true Christian doctrines and the conversion of European Christians to that doctrine.⁵² This restoration, for the LDS, occurred with the divine revelations reported by Joseph Smith Jr., whose teachings heavily stress notions of restoration and renewal. For Bautista, this made the redemption of "his people" possible, as he could simultaneously embrace Christianity while explaining the centuries of discrimination and destruction that Catholic Christians had carried out on indigenous Mexicans.⁵³ In his own mind, he was not only simultaneously indigenous, Christian, and Mexican, but he was the most authentic expression of all three.⁵⁴

Bautista's actions of intertwining theology and politics with group identity matches well with Mormonism, for, as scholar Jan Shipps points out, such an act is the very basis of Mormonism. Compare what Shipps says about U.S. Mormons to Bautista's actions:

> Just as the outcome of the American Revolution had left former English colonists without a usable political history, by designating all existing churches—not just the Roman Catholic variety— as corrupt abominations growing out of a "Great Apostasy" that began in the days of the ancient apostles, the Book of Mormon left the Saints with an enormous 1,400 to 1,800-year lacuna in their religious history.⁵⁵

Bautista was in the same position following the Mexican Revolution and with his conversion to Mormonism. He essentially had a clean historical slate on which he could fill in his ancestry—physical, spiritual, and political—and fit it comfortably to his *mexicanidad*, *mormonismo*, and *indigenismo*. The Book of Mormon, Mormon doctrines, and the modernizing nationalist rhetoric in Mexico allowed him to do so. This history paints Europeans not as authors of Christianity but as "corruptors that introduce chaos into society." According to Bautista, with the independence movement of Father Miguel Hidalgo in 1810, however, a free space was started where eventually the "Moses of Mexico," Juárez, would allow freedom of religion and set Mexico on the course to fulfilling its destiny as a base for the spread of true Christianity to the rest of the world. "Europe that never had the privilege to know true Christianity, only a copy," would then receive the truth from Mexican envoys.[56] In fact, the idea of Mexicans as descendants of Israel gave that group the rights of primogeniture directly from God, not Catholic Europe and those converted by its missionaries.[57] As for the Jews, they "expected a Messiah, but were sleeping" when Christ came and lost their position, though they could still repent and follow.[58] His road of historical convenience and construction of memory is very much like that undertaken by the Mexican national state after 1920 in their association with the liberal program of Benito Juárez (such as democracy and constitutional government) and denying any historical ties to continuity through the Porfiriato (the regime of President Porfirio Díaz).[59] Indeed, even Bautista referred to the revolution as a "restitution" of *juarista* democracy.[60]

Using LDS doctrine, Bautista established the superiority of his indigenous Mexican ancestors (or Lamanites, as he called them), explained away the domination of the Spanish via prophecy, and rejected the "stain" of European Catholicism without having to reject Christianity by making himself and his ancestry both Mexican and preconquest Christian. With the themes of the Mexican Revolution during the reconstruction period focusing on the future, renewal, and progress, Bautista easily situated his theology, race, and politics for the times. "Our sovereignty [indigenous and Mexican]," he proclaimed, "will be restored in all of its fullness."[61] Most of Mexico's concerns about the restoration of the nation's sovereignty lay squarely in conflict with the United States. During and after the revolution, the Mexican state relied heavily on the rhetoric of anti-Yankee sentiment as much as it did on the history of Spanish and Catholic domination—if only in word and not deed—as a powerful theme.[62] What position did Bautista and hundreds of Mexican Mormons have in a church whose headquarters was in the U.S. West on conquered Mexican soil, and whose highest local leadership, though formally Mexican in citizenship, was ethnically Anglo? As Mexican Mormon Abel Páez put it, "What a profound dilemma we find ourselves in: The discipline towards the Church and our duty to the *patria*."[63]

The Third Convention and the Seeds of New Jerusalem

When Margarito Bautista, in 1935, approached LDS leaders in Utah about publishing his book, he was soundly rejected. The polemical narrative, the hierarchy argued, overstepped official church doctrine, used apocryphal sources (though they did not indicate which ones), and made specific claims on the heritage and geography of North America and its inhabitants beyond the official church position.[64] Until that time Bautista felt he was squarely within LDS doctrinal positions, but the leadership's rejection of his book was a significant turning point for him. Dejected and disillusioned, Bautista retreated with his family to central Mexico to "instruct the members in his personal interpretation of Mormon doctrine."[65]

Bautista arrived in Mexico and fell in with Apolonio B. Arzate, a Mexican member of the LDS Church and owner of a printing press. Arzate was also a medical doctor (becoming director general of Mexico City's General Hospital) and a thirty-third-degree Mason with possible personal ties (according to his family) to every Mexican president from Emilio Portes Gil (1928–30) to Miguel Alemán (1946–52).[66] Arzate agreed to publish Bautista's book, and with donations from key church members in the Central Valley and Puebla, the book went on sale to the public between 1935 and 1936.[67]

By 1936, however, the Mormons of central Mexico and the hierarchy of the LDS Church were on a collision course. In that year the LDS Church placed the Mexican Mission under the direction of Harold Pratt—a Mexican citizen of Anglo descent from the Mormon colonies in Chihuahua and an opponent of Bautista's book. It was Pratt who suggested the leadership in Utah reject Bautista's book, and by April 1936, the popularity of the book prompted Pratt to issue a circular proclaiming that the book was "not in any way church doctrine."[68]

Pratt timed his offensive poorly, for in April 1936, a group of Mexican saints (Mormons) gathered in the capital to discuss the denied requests for a mission president of *raza y sangre*, or of Mexican "race and blood."[69] They assumed that Salt Lake City was unaware of the résumés of Mexicans qualified to fill the position of mission president and debated several people they could suggest to the central leadership in Utah (including Margarito Bautista, who later removed his name from nomination).[70]

This Mexico City LDS meeting, the third of its kind, was known as the Third Convention. The following year found the *convencionistas* and Harold Pratt in a series of negotiations in which both sides grew gradually more radical in their positions. This included a letter from J. Reuben Clark Jr., a member of the First Presidency of the LDS Church, stating that the Convention was out of line. The letter from Clark probably deepened the anti-U.S. feelings of Mexican Mormons as he was also former

U.S. undersecretary of state for Calvin Coolidge and ambassador to Mexico from 1930 to 1933 (between famed ambassadors Dwight Morrow and Josephus Daniels). In May 1937, the mainline LDS Church excommunicated the leaders of the Third Convention and the *convencionistas* took one-third of the nearly three thousand members in central Mexico with them.[71] The Convention eventually returned to the mainstream church (after ten successful years of growth and stability) in 1946, after intense negotiations that even brought the head of the LDS church to Mexico.[72] For Margarito Bautista, however, the break from the church in Utah was final.

Within weeks of the split from the mainline church in 1937, Bautista advocated that the Convention take a divergent path from the U.S.-based church and its adherents. He argued that the practice of plural marriage and the economic cooperative community practice called the Law of Consecration (and called by Bautista the United Order) be foundational doctrines of a Mexican Mormon Church.[73] According to Bautista's book, the Mexican members of the LDS Church had a special blood tie to Israel as descendants of the Lamanites, while the "gentiles" (now meaning Anglo Mormons to Bautista) were less favored in God's eyes. For Bautista, the mainline church's turn away from these early doctrines was only a sign of the Anglos' second-class spiritual state. Bautista points out, in his own book, a prophecy in the Book of Mormon describing the consequences if the gentiles sin:

> Then shall ye, who are a remnant of the house of Jacob, go forth among them; and ye shall be in them who will be many; and ye shall be among them as a lion among the beasts of the forest, and as a lion among the flocks of sheep, who if he goeth through both treadeth down and teareth in pieces, and none can deliver.

> Thy hand shall be lifted up upon thine adversaries, and all thine enemies shall be cut off.[74]

For Bautista, the Anglo Mormons had sinned, and the time had come for Mexican Mormons, as descendants of the "house of Jacob" (Israel), to punish the Anglos for their transgression. Mexicans must not only distance themselves from the Anglo Mormons, but also needed to return to the nineteenth-century practices of Mormonism no longer practiced, such as plural marriage and shared community resources. By doing so, Mexico could only benefit, and then, "as a lion . . . among sheep," Mexico would triumph over the United States. Indeed, Mexico could even be the birthplace of spiritual Hidalgos who would lead the world to unity.[75] According to Tullis, some *convencionistas* saw Bautista's rhetoric as a play for personal power, while others felt that his actions would take them too far outside the ability to return to the mainline LDS Church, as they hoped one day to do. As tension mounted, the rift between Bautista and the Third Convention grew until the group expelled him.[76]

Bautista, however, did not waste time licking his wounds. In October of 1937, he sent a letter to Mexican president Lázaro Cardenas, requesting an audience to review a proposal for land use. The return address he used was 185 Dr. Balmis—the home of Apolonio Arzate, his publisher, a firm *convencionista*, and, as mentioned above, a personal friend of the president. The letter requested that Cárdenas review a proposed community "en las tierras saladas de Texcoco" (in the salty lands of Texcoco).[77] Unfortunately, the meeting was denied and plans for the community were forwarded to the secretary of agriculture.[78] Neither the colony nor any other of the grand agricultural projects and individual agricultural efforts planned for the area were ever carried out. Due to the profitability of urban land speculation over agricultural projects, the drained land of Texcoco simply passed into the real estate market.[79]

Bautista's request, however, makes for interesting speculation using the tantalizing clues left behind. The name of the community proposed by Bautista was the "Colonia Productora Industrial." Settlement projects known as *colonias* appeared all over Mexico after the revolution, most subsidized by the state and dedicated to specialized groups, such as the railroad workers of Guadalajara or the various educators' *colonias* in Mexico City. Did Bautista wish to create a special "community" for his own group—Mexican Mormons? It appears so. According to his diary entries, as early as August 1937 he was "preaching the movement" to various Mormons in the central valley and states that several expressed interest in forming a colony with Bautista. He then spent the rest of August and September meeting with bankers and congressional representatives as well as drafting plans, clauses, and conditions for being a member of the *colonia*, though the diary does not reveal specifically what they were.[80]

Given Bautista's preoccupation with the early Mormon doctrine of the Law of Consecration, perhaps he conceived of a community in which members placed the ownership of all their property in the hands of the bishop.[81] In return they would receive a "stewardship" or "deed" of property to care for. From that, if any surplus beyond the comfortable needs of the family was produced, it went back to the bishop's storehouse for redistribution to the poor (both in and out of the group) and new members of the community. All other produce could be sold on the open market.[82] It is likely that Bautista's colony was to be a self-sufficient model of agricultural production and industry (*productora industrial*) to contribute "our grain of sand for the speedy reconstruction of our *Patria*."[83]

Bautista's selection of land, however, is most intriguing. In one respect, his choice is logical considering telegrams and letters to the president from other Mexicans requesting jobs and land in association with water control and land reclamation projects in Texcoco. In another respect, it reflects his theological plan as well. Just as Brigham Young led Mormon pioneers from Illinois to the Great Basin in 1847, "making the desert bloom," Bautista apparently had a rival Salt Lake City planned for the brackish waters and baked desert flats of Lake Texcoco.[84] This seems much in line with statements in his book demanding that the United States return former Mexican territory—a move that would have transferred the state of Utah to Mexico.[85] The gentile nations (the United States and Europe) "should return what they have overthrown by conquest and other tricks."[86] In a final nationalist twist, his diary reveals that he considered naming the *colonia* "Nuevo Tenoshtitlan" [*sic*], both usurping the U.S. Latter-day Saint seat of authority and restoring Aztec glory in a Mormon context.[87] Until his complete plans are recovered, we can only speculate. Such speculation, however, appears in line with the rivalry set up in his *Destiny of America* and in his increasingly anti-U.S. stand.

It also appears to be in line with pamphlets published by Bautista after his break with the Third Convention. Though the convention expelled Bautista, he continued as an active member of the Mormon community in Mexico City for several years (from 1937 until the early 1940s), until it became increasingly apparent that he was a total outsider.[88] During this period he produced theological pamphlets to encourage more Mexican Mormons to abandon the mainline LDS church and adhere to the Third Convention—to which he apparently still felt connected.[89] In the pamphlet, he takes exception to a statement by the president of the LDS Mexican Mission, Arthur L. Anderson, that Anglo-Saxons were themselves also descendants of the ten tribes of Israel that slowly migrated to England during the Babylonian captivity. Such a belief, popular among many British Protestants and not exactly Mormon doctrine, was a direct affront to Bautista's Mexican claim to Israelite descent and, therefore, superiority over the Anglos. At the end of the pamphlet, he chides any Mexican who would side with the Americans: "What do you say, Mexicans? Unfortunately, among us there are those walking in the light and indoctrinated that still say NO, IT IS STILL NOT TIME. When will Israel TEAR THE VEIL FROM YOUR EYES?"[90] To give up the birthright of Israel to the Anglos not only violated religious law, but the nationalist birthright as well.

When he learned that the Third Convention had returned to the LDS Church altogether, he put together a seventy-five-page pamphlet condemning the returning *convencionistas* as "false prophets," "devils," and "Iscariots," who had never understood the mission of the Convention to "redeem Mexico." He includes in the pamphlet a hypothetical prayer by an "Indian":

> Hear me, Thou, Oh God of my fathers
> Listen to the sad Indian
> For so long you have withheld
> Your anger—when will you cease to listen?
> THE AMBITION OF THE WHITE MAN—WHEN WILL IT CEASE?
> When will our interred remains know peace?
> Oh, IMPEDE HIM, GOD OF ABRAHAM![91]

Even the bodies of deceased Mexicans were offended by the return of the Convention caused by the "ambition" of the white man.

Margarito Bautista began as a rising star and exemplar of the universality of LDS doctrine. By rejecting both Catholicism and Protestantism, he served as a standard that could be displayed for LDS missionary work in Latin America and the redemption of the "Lamanites."[92] But Bautista was not a passive player. Exposed to early leadership directly after his conversion, religious doctrine that placed no limits on the possibilities of divine communion, and a theology that focused on the future of the Americas and its indigenous inhabitants, Bautista took things to their logical conclusion. Rejected by the mainstream LDS Church, he used his training to establish a parallel belief system based on LDS doctrine but that emphasized the future of Mexico and elevated his ethnicity. For Bautista, his assumption of leadership was natural, for could not God call whomever he wanted, especially a descendant of the chosen Lamanites to fulfill prophecy?[93]

Margarito Bautista was a new kind of Mexican with an identity formed by being more Christian than were Europeans and more Mormon than the Anglos. Bautista's vision, though, was not embraced by the urban Mormons of the Third Convention in Mexico City, and he fell back to rural central Mexico and the market town of Ozumba, just several kilometers from his childhood home. This move, however, was no retreat but a stand for his beliefs on ideal communities and the culmination of his life's work.

Symbolism and Membership in New Jerusalem

The town of Ozumba, Mexico State, is still the same bustling market center today that it was when it attracted Margarito Bautista in the 1940s. Pressing through the crowded *tianguis* (market street stalls) of the town of thirteen thousand inhabitants, visitors discover rows of flowers, fresh fish, beans, and endless mounds of walnuts as they wind through the streets for nearly two kilometers—not including the large and spotless municipal market. Trucks of fresh corn abut rows of fighting cocks, and turkeys screech as wrinkled Nahua women prod them and haggle in their native tongue. At the plaza, the Franciscan church dominates the center and a half dozen smaller chapels are found in the surrounding streets of this bustling village at the base of Popocatepetl, declaring the faith of Ozumba: Catholicism dominates and traditional Mexico plays on every corner.

But Ozumba is no monolithic relic of the past. Boasting as many Internet cafes as devotional chapels to the Virgin Mary, this is a town with a colorful recent history as well. During the revolution, *zapatistas, constitucionalistas,* and federal forces fought continually through the area. After the revolution, radical farmers' leagues, such as the Liga Ricardo Flores Magón, and other citizen groups vocally opposed imposed candidates and rigged elections, drawing a military occupation of the pueblo for a time.[94] This seemed to bring the community in line with the state, and future revolutionary agitation was directed into improvement projects, such as the Women's Civic Organization bridge, still a source of pride for the community.[95]

It was to Ozumba that Margarito Bautista retreated in 1942 to play out his dreams of founding a community of chosen people, finally doing so in 1947. For the preacher, his community had a future equally as bright

as Mexico, and in his mind, equally yoked together, as seen in his selection of the name—Colonia Industrial de la Nueva Jerusalén, often referred
to in Bautista's pamphlets as La Colonia Industrial de la Nueva Jerusalén
Mexicana.

Although New Jerusalem is an infrequently occurring scriptural concept—found only twice in the New Testament and then only in the visu-
ally enticing Book of Revelation, with all of its millennial associations—it
resonates strongly in the New World. The third chapter of Revelation
refers to a Christian who endures persecution before the Second Coming
of Christ as "a pillar in the temple of my God" who will be made part of
the New Jerusalem that "cometh down out of heaven." The second reference is even more specific:

> And I saw a new heaven and a new earth: for the first heaven and
> the first earth were passed away; and there was no more sea. And I
> John saw the holy city, the new Jerusalem, coming down from God
> out of heaven, prepared as a bride adorned for her husband.[96]

Understandably, the New Jerusalem receives a great deal of attention
from millenarians for its tantalizing appearance with little explanation.
For Mormons, the idea receives special emphasis as a city to be built in
North America at a sacred site in Missouri and is also associated with
Zion, a word that has multiple geographical and spiritual meanings associated with good community and the Second Coming.[97] For Mexicans
in the 1940s, raised with the promise of Mexico's bright future but faced
with the reality of constant public corruption, the idea of a society with
divine guidance and community support might well have been appealing.[98] Bautista often calls the colony the *Mexican* New Jerusalem (italics
added), to set it apart from other New Jerusalems, and in his book he
avers that the New Jerusalem will be "built by aborigines" and become
"the supreme capital of the world."[99] What brighter future could a Nahua
Mexican paint? In fact, Bautista even sees a future of pan-Indian unity
that will sweep the Americas. "Like Joseph's coat of many colors," Native
Americans are different, but are "one people."[100]

Many inhabitants of Colonia Industrial de la Nueva Jerusalén did not
begin life as Mormons nor did they exist in a vacuum of LDS beliefs. The
idea of the New Jerusalem has a long and established history in Mexico and
Catholicism, especially in those areas, like Amecameca and Ozumba, first

contacted by the Franciscans. Sixteenth-century European friars viewed the New World as a New Jerusalem, full of millennial and divine promises—as much for the conversion of the people they met there as for themselves.[101] Such millennial notions of New Jerusalem led Franciscans to consider their Mexican mission as bringing about utopian self-improvement and lead, with the discovery of these possible descendants of the Jews, to the establishment of God's thousand-year reign on earth.[102]

And what connection does this have with the Mormon Margarito Bautista and his followers? As historian Eric Van Young points out, a pattern of millenarian thought pervaded areas where Franciscans exerted an influence, sometimes centuries after the initial missionary fervor had worn off.[103] And while we cannot assume direct causation, we see an example of tactics and beliefs that mirror those of Margarito Bautista and illuminate his and his followers' choices beyond the ideas of Mormonism. Indeed, the millenarian concepts found in Mormonism may have been more appealing to Bautista and his followers, coming as they did from areas with a history of exposure to Franciscan millenarianism and highlighting similar desires. As noted above, the New Jerusalem is a symbol of possibility and the future, promising divine relief from present worldly cares. A prolific pamphleteer, Bautista gives some insight into his hopes in his 1950 pamphlet, *Will the Kingdom Be Restored (Acts 1:6,7)*, and his 1951 *Is a Discipline a Law?* Many of these beliefs merge the religious and the political and have their hopes in the millenarian future, though germinated in the hothouse of revolutionary experimentation.

For example, in the 1951 tract *Is a Discipline Law?* he argues that the "immortal Morelos" (José María Morelos) said that "dying is nothing when you die for the Patria. If dying for the Patria is nothing, then how much value would our pitiful sacrifices or life given for the Kingdom of God on the earth and the betterment of the Patria have?" His new colony was to be built both for the glory of the Kingdom of God and the Republic of Mexico. He then launches into several celebratory pages of the concept of Zion and the New Jerusalem. He goes on to state that in his colony he can offer those who strictly and completely obey all the "principles and ordinances" of the gospel not only a glorious participation in the Kingdom of God in this life but also access to the highest levels of the "Celestial Kingdom" after death. Throughout all of this he makes frequent reference for his hope of the "Millennial Reign" of Christ on the earth.[104] This coincides with his earlier writings where he declared that when the "Gentile" dominance of "Japeth" (United States/Europe) ends, then Christ can come and "dwell among his people."[105]

If there was any doubt that this New Jerusalem was to stand in opposition to the United States and Anglo Mormons, Bautista's hymns, pamphlets, and allies quickly suppress such a doubt. Members of the Mexican colony would even sing about one day going to the New Jerusalem in Missouri where they would receive their inheritance, taking land back from both their religious and political enemies.[106] Interestingly, the hymnbook used by Bautista and his group is titled *Himnos de la dispensación Lamanita* (Hymns of the Lamanite Dispensation). Again, we see the use of the term "dispensation" as we did with Aarón Joaquín and LDM, marking the beginning of a major and glorious new era of Christian world history—one dominated by Lamanites and not the Anglos of the United States. In addition, a member of the community, Alma de Olarte, claims that Bautista sought association with another polygamist Mormon splinter organization headed by Joseph W. Musser. Among the two prominent members of this group were two Anglo-Mexican Mormons named LeBaron, converts from mainline Mormonism by Margarito Bautista.[107] Although Bautista eventually rejected the LeBarons for their attempt to make him a subordinate and create their own church, he was initially intrigued by their anti-U.S. writings. Just like Bautista, they claimed that the United States would fall because of its rejection of Mormonism (and the Anglo-Mormon rejection of plural marriage), as well as because of its racial and religious discrimination (a "hatred based on a foolish tradition"). This U.S. style, said the LeBarons, stood in stark contrast to the noble Mexican Constitution and traditions that allowed true religious freedom.[108] The reluctance of Bautista to associate with the LeBaron brothers probably saved the lives of his followers as the LeBaron organization disintegrated in to a tangle of blood feuds and murder during the 1960s and 1970s.[109]

And what were these laws, principles, and ordinances that Bautista planned for his colony? He clearly lays them out in his 1951 tract, *Is a Discipline a Law?* as a reprint of the pact made by the colonists in August 1947. Primarily, Bautista was concerned with the laws of plural marriage and the United Order (the economic plan of mutual welfare), as explained above. The rules for Bautista's program, however, are quite interesting and differ greatly from the pre-1890 plural marriage laws of the LDS church. The Bautista laws restricted plural marriage to older married men of the community who had already undergone the sacred marriage ceremony known as "sealing." These men were allowed only to request plural wives from young women whose parents were also members of the United Order in the colony. In addition, the man and women requesting the "honor" of entering into plural marriage had to adhere to a strict thirty-seven-point plan designed to vet applicants before allowing them to participate. Most of the points hinge on the ability of the couple to prove they can live harmoniously in the community, their abstinence from adultery, and the patriarchal ability of the man to "keep his house in order." This last point included making sure his wives dressed respectably, appeared clean in public, and did not gossip.

Young men not previously married were not allowed to choose their first bride from the young women of the colony, but had to go outside the community to find a wife. Though the text offers no explanation for this practice, considering the deference to older men in the community, it might have served to insure brides for the older men. This new bride from outside then had to stand up to rigorous investigation by the colony's authorities, including the bishop and the president of the women's organization known as the Sociedad de Socorro. Finally, after five years of clean living and proven harmony in the community, the young man would be allowed to request a second wife. Indeed, a proven record of harmonious living is a constant requirement for participation in many duties in the community—probably a reflection of the absence of both. At any rate, the marriage request would be denied if the authorities discovered the young man had been courting the women during the five-year trial period, in which case he would have proven himself unfaithful to his first wife and a disruption to the community. He would have to wait another five years before making another request.

It appears that the laws for plural marriage in the community are weighed heavily in favor of the older members, who, as discussed below, were also in the minority. The say of women in the process seems severely limited, especially since their ability to refuse marriage is not laid out in the guidelines. The focus of the program, however, was not individual bliss but to build a tight-knit *colonia* that would be "a happy community where we can be the leavening lump to raise up our Lamanite brethren."[110] Bautista uses a New Testament reference in Matthew to the Kingdom of God being like leaven that, when placed in among the meal, raises the lump of dough "until the whole was leavened."[111] The community harmony found in Bautista's colony (the leaven, or yeast) would have an uplifting affect on their non-Mormon neighbors (the rest of the ingredients) until his "Lamanite bretheren" (those indigenous citizens of Mexico he called descendents of Israel) were improved both spiritually and temporally by the example of his colony. From correctly practiced plural marriage to shared community resources, Bautista hoped to inspire and improve the world around him.

However, despite all the language of community and harmony, it did not long stay a cohesive group, especially in the first years of its existence, with many of the older men abandoning Colonia Industrial after two or three years. What drove the older men from the community, even with the laws weighted in their favor, and what inspired the younger members to stay? A sample of the membership through their memoirs as well as the public record might shed light on the founding principles that both attracted followers and failed to hold some.

To explain this division within the group, I now turn to Alma de Olarte, a man who was a lifelong devotee of Bautista, and Don Felipe Burgos, the first bishop (head of the congregation) of Colonia Industrial and later a bitter rival of Bautista. Through them, we can sample who was willing to participate in Bautista's social and religious experiment in the shadow of Popocatepetl. This section will examine the founding and mission of La Colonia Industrial de la Nueva Jerusalén Mexicana as a means of interpreting community formation, piety, and reconstruction in post-Cárdenas Mexico. By carrying out this sample, we can also gain the insight that historian David Hall calls for, saying, "No one has or believes a 'religion.' Instead, the religious lies in what we do—in practices and in meaning that energizes such practices."[112] Given that theory, what energized people to follow Bautista, and others to later reject him?

Alma de Olarte Analco hailed from Puebla State, the village of Santiago Xalitzintla, south of Cholula. Born in March of 1930 as fourth of eight children, Olarte attended the *escuela rural federal* (one of the state-run rural schools) until third grade, where he "received good marks" and learned to dance in community festivals.[113] By age eight, Olarte Analco reports that he and his younger brother Nefi labored in the mountains near Xalitzintla cutting firewood to help the family. By 1940, Carmen de Olarte Hernández, Alma's father, was serving as secretary of the *ayuntamiento*, a position that required much of his father's time and forced the two boys to work for the "support of the family" and took them permanently out of school.[114]

Alma de Olarte's family may have joined the LDS Church sometime after his birth, as he recounts that he was baptized in the Catholic Church in May of 1930 but that he was "blessed" in a branch of the LDS Church in San Gabriel Ometoxtla, Puebla, in May of 1932.[115] This places Olarte's family in the LDS Church before Margarito Bautista's final return to Mexico and later during his solicitation of support for his book from Pueblan Mormons. In fact, according to Olarte, by 1938—less than a year after Bautista's split from the Third Convention—Margarito was in Puebla actively drawing away members of the LDS Church. In combination with local members from San Buenaventura Nealtican, Bautista approached the Olarte family about living the Law of Consecration and plural marriage. According to Alma de Olarte, his parents agreed, and in that year his father agreed to enter into a plural marriage that never occurred. Olarte does not say why.

Bautista formed other bonds to Alma de Olarte's family. Alma notes that by the fall of 1942, Bautista was established in Ozumba, Mexico, on four hectares of land, and in that year, "Brother Margarito Bautista brought me to Ozumba to help build a garden." In addition, while he was there he joined with several other men to build Bautista a house of *zacate* and *cuilote*, or wattle and daub.[116] In 1943, the sixty-five-year-old Bautista asked Juven de Olarte, Alma's older sister of perhaps fifteen or sixteen, to marry him—a transaction formally completed in 1947, though Alma de Olarte refers to the older man as his "brother-in-law" as early as 1946. By 1945, with their father dead, Alma de Olarte and his brother Nefi opted to move their family to the "rancho" of Margarito Bautista. Here they raised flowers, selling them in the markets of Mexico City for an income Olarte calls "very satisfactory."[117] That year yet another family settled on Bautista's land and joined the Olartes in selling flowers. The formation of a community was in process.

However, this was no haphazard coincidental community. Alma Olarte claims that in 1942, Bautista had actively urged his new followers in Puebla to build a "house of prayer" and live "independent of the [mainline LDS] Church" in a "celestial" community. *Celestial*, as used in LDS theology and by Bautista, refers to a heavenly order, or an idyllic community. The members agreed and Bautista solicited "the help of Señor Lázaro Cárdenas" in getting permission to cut trees for rafters for the chapel. In 1942, ex-president Cárdenas was serving as the commander for the Pacific Military Zone, but this request for aid might reveal several things about the group. Perhaps Bautista did solicit the help of Cárdenas in 1942, as the former president remained an influential *patrón* after he left the presidency—even though it is doubtful that in his capacity in the military he was involved in allocating forestry resources. Bautista had once before made an urgent request for an audience with Lázaro Cárdenas in January of 1939 that received a dismissive statement that the president was "aware of the request."[118] Did Cárdenas meet with Bautista in 1939? As Bautista never mentions a visit, it is highly doubtful.[119] Bautista maintained a fondness and confidence in Lázaro Cárdenas (Bautista once referred to him as "raised up by Heaven") and the associated meanings of egalitarian, agrarian populism.[120] It might even provide another explanation for the community formation: a community of people enamored of the ejidal cooperative land movement but unable to participate in that program, either due to the community rejecting them for their beliefs or the failure of the state to include them.

By April 1946, Alma Olarte reports that a members' council met in Felipe Burgos's house in Puebla to decide the direction of the colony.[121] He states that land and limitations in Xalizintla hampered living the Law of Consecration and so the group sought to relocate. Furthermore, in the nearby area of San Buenaventura Nealtican, the mainline organization of LDS followers was gaining ground against the Bautista faction, and in 1948 one mainline LDS man became so popular he became municipal president of the area.[122] In addition, if letters to Mexico City about Mormons in 1950 are any indication of the mood in the area, Mormons in general were poorly received in the Catholic town and land shortages could only exacerbate problems.[123]

Proposals ranged from moving to the Cortez Pass to the "colonia Zapta [Zapata?]" in Puebla. Bautista even tried to get the members to consider his decade-old plan of settling in the "vaso de Texcoco," to no avail. Eventually, Olarte reports that Bautista turned to him and asked the sixteen-year-old where they should settle. Olarte says that he opted for Ozumba because he lived there, and with its two large weekly markets and access to Mexico City via railroad and buses, it was ideal for the economic prosperity of the members.[124] On January 1, 1947, Bautista gave the dedicatory prayer for the colony and the project was officially underway.

We have seen the community formation through the eyes of Alma de Olarte Analco, a Pueblan peasant educated in the state-run schools of the 1930s that stressed socialist education. By his own words he was little interested at the time in scripture or religious things, but when asked what he most valued for the location of a colony, access to markets and good transportation were foremost in his mind.[125] Eventually, Olarte grew to be a confidant of Margarito Bautista, and when the young disciple became a printer, he edited and produced Bautista's later ecclesiastical works, many anti-Anglo and anti-mainline LDS. Olarte's view of Bautista is a loving one, and though his history of Colonia Industrial is also an account of the tensions and conflict of the small community, Bautista always ends in a good light. Indeed, the history carries through only until 1961 and the death of Bautista at age eighty-three, after which Olarte shows little interest and reflects sadly on the subsequent changes in the community.[126]

One of the arguments and disagreements that pulled at the integrity of the community was the loss of bishop and skilled carpenter Felipe Burgos González and his family in 1949.[127] Although Olarte does not explore the exact reason that Burgos left after being a formative part of the community, Burgos himself has his reasons and provides us with yet another profile of those willing to undertake this community experiment with Margarito Bautista—and then cast it aside.

Felipe Burgos was born in either Santa María Ocoyucan or Malacatepec (he gave two locations), near Cholula, in the state of Puebla on May 1, 1903.[128] A picture of his mother kept in his two-room home readily identified her as an *indígena* who, said Burgos, spoke Nahuatl. Burgos himself knew only one or two words of the language. His father, European in appearance and with a long, flowing beard, was a schoolteacher and store owner in his small village during the Porfiriato. Don Felipe himself self-identified as a *pobre indio* and *indígena* (poor Indian and indigenous).

As a child, Burgos remembers his father ending his home schooling in 1909 and taking him to Cholula to enroll in the government school. However, due to crowding he was unable to enter, and thereafter he enrolled in a "private school" run by two U.S. Americans. They soon departed for the United States and his aunt, with whom he was living in Cholula, attempted to enroll him in a Catholic school, but, as Burgos remembers, it was "too full of rich kids" to admit him. They even tried an evangelical Christian school but were turned down because he was Catholic. It was in these excursions around Cholula and Puebla that he remembers his first taste of the revolution, seeing rallies for Francisco I. Madero.

By 1914, the reality of the revolution came to Burgos's home village as his father's store was burned (he did not indicate by which revolutionary

faction), forcing the elder Burgos to rely on teaching alone—a grim pros-
pect as the salary was two pesos per day. At this point, Felipe's father appren-
ticed him out to a local carpenter for fifteen centavos a day. According to
Burgos, all the family funds went toward the maintenance of his sisters
so that they could "go about as señoritas," perhaps in an effort to marry
them well and improve the family situation through advantageous unions.
Eventually, Burgos recalls moving to Puebla as a barefoot child where he
lived with his aunt and talked his way into a large woodworking shop, per-
fecting his craft and rising to four pesos a day. On weekends he returned
to his family home.

While in Puebla, he passed a Baptist church and entered out of curiosity. He recalls that being called "brother" was an electric spiritual experience of inclusion that he had never felt before. From that point on he lied
to his family, saying he had to work on Sundays, and instead attended
Baptist services. Finally, the Baptists invited him to be baptized, but
Burgos refused out of fear of his father. The congregation sent missionaries—"North Americans," said Burgos—to his home. They left him with
a copy of the four New Testament Gospels in Spanish and promised to
return. The next week, however, they did not come but instead, by coincidence (Burgos did not refer to it as divine providence), two Mexican LDS
missionaries from Ometoxtla arrived and invited him to hear their lessons.
Eventually Burgos began attending LDS services, overcame the fear of his
parents, and was baptized.

And so his association with the LDS Church began, but would not
last. After telling his conversion story, Burgos jumped straight to a darker
tale, growing agitated as he remembered. "That man [Bautista] came from
the North . . . he came to deceive us . . . he didn't tell us 'I've committed
adultery' . . . he didn't work, he just came and lived off the good feelings
of the poor Indians, like me, of Xalitzintla—we gave him shoes and food."
Margarito Bautista had come to Puebla, and Burgos had little more to
say about "that man from the North." In his disgust for Bautista, Burgos
stripped his memory of all that Margarito prized about himself: piety,
indigenismo, and *mexicanidad*.

Apparently the initial relationship was not as bumpy as it later became,
nor were Bautista's beliefs impossible for Burgos to swallow. Before the
community moved to Mexico State, Burgos twice tried to contract plural
marriages with women in Puebla—neither of them Mormons, and one
who only agreed to be his second wife if she could still have a Catholic

wedding. The idea of being a second wife was apparently not as appalling as missing out on a traditional Catholic ceremony; Burgos declined the marriage. The other woman who agreed to marriage attempted to make Burgos her own by grinding up the rib bone of a human cadaver and putting it in his cup of *chocolate*, a variation on the native practice of securing a lover. Again, Burgos changed his mind about the union. The casual acceptance of Burgos's invitation, however, invites a question. Could many of Bautista's followers have come from Puebla because of a tacit acceptance of plural marriage and glorification of the indigenous image? According to anthropologist Hugo Nutini, islands of pre-Columbian "continued" polygynous communities did exist in rural central Mexico as late as the mid-twentieth century. The anthropologist points out that the polygyny served to bind multiple families together and strengthen household economies. Nutini's analysis of a Tlaxcalan village revealed a sub-rosa acceptance by local authorities of polygyny. He also states it was a secretive affair in regard to the state or federal authorities, but that it was accepted throughout the local community, with 9 percent (over two hundred) of patrilocal families participating.[129] Nutini's case study of San Bernardino Contla in Tlaxcala reveals that even local officials might be practitioners of polygyny.[130] While it is difficult to prove conclusively a direct causative link between indigenous polygyny in a neighboring region with acceptance of Mormon polygyny among the indigenous in Puebla, it is at least safe to conclude that acceptance by a community and local authorities of such a practice, while rare, is not unheard of in rural Mexico.[131]

Margarito Bautista (*center*) stands with an unidentified wife (*right*), one of his mother-in-laws (*left*), and her two children (Margarito's brother- and sister-in-law). Freedom to engage in the plural marriage practice of polygyny was one reason Bautista founded his community of Colonia Industrial (no date, photographer unknown). PHOTO COURTESY OF THE MUSEO DE HISTORIA DE MORMONISMO EN MÉXICO, A.C.

As for Felipe Burgos—who never successfully contracted a plural marriage—his tenure as the first bishop of Colonia Industrial de la Nueva Jerusalén lasted only two years, from 1948 to 1950, when he sided with a faction that said Bautista was "fallen." Burgos says he left because he was promised financial help from the community to start a carpentry shop in downtown Ozumba but never got the money. His family abandoned Colonia Industrial soon thereafter and went to Colonia Manuel Ávila Camacho, in Iztapaluca.[132] They later drifted back to Ozumba in 1953, and in 1954 he formed Colonia Alzate across the arroyo from Colonia Industrial.

While these two cases of residents of Colonia Industrial de la Nueva Jerusalén are only partially representative of the entire community, it shows a diversity of age and ability (young peasant to middle-aged skilled artisan) and a similar reflection of what benefits each sought from the colony. However, documents do exist within the municipality of Ozumba that illuminate further who participated in the community, allowing a glimpse of the larger community.

According to a June 1951 Padrón de Personal de la Colonia Industrial, or register of men able to work in the polling place, twenty-four men were listed as available.[133] Of those, all were labeled as literate. The bulk of the men, 54 percent, were married and between the age of thirty and fifty, with only one man in that age bracket listed as unmarried. Eighteen-to-thirty-year-olds represented 37 percent of the group, one man between fifty and seventy (age fifty-one) appeared on the roll, and one over seventy—Margarito Bautista, at seventy-two. The number of men who reasonably participated in the revolution as armed combatants is around five, one of those being Bautista, who we know was in the United States during the conflict.[134] The others would have been thirteen, sixteen, seventeen, and twenty in 1920, and all but Bautista were probably too young for combat (under twelve) in 1910, though child soldiers did fight in the revolution.

The 1951 Padrón de Personal also lists the occupations of the men of the colony. Four men called themselves *jornaleros*, or day laborers, and an additional seventeen called themselves *campesinos*. While *campesino* implies some form of access to land and *jornalero* implies landlessness, both had equal access to the colony's lands. The list also states that there were four men that called themselves potters. After these categories with multiple entries, the list gives one each of a cobbler, baker, printer, and flower grower. Unfortunately, the record does not indicate the level of production or capital associated with the artisans in the community, and we do not know if they owned their own tools or had only their labor to sell.[135] What we can see by the number of laborers and *campesinos* is that those attracted to Colonia Industrial were neither particularly wealthy nor were the majority skilled laborers. Margarito Bautista declared himself a *jornalero*, despite being the original owner of the colony's land as well as an author, lay clergyman, and flower grower.

By 1953, the city of Ozumba took a census of all members of Colonia Industrial that provides a view of women and minors in addition to the men.[136] Though the collection indicates no month, the census could have been taken in conjunction with the 1953 women's suffrage decision. The census shows a 14 percent decline in the community from the official 1950 census rather than an increase, as seen in the rest of Ozumba, and lists eighty people as living in the colony.[137] Of those eighty people, 62 percent were under nineteen, eight of those being eighteen to nineteen years old. Just 20 percent of the community was between the ages of twenty and thirty. Fully 82 percent of the community was not even born at the cessation of the armed revolution in 1920. Of those between eighteen and thirty years old, women represent 55 percent. Unfortunately, the inattention paid to the "single" column, and the possible confusions caused by plural marriages, renders the document impossible for gaining a perspective of how many of those young people were married and to whom.

For those over thirty, 17 percent fell between the ages of thirty and fifty, with an equal division in men and women. Of the fifty- to sixty-year-old group (2 percent), we see one man and woman, the woman a sixty-year-old widow and the man married to a woman of forty-five. There is no one listed between sixty and seventy years old, and once more Bautista is the lone septuagenarian, at seventy-five. Bautista shares another singular position, having been born in the state of Mexico; for of those over eighteen, all but three were born in Puebla.

While my focus on Olarte and Burgos is due to the availability of sources, the two also represent the group and what would energize their belief in Bautista. Neither the older Burgos nor the younger Olarte participated in the armed conflict of the revolution, the one a *pacífico* and the other born after the end of fighting. In addition, both come from Puebla and express an interest in their indigenous ancestry. Olarte and Burgos had strong material reasons for associating with or abandoning Bautista, with Olarte's dream ending in a locally successful printing operation and Burgos leaving the colony in disgust at the community leader's failure to fund his proposed carpentry shop. As we see from the voting roll, not many of the colony's men listed themselves as skilled artisans, and they may have opted for a community that provided them a safety net for the vagaries of the economy. Olarte himself began as a laborer and flower grower before using community funds to become a printer.

In conclusion, the concept of communal living—and thereby participating in a community that provided both a social safety net and a market for their talents—may be one reason some chose to participate in the intentional religious community. Olarte's initial interest in locating the community where he did, as earlier discussed, was based on access to markets—and Burgos would leave the community when he felt his economic interests were threatened. Neither was apparently disturbed by the concept of plural marriage—the marriage of Olarte's sister to Bautista gave him a kinship connection to Bautista, and Burgos attempted to contract plural marriages several times. In the end, this too may have been another example of maximizing household resources—polygyny as a means to multiply household wealth is a debated yet accepted motivation for polygyny in the anthropological literature.[138] Finally, while Olarte began with little religious interest, he ended his life a staunch defender of Bautista and his mission—like many of the younger members who remained in the community. Burgos, on the other hand, began as a key player in the formation of the colony but soon grew disillusioned and disgusted with the project—a trend that held for older males in general.[139] Both reflect a tendency toward factionalism in the community, though expressed at different levels.

The lack of older men in the community in the 1951 census, however, does not mean that they were not present in the colony in 1947, as we can see by Felipe Burgos. One member of the community who came with two wives and a sizable extended family and friends (twenty-six altogether) was Melesio Hernández, from Libres, Puebla.[140] Another family of somewhat equal size was the Casildo Santamaría family—consisting of two wives and perhaps eight children and assorted relatives (including one Anastacio Zacarías with plural wives). In the case of Melesio, he had no children by his multiple wives, but he did claim a son from another relationship that was at least as old as one of his wives, though given his lack of offspring with his wives, that he fathered the boy is questionable.[141]

By April of 1947, Anastacio Zacarías was accused of torching the community storehouse and Casildo Santamaría had abandoned the area with his entire family. Alma de Olarte says that the man could not "endure the poverty," but a 1953 complaint to the municipal authorities, listing people exiled from the community, says he was removed for "claiming his rights," though the complaint was not specific as to his losses.[142] Melesio Hernández remained in the community for two more years, but by 1949, he and his brothers had formed a schismatic group within the colony that rejected Bautista. It was to this group that Felipe Burgos adhered, but the later impregnation of one of Hernández's wives by the man's alleged son from a premarital relationship scandalized the group and it broke up.[143]

Why did these established men with multiple wives reject Bautista? Certainly not for lack of leadership opportunities, as evidenced by Felipe Burgos. Perhaps talk of sacrifice and blessings for the Kingdom of God had little pull when faced with the reality of feeding a larger family in a poor community. Ilene V. O'Malley posits that postrevolutionary Mexico was saturated with hierarchy and patriarchy as the state infiltrated popular culture with macho hero cults. These actions, she said, moved Mexicans to look for revolution and social action from patriarchal leadership and not from themselves.[144] Could younger Mexicans, like Alma de Olarte, who were educated in state-run institutions, have looked for guidance in patriarchal figures like Bautista, while older men rejected such social controls as antithetical to the revolution they had lived through?

While the idea of the New Jerusalem and the promise of security—both present and future, spiritual and physical—likely helped attract believers of all ages to the community, a system of economic equalization perhaps threatened the older members of the community, who entered with more resources, while younger, less-established men felt protected. The practice of polygyny could strengthen the household economy, and the Law of Consecration provided a safety net for a time when land distribution and benefits to agricultural Mexicans fell to record lows compared to the previous decade, but it also made the older men the constant target (as evidenced by Melesio Hernandez) for "predatory" younger males.[145] Clearly, while Bautista's rhetoric provided members with an uplifting doctrine of self-identification that legitimized their efforts as both Mexican and Christian in a time of rapid modernization and change, the community was hardly free of interpersonal conflict.

And what of conflict with the nearby residents of Ozumba? With such practices as polygyny, church-owned goods, and the dispossession of land leading to divisions in Colonia Industrial, how did the municipal government respond? The lack of response by municipal authorities reveals yet another reason why Colonia Industrial survived and reflects how some Mexicans carved out their space on the local level.

Controversial Religious Practice and Local Secular Leaders

The relationship between Colonia Industrial de la Nueva Jerusalén and political entities provides an interesting exploration of state power at the local level in the late 1940s and early 1950s. The illegal practices of church-held land and buildings, plural marriage, and displacement of community members from land were common activities in Colonia Industrial de la Nueva Jerusalén. Given the many portrayals of the Mexican state as wielding absolute power, one would tend to imagine a short life for this intentional religious community. The experience of Colonia Industrial, however, shows a pliant state government and an accommodating municipality that allowed legal flexibility for those seeking a spiritual path seemingly opposed to constitutional principles but that in practice and influence posed no threat to local leaders' ability to govern. As historian Alan Knight argues regarding popular movements, "It is empirically almost impossible for popular movements to avoid the embrace of the state; indeed, it is only by entering that embrace (cautiously, with eyes open, and passion stilled) that popular movements can achieve positive results. In other words, the relationship between the state and popular movements is a mutually conditional one, albeit rarely if ever an equal one."[46] Though Knight makes his argument about Mexico between 1934 and 1940, historian Jeffrey Rubin argues that popular movements in Mexico have a long history of avoiding the control of the central state—despite its growing reputation after 1940 as a centralizing, corporatist power.[47] Though Colonia Industrial held none of the political influence of Cárdenas-era *campesino* unions (see Knight on Cárdenas) or leftist political movements in a powerful regional market center (see Rubin on Juchitan, Oaxaca), this tiny movement developed a relationship with local leaders that allowed it to carve out its own working space for the practice of beliefs that otherwise would have landed many of the group's adherents—including its founder—in prison.

In 1951, Mexico State faced an election to fill the governor's seat. If the municipal records of Ozumba are any example, the conclusion in favor of the PRI's candidate, Salvador Sánchez Colín, was a given. (Although there was an opposition candidate, he apparently didn't merit a meeting with Ozumba residents—or at least a record of it.) The *municipio* scheduled a round table discussion with Sánchez Colín for April 1951 with every political entity in its boundaries submitting requests of what they wanted from the candidate. School repairs, water pipes, a new market—the submissions are a typical shopping list of municipal improvements, and Colonia Industrial made its request alongside its fellow entities. Due to its distance of two kilometers from the town market, the residents of Colonia Industrial de la Nueva Jerusalén wanted a *carretera* or *camino vecinal* (a quality road instead of a path) to connect the colony to the *cabecera municipal* (main town) of Ozumba.[148] The signatures on the letter? There were four: Felipe Burgos and Melesio Hernández, representing the anti-Bautista faction, and Candido de la Cruz and Nazario Reynoso representing the pro-Bautista faction. Apparently, when it came to access to markets, the men put matters of theology aside. In addition, while all other submissions from *colonias* and villages came with descriptions of their duly elected offices, the submission from Colonia Industrial carried none. Apparently elected representation was not a concern, and if it was, it is an interesting legal twist to see Reynoso acting as that authority, since he was the bishop of the congregation, making him a clergyman and therefore illegal to hold public office. But Colonia Industrial got its road. A similar request for a cemetery, however, was denied (though no reason was given), and Colonia Industrial appears to hold neither a special or negative position.

Later that year, in November of 1951, Margarito Bautista was summoned to the town hall on charges brought by Melesio Hernández. Upon arrival, authorities took Bautista into custody and put him before the municipal judge on charges of "swindle, adultery, fraud, deception, and rape." Alma de Olarte claims that when the members of New Jerusalem tried to testify, they were unable because the courtroom was packed with a "chusma [y] de los lobos," or "mob and wolves." We see Olarte using language that sounds alarms for Mormons—Joseph Smith Jr.'s death also involves the image of mobs and invokes the language of persecution.[149] By taking on the mantle of the persecuted prophet, Margarito attempted to once more eclipse the U.S. American Mormon experience and reinforce the identity of his Mexican group as the "persecuted chosen people." Unable to defend their leader, Olarte reports that Bautista was jailed and sent to prison in Chalco to face the district judge, but not before arranging for five of his six wives to be spirited out of Ozumba to Mexico City.[150]

The actual trial in Chalco is an exultant moment in the memoirs of Alma de Olarte. The first blow to the charges occurred when the doctor

examined the victim of the rape—the sixth wife of Bautista and niece
of Melesio Hernández, Raquel Hernández. According to the doctor the
victim had been "violated" in the "last three days"—making it impossible
for Bautista to have carried out the act as he was imprisoned in Ozumba
at the time.[151] On this point Olarte's narrative is unclear, for he stated
that Bautista was arrested with rape as one of the charges, but later he
states that the rape charges were dropped because the rape, according to
the doctor in Chalco, would had to have happened during the time that
Bautista was already incarcerated. While Olarte could simply be confused
on the chronology, it is also possible that the doctor misdiagnosed the
situation or that the charges of rape were fabricated. No matter the reason
for the confusion, Bautista was never convicted of rape, and once cleared
of those charges he appeared before the public ministry agent to answer
for the remaining charges.

The first accusations were swindling, fraud, and deception. Upon
questioning Bautista about the whereabouts of fourteen thousand pesos,
the aged man indicated that Felipe Burgos, one of his accusers and former
bishop of the colony, took receipt of the money, and not he. Burgos then
took the stand and produced his account books showing that the colony's
money was spent on corn, beans, sugar, lard, chilies, tomatoes, various
foodstuffs, and community expenses. The judge asked with what authority he had taken control of the community fund, and Burgos answered
that he did so as a bishop.[152] In the middle of a Mexican courtroom, a
clergy member admitted that he had total control of the funds of a legally
incorporated colony of a Mexican municipal entity that also existed as an
unincorporated church—and suffered no penalties. Bautista was cleared
of the fraud, swindling, and deception charges but still faced the final
test—adultery by virtue of having multiple wives.

Alma de Olarte reports the conversation on adultery as follows:

> The judge took charge and said: "Señor Bautista, you are accused
> of adultery," then, directing his words at Brother Bautista, he asked:
> "Sr. Bautista, are you a Mormon?" Brother Bautista did not answer.
> The judge asked once more, "Are you a Mormon Sr. Bautista?
> Speak, tell me if you are a Mormon." With fear, Brother Bautista
> answered "Yes, sir, I am a Mormon." Then, the judge, with com-
> plete authority and solemnity looked at his secretary and said:

"Miss, please take this down. Señor Bautista is a Mormon, and Mormons have the right to have many wives."

Olarte follows with "Brother Bautista was freed."[153] The day was not entirely without punishment, though. Members of the Bautista group were fined for walking on the grass of the municipal offices. The discussion of polygyny with local authorities was not over, however.

In 1953, the municipal president of Ozumba, Roberto Rojas Grau, summoned "all the colonists" to the Ozumba town hall. Rojas Grau was concerned with stories that the colony practiced polygyny and, after ascertaining that Isidro Olarte had two wives, made the following statement: "We are not upset you have several women, what's upsetting is when they don't get along. You can have as many women as you want, but only one in Ozumba, another in Cuautla and another in Puebla, to avoid problems."[154] Harmony trumped the enforcement of laws on marriage by the state and placed tranquility ahead of the rule of law.

Beyond the municipal level, Colonia Industrial de la Nueva Jerusalén came to the attention of state and national organizations as well. For example, in 1953, Governor Sánchez Colín ordered its removal by, according to Olarte (and Olarte alone, calling into question its accuracy), bombardment ("ordenó la exterminación de la colonia a través de un bombardeo").[155] However, after an urgent telegram from Margarito Bautista's lawyer explained that the colony was on private property and not state or ejidal land, the governor withdrew the order to exterminate Colonia Industrial. Even federal entities such as the National Campesino Confederation (CNC) were aware of the situation of controversial land use in the area, but only ordered the investigation of the removal of several families from the colony (that came to nothing) and never moved to halt the corporate holding of resources and land on the edge of the village of Ozumba.[156]

Despite investigations, summons, and some harassment, the state made no concrete moves to disband the colony—including the governor's aborted "extermination order" rescinded soon after its issuance. As far as Ozumba was concerned, Colonia Industrial was legally incorporated into the community in September of 1947 (followed by an independence day parade on the sixteenth), after which they petitioned the governor, paid taxes, served in the military, sold in the market, and worked for the community. The existing partial list of PRI membership in Ozumba reveals no members of the Colonia Industrial inscribed in the official membership, but as the voter roll reveals, they were expected to participate in voting like anyone else. It appears the group posed no significant threat in voting power, as they pertained to voting district one, and their initial twenty-four male votes would hardly prove pivotal compared to the several thousand other votes in the district. While the list of PRI members for Ozumba was partial, if one assumes that the missing portion of the list shows no members of Colonia Industrial enrolled in the party, several possibilities exist—all of which require speculation. Perhaps the community encouraged members not to join the party as a way to avoid drawing attention to the community. Considering Bautista's imprisonment in Ozumba, as well as his encouragement of community members to be involved with the party (as well as the participation in city government to the present day), that option seems unlikely. Perhaps local PRI bosses banned citizens from Colonia Industrial from the party roles as their presence might cause tensions with other local residents, particularly those opposed to the religion practiced in the colony, in an era when the PRI was reconciling with Catholics and Catholicism in Mexico.

Regarding taxes and community participation, the group did not represent a major source of income with initially four and then later eight hectares of land. Continuous references to poverty by community members also shifts the argument away from the *colonia* being a strong income source for the municipality. When charges were leveled against members of the Ozumba populace for failure to contribute to the construction of a community water system, none of the small handful of rebellious community members was listed as living in the colony, though they did contribute to and receive the same water service. For the New Jerusalem of Colonia Industrial the pattern seems clear—as long as they proved no threat to those outside the community, whatever they did inside was fine with the state, even if the actions taken within the *colonia* hampered the rights of Mexican citizens within the group. With full knowledge of the local secular authorities, Colonia Industrial operated under its own rules.

Conclusion

The death of Margarito Bautista in 1961 at age eighty-three caused a shift in the colony, according to Alma Olarte; and those closest to the elder religionist soon found themselves on the margins of the community. The group modified its stand on the Law of Consecration to lessen the rigors of community membership and participation in the economic order. Even the rules governing plural marriage became less stringent, removing some of the age and residency restrictions first laid out. Much like the religious towns of New England, the enthusiasm of the first generation of religious settlers was dissipated in the second.[157] The community, however, continues to play its balancing act of law and religious freedom as the group finally received official recognition by the Mexican federal government in 1993 as the Iglesia del Reino de Dios en su Plenitud.[158] This recognition came fast on the heels of the efforts of President Carlos Salinas de Gortari to reconcile religion and the Mexican Constitution—though the state certainly did not legalize plural marriage in the process, and the inhabitants of Colonia Industrial have certainly not rejected it, even emerging unscathed from a 2003 investigation by the office of the attorney general of Mexico.

Despite the changes, the longevity of the Colonia Industrial de la Nueva Jerusalén invites questions as to how a community so outside of state control and law could exist for so long. First and foremost, the community owes its existence to local authorities and judges who valued the principles of religious tolerance inferred by the anti-Catholicism of the state, though not enshrined in practical laws or carried out by federal officials. While the community stayed large enough to affect the governability of the municipality to which they belonged, but small enough to avoid a broad popular challenge to local authorities, they avoid, time and again, regulation. While the absence of the rule of law in Mexico may have opened Colonia Industrial de la Nueva Jerusalén to harassment and persecution by Catholics and other Protestants, that same absence of law enforcement allowed the group a space for religious practice that their persecutors found offensive. The foundation of the colony and its "Mexicanized" form of Mormonism came hand-in-hand with a devotion to the creation of a new society for Mexico—but one that came with their own local definition of a "Mormonized" Mexican identity.

CHAPTER THREE

Sinarquismo and the María Auxiliadora Colonization Experiment

❧

✦ THE FINAL CASE STUDY IN THIS WORK departs dramatically from the first two studies, which focused on non-Catholic Christian movements sympathetic to the Sonoran revolution and the later power of the ruling Institutional Revolutionary Party (PRI). Not surprisingly, Catholics also desired to participate in the reconstruction of Mexico after the revolution and take advantage of the moment to create communities that followed Christian ideals combined with Mexican nationalist fervor. In this chapter, however, I explore the contrasting case of the Unión Nacional Sinarquista (UNS), or the *sinarquistas*, a right-wing Catholic movement that sought to counter the influence of the revolutionary state and to organize Mexico according to communities united around their shared faith. Despite the label of "counterrevolutionary fascists" placed on the group by the ruling PRI, the *sinarquistas* are as much a part of the flood of community and religious experimentation set loose by the Mexican Revolution as the less traditional movements of the Luz del Mundo or the Mormons of Colonia Industrial discussed in the first two chapters.

In particular, this chapter utilizes the writings of Salvador Abascal, *jefe nacional* of the UNS (1940–41), to focus on the *sinarquistas'* colonization project in Baja California Sur as a means of rebuilding Mexican society on a local level and reject the blueprints laid out by the ruling party. Abascal's openly counterrevolutionary position posed its own social revolution to turn the new state on its head and revive the halcyon days when church and state ruled together as the "Two Majesties" of Hispanic life. More importantly, this desire for an idealized fantasy of medieval Catholicism was founded in a drive to drastically reduce the power of the central state and increase the power of the local community—a project played out in the UNS-Abascal project to create an alternative model to the "official" revolution. Nevertheless, Abascal's Catholic utopia mirrored many of the goals of the revolution after 1940, including rural colonization instead of land redistribution, literacy, and agricultural production. Such shared missions earned Abascal allies from both the Mexican right and the left and demonstrated the national desire to solve some of the great problems of Mexican society through efforts in community formation, regardless of political leanings.

Salvador Abascal and the Unión Nacional Sinarquista

"My first memories are of the revolution," wrote Salvador Abascal Infante in his 789-page memoir, *Mis recuerdos: Sinarquismo y Colonia María Auxiliadora.*[1] These memories, however, did not match the glorious struggle for freedom and progress perpetuated by the ruling party, and instead focused on the loss of his home, forced migrations, seeing his first dead body at age five, and his mother rescuing his father from *villista* soldiers. As Abascal recalled:

> The Carranza mob came and Carranza-ized us as soon as they could—from taking the good mare, our mauser and even our new little house we had not even moved into yet—all because my father was [alleged to be] *villista*; then came the *villistas*, who arrested my father . . . because he was [alleged to be] a *carrancista*, and my mother . . . went twice to pull him away from the firing squad wall. Life became quite impossible.[2]

Robbery, kidnapping, and chaos from the child's point of view are what Abascal recalls best about the first great social revolution in the twentieth century, and he describes his formative years as short bursts of joy found in family and community life in the small village of Santa María, Michoacán, interrupted by the intrusions of politics and revolution.

By 1916, Abascal's father opted to move the family away from the poverty of Santa María to Morelia, Michoacán, where his sons could receive an education. Once in Morelia, however, the family was schooled in more than just arithmetic and reading. Abascal's father, Adalberto Abascal, kept them on a strict regimen, even bathing them in the middle of the night every day because he had read that "the children of aristocrats" did so in order to "gain the strength necessary to destroy their effeminate enemies."[3] His education in the tensions between church and state also came in Morelia where his father became a member of the secret Catholic organization known as the "U." The group organized members of Morelia's Catholic society for the defense of Catholicism, particularly the looting or seizure of Catholic churches, convents, and schools by the leftist governor of Michoacán, Francisco Mújica. For example, in 1921, "U" informants discovered that Mújica was planning to seize the Teresian order's convent. Abascal's father organized a group of "hundreds of followers" to surround the building and deny Mújica easy entry into the convent without provoking a riot.[4] Abascal became well versed in the standoff between the revolution and the Catholic Church.

Salvador's traditional Catholic background made the priesthood a natural choice, and he entered religious education and seminary, where he remained for five years before deciding at fifteen that he was leaving. He found his "fascination" with women undeniable and decided he did not want to become "encumbered" by the priesthood, stating that he "rejected it [the priesthood] without difficulty."[5] Faced with choosing law, medicine, or engineering—"almost the only jobs available in those days"—Abascal opted for law, as it seemed the one he disliked the least. From there he opted for criminal law, as it fascinated him because it dealt with "liberty and honor."[6] He dismissed commercial law as a defense of the rich and constitutional law as an empty and romantic study.

By 1931, Abascal was serving as a justice of the peace, or known as the office of the *juzgado mixto de primera instancia* in Ayutla, Guerrero, and later in other towns throughout the state. Here, as an employee of the government, he became painfully aware of the system in place in Guerrero.

Among the things that angered him were the constant offers of bribes to sway his decisions (which he claims never to have accepted) and the grinding poverty throughout the countryside. At one point, Abascal took on a town council for having a prominent local resident and former *zapatista* general gunned down, only to have the governor of Guerrero transfer him. On another occasion, a murderer he was prosecuting was released by local authorities and headed to Mexico City. It had to be a conspiracy, wrote Abascal; it must be "the power of Masonry" combined against him to release his prisoner.[7]

Above all, however, he felt "a profound ache" about the division of villages due to crime. Called to investigate a fatal gunshot incident, Abascal arrived minutes before the victim died. Though he tried to get information from the wounded man about the shooter, the victim was unable to speak. Seeing that the man was dying, Abascal pressed on, saying the man should tell him who shot him and also forgive the assailant. The gunshot victim, however, responded with an angry "no." Abascal persisted, insisting the man forgive his assailant and ask God for forgiveness, but could only watch as the man died in agony, refusing to forgive his assailant. This rejection of forgiveness, mercy, and God left a lasting impression on Abascal who saw it as a result of the secular state and the division caused between Mexicans by the official revolution.[8] Mexicans shot down by other Mexicans was bad enough, but to then have them reject divine forgiveness and mercy was too much for Abascal to comprehend.

By 1935, Abascal was back in Morelia practicing law and was approached by a member of the National Defense League of Religious Liberty (*la liga*) to work against sitting president Lázaro Cárdenas. The secret organization only contacted him once, and he never heard from them about the matter again. However, the next day he was contacted by a friend of his father (named only as Dr. X, even after forty-five years) and asked to join the supreme council of the Michoacán division of the league. At the time, Abascal recalls, he saw it as a secret Catholic state within Mexico fighting against what he termed the "atheist revolution," "international Judaism," and the Jewish conspiracy to take over the world. However, he follows the remarks on the mission of the legions by saying it was only "beautiful illusions!"[9] Whatever his later reflections on the weakness of the league, the group familiarized him with the Catholic counterrevolutionary movement and put him in on the opening formation of the Union Nacional Sinarquista in 1937.

As part of a tradition of politically active Catholicism, the Unión Nacional Sinarquista appeared in 1937 during the heyday of the populist president Lázaro Cárdenas. Formed as the public face of the secret Catholic society known as La Base, the UNS was one of several cells that campaigned against the secular state by encouraging religious community organization and rejecting federal programs such as land distribution and secular education.[10] In this, the UNS arguably draws on the traditional conservative posture of the Catholic Church to oppose what they saw as the state's attempted domination of everyday life. The UNS is certainly part of a long and traditional debate about the relationship between the Catholic Church and the state in Latin America, as discussed in chapter 1.

The other tenets of the UNS are rooted in Catholic social doctrine as espoused by Pope Leo XIII's 1891 encyclical *Rerum Novarum*. The papal pronouncement castigated unbridled capitalism, encouraged worker organization while maintaining private property, and supported the social safety net of private charity. The UNS also drew heavily from the 1931 follow-up to *Rerum Novarum*, the encyclical *Quadragesimo Anno*, issued by Pope Pius XI. Feeling that the social questions of the day, especially what he saw as the corrosive effects of individualism and the overburdened state, had not adequately been resolved by *Rerum Novarum*, Pius XI hoped to encourage a return to the "rich social life which was once highly developed through associations of various kinds."[11] His approach to resolving this issue of individualism and the distorted role of the state was to devolve certain social functions back to corporate bodies to administer, a strategy known as corporatism (*corporativismo*). These bodies were to be "essentially self-governing bodies, with the door opened to the state intervention only in cases of unresolvable [*sic*] conflict."[12] As political scientist Howard Wiarda phrases it, "In the corporatist tradition we are treating a distinctive, alternative, and in many ways peculiarly Iberic-Latin way of coping with and managing the great modern issues of industrialization, mass society, and accelerated social change."[13] Such a description fits exactly the concerns of the UNS as well as Mexican society in the Cárdenas years.

In fact, this corporatist approach was highly popular in southern Europe and in Latin America (in places such as the Dominican Republic, Brazil, Chile, and Colombia). However, unlike the vision of the pope, many nations (such as Italy under Mussolini) used the corporate idea not to allow activity free from the state, but to dominate the state by dominating the corporate structures. Wiarda characterizes this as the difference between "corporatism of association," which first inspired nations to move in this direction, and the "state corporatism" that in many (but not all) cases devolved into fascism.[14] Faced with the secular state corporatism of Cárdenas and the ruling party, the UNS was far more enthusiastic about the "corporatism of association," very much reflected in their unwillingness to form a political party or enter into any form of politics and participation in the state.

The UNS declaration of June 12, 1937, reflects the teachings of *Rerum Novarum* and *Quadragesimo Anno* in that it calls for individual liberties, a spiritual attitude of service and generosity, aid to the poor instead of money for party politics, opposition to hate and violence, justice, and relief of human misery. It also advocates order and organization, devolving duties to nonstate organizations to handle many of the social questions of the day, such as poverty or labor tension. The path designated by the UNS, is not based solely on long-standing debates about the position of the Catholic Church in relation to the liberal state in Mexico, but also on global Catholicism's concerns about faith in the face of modern capitalism and competition for hearts and minds from socialism and strong central states.[15] Despite leaving his seminary training early, Abascal was still destined to become a priest of sorts—or at least a missionary—for the National Union of Sinarquistas (UNS) and their interpretation of Catholic social doctrine. And indeed, Abascal and other proselytizers were extremely successful, as by 1941 the UNS grew to over a half million members, mostly in the western and central Mexican states of Michoacán, Jalisco, Guerrero, Guanajuato, and Querétaro.[16]

The revolutionary position and language of the UNS is readily visible in some of the available sources on the movement. Principles such as caring for the poor, rule of law, democracy (though some in the UNS found democracy merely a prelude to chaos), Mexican nationalism, localism, and land reform all appear in the UNS position—many of the same items fought for by the liberal revolutionaries in the early stages of the revolution.[17] They also express a deep concern for the reconstruction of Mexico after the destruction of the revolution, but this often meant the preservation of not only Spanish architecture but the perceived values of "hispanidad."[18] They also employ a language of land reform that is most interesting.

Take, for instance, one occurrence from the memoirs of Salvador Abascal. The scene is easily imaginable. A line of peasants, heads bowed, stood in a line to discuss their grievances with the president of Mexico.

Hats in hand and wind tugging at their homespun cotton clothing, the men have never met the president of their country face-to-face. He is their great leader—some call him their father—and the peasants mumble gratitude, some smile, and all shake hands with the president. All, that is, but one. One holds his head up, and when the president stops to speak with him, this man does not mumble words of gratitude, but demands the removal of the U.S. presence from Mexico, respect for the national flag, and, above all, land. Land, he says, will make him a truly free man—a free Mexican.

A scene from Elia Kazan's 1952 *Viva Zapata?* one might think. But this is no Steinbeck screenplay, though the symbolic players may be the same. In this case the peasant is a *sinarquista*, Eusebio González (not the same Eusebio from chapter 2), and the president is famed land reformer Lázaro Cárdenas. And like the very Catholic Emiliano Zapata, this peasant wants land. "Now that the Revolution offers you a bit of land," says Eusebio, "you must struggle so they [the state] give(s) you title to that land so that you can be free."[19] But what is the land that these Catholics want? Hardly the ejidal land system of state-sponsored collective ownership, but individual plots that are privately owned. Essentially, Eusebio demanded the right of the individual farmer, celebrating producer ideology, while Lázaro Cárdenas comes off as the conservative, paternal figure standing for centralized, orthodox authority.

In his fieldwork, carried out in rural Querétero, political scientist Lorenzo Covarrubias gives us another example in the small agricultural village of Santo Niño de Praga. As Covarrubias points out, agriculturalists found representation outside of the state in the UNS. This community rejected overtures by the ejidal land program to expand its holdings and own property in common, allowing them access to both financial and technical resources. The reason? This pueblo did not want to "be in servitude to the state."[20] The language of rejection of the central state also points to another revolutionary aspect of the UNS related to land hunger—localism.

The localist notion is a combination of two particular forces: antimodernity and local culture, particularly the binding ties of shared religious culture. Such ideas present in the revolution (and the reaction to it) and in Mexican society are neither surprising nor new. The village and its people communed through "shared religiosity—by the religious landscape of shrines and pilgrimages that surrounded them, and by the calendar full of saints' days and other sacred occasions that brought them together in celebration," as was the case with the followers of Emiliano Zapata in his struggle against the powers of Mexico City.[21] As historian Alan Knight has pointed out, displays of loyalty to the *patria chica* (local community) in conjunction with the revolution are not unthinkable, as revolutionaries could simultaneously maintain ideas of "a lively notion of the nation" while still maintaining a "strong identification with the *patria chica* [that was] inherently decentralising, even anarchist."[22]

Even the liberal and anticlerical thinkers of Mexico's reform movement to limit the role of religion in society waxed nostalgic about the superiority of Mexican village life, including religion. Historian E. Bradford Burns cites liberal Mexican thinker Ignacio Altamirano's *Christmas in the Mountains* (1871) as a triumphant salute to the stability of patriarchal village society that is "a simple but good place, [with] morality, harmony, and a patriarchal society, in which priest, mayor, school teacher, and village elders guided the local inhabitants." As Burns argues, the story of the jaded military officer escaping the cares of the world in order to find solace in "simple virtue, and true, modest happiness, which in vain I had sought for in the midst of opulent cities" is a fairly standard response to modernization in nineteenth-century Latin American society.[23]

Considering the presence and tradition of the exaltation of the local village and its religious life in even the most liberal and revolutionary corners of Mexico, it is easy to understand such a presence in a movement as conservative and Catholic as the UNS. Following their own spirit of localism, the UNS made building plans available to their members on how to construct the ideal small farmstead—down to the location of fruit trees and animal sheds—and a local schoolhouse.[24] For those forced to live in cities, membership was divided into zones based on *barrios*—defined as "a part of the city that is distinguished from the rest by its chapel, market, customs, [and] particular traditions."[25] The description sounds more like villages or seventeenth-century cities than the modern cities of 1940s Mexico. It is precisely this type of focused response to local needs combined with a preservation and even elevation of rural culture that made the UNS so popular in areas such as agricultural Querétaro.[26]

The antimodern position of the early UNS is readily apparent in much of its literature. Take for example the reflections of *sinarquista* Salvador Abascal on the growth of movie houses in rural Mexico after the revolution. "Movies are miserable wastes of time . . . a corrupter of minds and customs. *El Cine* is a drug."[27] Rather than using technology to look to an imaginary outside world, Abascal wanted Mexicans to look inward at the "customs" of village life for the foundation of Mexican society. In his view, other usurpers of Catholic village life included alcoholism, Protestantism, sex education, and unions. The UNS also identified *caciquismo*, or local political bosses, in its list of outside invaders that needed removal from village life for their tendency to act as co-opted puppets of the central state.[28] By rejecting politics and establishing order in villages based on Catholic morality, the UNS hoped to mobilize every village in Mexico toward ritual and community to "convert the people of the *patria* into a people of morality, culture, and the habit of work, abundance of goods, and a civic spirit. We want to be part of a people full of spiritual peace, full of knowledge, and full of bread. Only with such a people can the *patria* begin to rise to true greatness."[29]

And what did such unyielding localism mean for UNS perceptions of foreign powers? While the official revolution bought arms from and made deals with the United States, or imported intellectuals and military manuals from republican Spain and the Soviet Union, *sinarquistas* argued that the triumph of Mexico needed to come from within, not through importation of culture, goods, and ideas.[30] As expected, the United States and Britain were special targets of the UNS, particularly the two empires' market capitalism and democracy, or, as the UNS put it, their false democracies. Wrote Abascal, "No democracy really exists in the modern world— not in England or the United States—because International Finance rules with an iron hand."[31] The evidence of this statement, argues Abascal, is found in the observation that "the Jew Roosevelt" only brought the United States into World War II to make sure communist Russia did not fall, and that England fought for power, prominence, and the desire to maintain its empire.[32] To him, the entry of Mexico into the war on the side of the Allies was a sign that the United States was moving to swallow up Mexico. The presence of U.S. military personnel in Mexico, pro-Allied sentiment in the press, and Mexican labor in the United States to aid in the war effort could only serve to distract Mexicans from U.S. imperialism. Blinded to the truth of U.S. behavior, Mexicans would never see the infiltration and preparation for invasion of their nation by the United States. On an ironic side note, however, Mexican *braceros* in the United States constituted some of the most generous donors to the UNS transnational organization.

An official *sinarquista* declaration issued in 1941, titled *Guerra, No,* argued: "We are radically and resolutely Mexican and nationalists. We indignantly repudiate this colonial mentality that conceives of Mexico as no more than a satellite state, destined to spin eternally in a subaltern orbit of darkness and misery." In an interesting follow-up it states, "We [Mexicans] have been able to kill each other for thirty years of revolution but we still do not have the valor to give our lives in defense of the *patria*."[33] Even in 1941, the UNS still felt it was engaged in a struggle for the direction of Mexico.

In an interesting twist, President Cárdenas posed a question to the above-mentioned peasant, Eusebio, regarding nationalism. Asked Cárdenas, "How do you view this business of clergy that come and impose their laws and have their head in Rome? I warn you that the *sinarquistas* are provoking the revolution because they are bullied by the priests, and you will see that you will have to take up arms." To which Eusebio responded, "If *sinarquismo* were run by the clergy, as you say it is, it wouldn't be what it is. You should know that *sinarquismo* is not a dividing party . . . perhaps the majority is Catholic but that does not mean it is bullied around by the priests. Ultimately, this is not a question of religion but of civics."[34] For this peasant, the focus and momentum of the movement originated in Mexico alone, and not even the Vatican could control it.

Indeed, one anonymous *sinarquista* even explicitly laid claim to its being the most authentic, revolutionary, nationalist movement in Mexico. Said the speaker, as recorded in a transcript:

> *Sinarquismo* coincides with the revolution because we desire to transform the conditions in which many Mexicans live. We want harmony, unity, and social equilibrium—in other words, we want a common good. For this, because we are not in agreement with the present conditions, because of this *sinarquismo* is revolutionary: but we are contradictory to those mystifying charlatans and we condemn their demagoguery that stirs up the masses and stirs up in men their most vile passions.

He then goes on to condemn a whole list of foreign symbols employed by the revolution, such as red banners or hammer-and-sickle designs.[35] For the UNS, the PRI leadership in Mexico City was not "authentically Mexican," but was composed of false Mexicans "contaminated by the gold of Moscow."[36] Though they rejected the "official" revolution as constructed by the ruling party, the *sinarquistas* certainly saw their movement for the agricultural and localist good of Mexico as far more authentic than that of the ruling party.

This struggle to define and control Mexican authenticity in the UNS often took the form of a racial celebration of *indigenismo* and *mestizaje*. While the *sinarquistas* are often labeled as fascists for their authoritarian, nationalist, and right-wing views, this certainly does not exhibit the same connotations of racial purity as that of German fascism, despite their strident anti-Semitism. When President Manuel Ávila Camacho (1940–46) labeled the group "exotic" in a public speech, Abascal fired back a telegram naming *sinarquismo* as the most Mexican of social movements, one reason being that the majority of members were "indígenas y mestizos" and that they existed to fight "racial, economic, and social" problems.[37] Racial problems even provided another reason for the UNS to nationalist claims of superiority over the United States. Next to pictures of a race riot in Detroit, *El Sinarquista* ran a story condemning racial purity theories in Germany and the United States, as well as the attendant discrimination that accompanied it for blacks, Mexicans, and Jews.[38]

The UNS's nationalist authenticity, land policy, and antimodern stance, all reflect how much the official revolution had still not "institutionalized" all of the alternatives that sought to remake society after the disappearance of Porfirio Díaz. Clearly the *sinarquistas* still engaged in the struggle for a better Mexican society. And, despite the great success they had in the 1940s—or perhaps because of it—the UNS and Salvador Abascal dreamt of taking the movement to a higher level, not only by constructing society via ideology but by physically building it with colonies.

Planning a Christian Community

By 1938, Abascal was a rising star in the UNS, even traveling to the radically anticlerical southern state of Tabasco to combat the socialist governor of the state, Tomás Garrido Canabal.[39] Indeed, he gathered huge crowds all over Mexico and recruited thousands to the cause of *sinarquismo*. He even seems to have carried an aura that caused one scholar to observe that people were "attracted by his mystical power."[40] Abascal himself refers to the momentum of the movement in 1940 as "advanced by a mystical power that not even we could articulate."[41] Finally, due to internal divisions, Abascal was invited by the governing council to take control of the UNS in August of 1940. At thirty years old, Abascal headed the largest, and perhaps the only, viable opposition organization to the PRI in Mexico with over 500,000 members.

Their goals, as stated above, were to put Mexico on a path toward economic self-sufficiency, unite the nation under one religion (Roman Catholicism), and eliminate political bickering. Most importantly, the UNS sought to return land to private and peasant ownership, distance Mexico from foreign influence, and make the local village or neighborhood the center of life. With the movement surpassing half a million, Abascal boldly moved to capture the attention of the government and the imagination of Mexicans: Like colonial-era Jesuit missionary Eusebio Francisco Kino in northern New Spain, the UNS would send *sinarquistas* north to establish a cordon against the barbarians. In this case, the project would be colonies, not missions, and the barbarians were the *gringos*, not the *indios bárbaros*.

While Kino is certainly mentioned in Abascal's memoirs, he links his idea for colonization to a 1936 conversation with a Baja California Norte resident. According to his contact, Baja Norte was a moral and economic appendage of the United States with vice and corruption being the most noticeable features of the relationship with their northern neighbor, especially evident after Prohibition in the United States. With so few people living in Baja and with poor physical connections to the rest of Mexico, Abascal truly believed that the United States would move to annex the peninsula within ten to thirty years. The United States would then use their new base to dominate the culture and economics of the northern states of Sonora, Sinaloa, and Nayarit. "Such an enormous amputation," lamented Abascal, "would be the death of the Mexican *patria*. Mexico, the soul of Mexico, would die of shame."[42] Clearly, patriotism demanded action, but how could such a grand project come to fruition? The *sinarquistas* did not advocate moving to the cities of Tijuana, Loreto, or La Paz to convert the urban centers of Baja and seize political control or settle on the coast and become fishermen. Instead, Abascal's plan was to create a traditional central Mexican agricultural village in the middle of the desert, much as Kino or Junipero Serra had tried.

Through the spring and summer of 1941, the official newspaper of the UNS, *El Sinarquista*, appeared to be preparing the membership for the possibility of colonization without mentioning the actual plans. In June of 1941, the UNS opened its first affiliate in Baja California. Then, through July, the paper ran a series of stories such as "How We Lost Texas," "The Invasion of [18]47," a story on U.S. piracy, and finally, a "Close Focus" on the territories of Baja California Norte and Sur, especially their mineral wealth and agricultural potential.[43]

In August of 1941, Abascal headed for the Baja Peninsula to scout the area from La Paz in the south to Tijuana in the north for colonization zones. *El Sinarquista* for August 14 only mentions that he is on a visit to the northeast, and making an "exploration," but with no further information. Selections from Abascal's diary make one wonder if he traveled to the same place he describes in his later letters to UNS headquarters. During the trip he simply gushes about the possibilities for colonization with the presence of ample water, cheap land, room to expand, natural resources, such as minerals, for mining, business, and industry—all the things for a large-scale introduction of families into a wilderness—even a desert wilderness.[44] Abascal's journal reads like the biblical Joshua returning from Canaan with a bundle of grapes (substitute grapes for the seven-kilo sweet potato Abascal uses), to induce Israel to cross into the Promised Land.

With the cry "Salvaremos Baja," Abascal put the organizing process in motion to form the colony later known as Colonia María Auxiliadora.[45] La Base required little convincing to back the proposal, and Abascal approached the Manuel Ávila Camacho administration on September 2, 1941, to approve the plan and provide land. Arguing that forming the colony would be an act of supreme dedication to Mexico, Abascal also requested that his colony be allowed religious education and no regulation on clerical activity. In a September 11, 1941, meeting, Ávila Camacho, a believing Catholic himself, approved the idea, adding that the central government would provide free land as well as pay for the transportation costs of the colonists.[46] In a grand convergence of patriotic fervor, the "counterrevolution" of *sinarquismo* and the central state, led by a former general bent on consolidating the power of the ruling party, sought to colonize the desolate Baja Peninsula.

That same day, *El Sinarquista* revealed their formal plans for colonization, announcing with the headline: "We undertake a gigantic work— The colonization of Baja California—Thousands of Mexican families to populate desert zones—Thus, Sinarquismo shows its profound love for the *patria*." The story goes on to say that colonization would "facilitate the establishment of federal soldiers in places lacking defense for the nation." Baja, as the least populated of Mexico's territories "and furthest away economically and in distance," needed protection from a possible invasion from the United States, claimed *El Sinarquista*.[47] In a September 11, 1941, letter to local leaders, the UNS called for "hard workers . . . farmers . . . intellectuals . . . and artisans" to join in the quest to "begin this great work . . . to create a model of society (that will be known by all for its morality, intellectual advancement, and material gain)." By 1946, the UNS wanted to see 150,000 people relocated to Baja.[48]

The response to the call for colonists was immediate. By September 25, 1941, *El Sinarquista* announced that "thousands" had volunteered to take up the challenge to "create a new type of society founded in the eternal Christian principles." These volunteers, says *El Sinarquista*, were clearly "animated by the spirit of missionary soldiers."[49] Donations also began to pour in, nearly 28,000 pesos by mid-December, as well as a large offer of agricultural plants, farming and construction equipment, and clothes from the *sinarquista* chapter in Fresno, California. In fact, over the next three years of the experiment, the various chapters of the UNS in the United States—from Indiana Harbor, Indiana, to Los Angeles, California—would consistently contribute more than the chapters of the UNS in Mexico, most probably because they were earning wages far higher than their Mexican counterparts.[50] Even "Anglo" Catholics in the United States applauded the effort, saying: "Their [the UNS] current project of peopling and making fruitful the barren stretches of lower California commands the respect of many in our country who know the difficulty and the general advantages deriving from this development."[51]

President Ávila Camacho also took possession of formal plans for the colony on October 6, 1941, of the same year, prompting fierce opposition in the Chamber of Deputies against supporting the proposal, arguing that Abascal would turn Baja into a Nazi republic on the Pacific.[52] Such protests, however, fell on deaf ears, and Abascal maintained an open channel of communication with the president on the colonization plans. In early November he informed Ávila Camacho that the secretary of the interior, Miguel Alemán, had been helpful in promises of transportation to the site in Baja, and that General Múijica, now governor of Baja Sur and one of Mexico's most radical leftists still in power, had also made promises of support—the same who as governor of Michoacán had battled Abascal's father in Morelia for the control of a Catholic convent. Abascal even notes—in an obvious last shot at the government—that the UNS eventually planned to build small factories for Catholic workers expelled from their jobs in El Salto and Uruapan, Michoacán, when those workers had not joined the state-sponsored unions. All in all, Abascal appeared confident in the project in November.[53] The fate of the Baja colony, however, was sealed even before departure, and not by the protest of Mexican deputies, but by a decision made thousands of miles away in Tokyo.

On December 7, 1941, the early morning strike of the Japanese Empire at Pearl Harbor, Hawaii, sent ripples throughout the world, including Mexico City. Though Mexico would not declare war on the Axis powers until May of 1942, President Ávila Camacho leaned toward supporting the United States immediately. Abascal, traveling in Michoacán, scrambled to return to Mexico City to reassess the situation as the scale of the war in the Pacific and its implications became apparent. According to his account, he was intentionally delayed by La Base from returning to Mexico City. This delay allowed La Base leader Antonio Santacruz to make a deal with the central government to phase out Abascal and sabotage his colonization project in exchange for a cessation of government attacks on the UNS and an opportunity for Santacruz to curb the power of Abascal. La Base, claims Abascal, saw a way to mainstream itself with the tolerant Ávila Camacho by sacrificing Abascal, the most vocal anti-Yankee member of the group. Abascal used State Department documents from the United States National Archive to show that the FBI and the U.S. embassy in Mexico saw him as a threat, and by La Base offering to push him out, they would give Ávila Camacho an immediate prize to offer the United States.[54]

Abascal returned to Mexico City on the December 9, 1941, and by December 11, he was no longer head of the UNS. He appears to have attempted a last-minute saving effort, sending a December 10 telegram to President Ávila Camacho saying that, considering the war in the Pacific, he could easily raise a thousand families (with enough funding) in two weeks' time for the settlement and protection of Baja California.[55] The offer, however, appears to have been ignored and Abascal was forced to work out an exit deal with La Base and Santacruz. In exchange for his peaceful resignation from leadership of the UNS, Abascal demanded that he be allowed total control of the María Auxiliadora project as well as guaranteed funding. Eager to be rid of the firebrand, La Base quickly agreed, seeing the colonization project as a way to dump Abascal in one of the most remote corners of Mexico.[56] Though he had not planned on going to live in Baja himself, the radical Catholic packed his bags and headed for Mazatlán to board a boat for La Paz, Baja California. It is not surprising that there is no mention of the power struggle in the pages of *El Sinarquista*, only a small note that Manuel Torres Bueno was now the new UNS chief. Abascal, it notes, had "volunteered" to lead the colonization effort.[57]

Living the Christian Community

With the colonization announced, and with the responsibility for the
project squarely on Abascal's shoulders, the events of December seem to
support Abascal's assertion that his dismissal to Baja was a planned failure, designed to remove him permanently from power in the UNS and in
Mexico in general. Settlement in Baja was an approved goal under the former administration of Lázaro Cárdenas as well as Ávila Camacho, and even
appears on official letterhead as the phrase "Cooperate with the progress
of Mexico and its efforts to prosper its territories of Baja California and
Quintana Roo."[58] However, such projects seem possible only with a large
investment of funds.[59] Indeed, the state received a number of letters from
Cárdenas-era *ejiditarios* in Baja begging the state not to send the *sinarquistas* since local resources were so few and state funds had been so lacking
that the *sinarquista* presence would only devour what little the local population had.[60] With that in mind, the actions of Secretary of the Interior
Miguel Alemán seem more sinister than they might otherwise.

On December 11, 1941, Abascal sent a telegram to the president
asking why Alemán had still not approved funds for transportation. By
December 16, 1941, his tone grows more desperate, saying that the families are waiting, having sold all they own, and still no money has arrived
for equipment or transportation. In addition, the previously approved
government boats had failed to appear, forcing them to charter their own
expensive boat. Nevertheless, the group departed without funds, and a
Christmas Day telegram by the new UNS *jefe nacional*, Manuel Torres
Bueno, describes the situation as rather bleak with no money for any agricultural equipment.[61] That notwithstanding, the new UNS leader ordered
the go-ahead of another colony in Sonora, under the direction of another
former UNS head, Manuel Zermeño, draining away valuable funds from
the Baja enterprise.[62] Even *El Sinarquista* dropped its usually sunny façade
to report that by January 1, 1942, the government withdrawal of support
as well as the reluctance of wealthy *sinarquistas* to contribute had left the
colonization effort in danger. "We cannot fail!" it proclaimed.[63] Despite
all of these setbacks, Abascal pushed ahead with his usual zeal.

Historian Jean Meyer avers that Abascal saw himself in the model
of a new Moses or a modern Padre Kino taking control of the north.[64]
While Meyer shows no evidence for Abascal's view of himself as a Moses
figure, the connection with Kino and the contact/conquest-era fervor
of the regular clergy is abundant in Abascal's rhetoric. For example, in

commissioning a Dutch engineer, Peter Wiegman, to begin construction and planning of the colony, he instructs the European to construct a "Paradise of God," reminiscent of utopian dreams from bygone colonial eras. Indeed, at the Sonora colony, called Villa Kino, Manuel Zermeño drew an explicit comparison between the UNS enterprise for "progress and civilization" and the colonial Michoacán hospital societies of Vasco de Quiroga.[65] Unlike the Franciscans or Jesuits, however, Abascal would take his "mission population" with him rather than establishing outposts to convert the heathen.

Who went with the former UNS chief? Abascal signed up eighty-five families or nearly four hundred people to settle the Santo Domingo Valley of Baja California Sur. Judging from pictures, the group appears to contain several middle-class families, but was mostly composed of poorer *mestizo* and indigenous agrarians. Meyer notes that most were day laborers, peasants, dissatisfied *ejiditarios*, and small landholders.[66] Abascal also sent entire families rather than just male heads of household. The reasoning at the time was that men separated from their families would relax their morals and children without fathers would lose proper respect for their elders. For even Abascal, as a bachelor (he would later marry in March of 1942), to participate in the project "[had] no honor."[67] The basis of the ideal community needed to be the family, conceived of as a father, mother, children, and associated blood relatives.

Reflecting back from 1980, after almost forty years, he justifies his decision to send whole families by pointing to the *bracero* program (a guest-worker program in the United States) as an example of men separated from morality as they worked for the *gringos* and left their families at home in chaos.[68] In his opinion, sending men to work for the "Jew Roosevelt" made Mexico a whore, whereas he proposed a unified Mexico of families working in Mexico, for Mexico. Abascal's reasoning is both nationalist and localist, insisting that the family order supersede all other needs. Abascal also admits that he judged the eighty-five families as sufficient to get the attention of the whole nation and stir their national pride.[69] The presence of children and the women who cared for them in Abascal's traditional model would eventually prove the undoing of the project as fifteen children and six adults starved to death in the desert and resources were diverted from building the colony to caring for the ill and dying.[70]

Before the colonists could arrive in Baja, however, they had to make the passage between Mazatlán on the mainland and La Paz on the peninsula.

For the agrarian colonists—most from the highland areas of Michoacán and Guanajuato—the open-water crossing proved extremely difficult. Seasickness left dozens unable to function due to nausea, dehydration, and diarrhea. By January 1, 1942, only 218 colonists of the original 400 (the rest abandoned the project) remained for the long, dry caravan up 300 kilometers of desert roads to the Santo Domingo Valley. *El Sinarquista* published photos of a military reception of the colonists and sunny reports of the colonists' prospects.[71]

For several days the party was delayed in La Paz, but that setback provides clues as to how Abascal envisioned society. Disembarking from the boat, the party formed a procession carrying crosses, images of the Virgin Guadalupe, and other banners—both political and religious—and marched in silence to the parish church.[72] The intent of the procession was to establish the divine solemnity of the project on which they were about to embark and focus the attention of the citizens of La Paz. This act of establishing a community for the defense of Mexico required a manifestation of their dedication to the divine—a dual purpose summed up well by the presence of the Virgin of Guadalupe, who serves as both a national and religious symbol.

Forced to wait in a large rented house for trucks to arrive to carry them north, the colonists lived together in very close quarters, an act Abascal found totally repugnant. "The communal life in La Paz caused great hardships to the *Señoras* and their husbands."[73] The problem was mainly families sleeping in close proximity to other families with no separation of walls—no sacred preservation of the sanctity of the home. Living "communally" represented a lower order of life. The only part of the "physical and social order" of La Paz that Abascal did find acceptable was the absence of army patrols or *agrarista* militias, "which made our people feel as if they were in a civilized atmosphere with respect of human beings."[74] For Abascal, society needed to be ordered, but not a Hobbesian society of violence forced to order by government troops, but rather one inspired by the respect instilled in the temple of the home and shared sacred experiences in the cathedrals of God. Nevertheless, it was one of Mexico's most noted *agrarista* leaders, Francisco Mújica, that provided the trucks to carry the *sinarquistas* north as well as a government-owned drill to punch a well in the Baja desert for the colonists. Mújica even started a road project from La Paz to Loreto—not far from the site of the new colony—to help facilitate the growth of the colony.[75] As Abascal reported of his La Paz meeting with Mújica: "He never tried to impede us in the least bit. On the contrary, he helped us whenever he could; though he could do little more for the limitations of the economic resources of the Southern District [Baja Sur]."[76] Armed with the hand of God on one side and an icon of the Mexican left on the other, the *sinarquistas* began their colonization in earnest.

Though the first wave of colonists arrived on January 3, 1942, and had begun planting crops, the founding day of the colony is recorded as Sunday, January 11, 1942. The arrival of the majority of colonists signaled the go-ahead for the necessary ceremony to establish the colony officially, and even though they had celebrated mass the day before, the January 11 mass was special. The visiting priest taught the colonists from the New Testament letter of Paul to the Colossians (Abascal does not mention a specific verse) "which appeared directly for us."[77] Colossians is a rebuke of Christians gone astray and exhorts them to return to their duties to Christ and society—a mission with which the *sinarquistas* would have identified closely. After mass, the colonists formed a procession under the cross and the "Capitana" banner, as well as national and *sinarquista* flags, and marched to the small chapel in Santo Domingo, at this point little more than a makeshift chapel of reed mats. There, in the chapel, Abascal delivered the flag of Mexico to the feet of "la Reina," Mary, the Queen of Mexico, and declared "solemnly" the foundation "for the honor of God and the good of the *patria*, the *sinarquista* colony María Auxiliadora, in Santo Domingo, Baja California, this day, Sunday, January 11, 1942, at thirteen hundred hours and fifteen minutes."[78] Nothing short of a ceremony culminating with the union of Agustín Iturbide's tricolor and the Virgin Mary, recorded down to the exact minute, would do for Abascal and the colonists.

As Lewis argues of the "critique" of society generated by revitalization movements, that same critique must be powered first by a perception of society as a whole as well as a new "mental image" (or "mazeway") of the society that the movement seeks to form. As the group seeks to transform society under the guidance of a charismatic leader, "a noticeable social revitalization occurs, signalized by the reduction of the personal deterioration symptoms of individuals, by extensive cultural changes, and by an enthusiastic embarkation on some organized program of group action."[79] In other words, only by following the guidance of their leader, and working together as a group, can the members of the movement find relief from the stress imposed on them from the society they no longer agree with or desire to adhere to. Such was the case of the María Auxiliadora colony, where colonists attempted a Catholic community rigidly guided by a village patriarch—Salvador Abascal.

Even the choice of the name, María Auxiliadora (Our Lady, Help of Christians), is revealing for the social mazeway that Abascal and those that followed him hoped to form. Of all the appearances of the Virgin he could have chosen, Abascal chose one directly connected to the pope as well as with a martial history in the Catholic struggle with Islam and the secular state rather than the more common Mexican Virgen de Guadalupe or La Virgen de los Remedios. During the 1571 battle of Lepanto between Christians and Ottoman Turks, Pope Pius V ordered the rosary recited in Rome, and after the surprising Christian victory, he attributed the win to the rosary recited during the battle. The pope then called for a celebration of the Virgin of the Rosary, calling it a celebration of Our Lady of Victory in Christendom's struggle against Islam.[80] In 1814, Pope Pius VII claims to have been released from Napoleon's captivity due to María Auxiliadora's defeat of the French emperor in Russia and later at the battle of Waterloo.[81] For the UNS, an organization of poor, devout, agrarians battling the powerful central state (at least in their perception of the situation), María Auxiliadora stood for the construction of a society out of few resources with the potential to bring victory over incredulous adversaries.

The daily life of the colony follows Wallace's assertions about revitalization to the letter, seeking to create an improved group system, particularly with a more spiritual foundation. As one *sinarquista* from Querétaro declared: "We have mass . . . peace . . . charity . . . conformity . . . fraternity. What we don't have are rifles (and we don't need them); no rifles, no hate, no resentment; no leaders; no *comisariados* [government supervisors] taking 30 percent."[82] Abascal's intention was to set aside the contention of the revolution in favor of the village where they could "revive in all forms the traditional liturgical celebration of the [Catholic] church." Thus, of Abascal's first letters asking for aid from the UNS leadership, he not only requests ten tons of corn a month to keep the colony fed, but song books filled with traditional Catholic compositions such as "Las Pastorelas," or songs for Christmas.[83] To add to the spirit of cooperation, the colonists also ate communal meals together, building a sense of community but also allowing leaders to maintain tight control of the limited food and water resources. In addition, labor crews daily divided up construction duties

Además de chivas y ajonjolí también se cosecha maíz en María Auxiliadora.

Pero no sólo chivas, también se produjo en abundancia ajonjolí.

221

Pictures from *El Sinarquista*, the official newspaper of the UNS, celebrated the productivity of the soil in Baja, California. These pictures were later pasted into a scrapbook "historia gráfica" of the movement in 1947 as the movement was entering into a steep decline in influence and membership. HISTORIA GRÁFICA DE SINARQUISMO, 1947. THIS EXAMPLE COMES FROM PAGE 221.

as well as agricultural endeavors to grow wheat, corn, potatoes, assorted vegetables, and chilies.[84] Each family experienced in farming received twenty-five hectares of land, and each nonfarming family received three hectares—though it appears each family had to rely on the collective labor of the group to survive in the harsh environment.[85]

Religious education also comprised part of the plan for the community.[86] Lacking priests to take charge of the children, Abascal himself took charge of one school while Juventina Morales took charge of the other. Why two schools? The Escuela María Auxiliadora was dedicated to the education of young boys—not only separated from the girls but from older boys as well. The Escuela Madre Santísima served for the young women—again divided by age—of the community. Though divided by sex and age, each school displayed the only unity that mattered: a prominent cross stood above the entrance to each building.[87] Isolated in a small village of no more than two hundred people, the children found themselves further divided from their siblings and playmates of a different gender. This is likely due to the colony's desire to train them to later live an ideal, conservative, Catholic adult life free of unseemly relations between the sexes. As Abascal told his colonists, the colony existed to "form a Catholic people [and] perfectly educate our children."[88]

That strict gender division was part of his vision for a "Catholic people" appeared throughout Abascal's memoirs, with women almost always engaged in a separate sphere of existence than the men—washing, cooking, educating, and sewing. As he describes one idyllic afternoon in the colony: "All the men were working, the women inside their houses, and the children in school."[89] Considering the overwhelming presence of women in the UNS movement, it is hard to imagine that the rigid division of the sexes went beyond only the idea of segregation.[90] Yet that is Abascal's goal. From his diary in April of 1942 he writes: "Once a week I teach classes on religion, required of all men, with the authorization of the parish priest. Separate from them I also teach an obligatory religion class for women."[91] Such a revitalizationist approach to gender and separation was well situated for the revolutionary era. While athletic, educated women with modern clothing, bobbed hair, and a public presence were associated with the revolution and attacked by both conservative citizens and the Church, Abascal sought a more "traditional" role for women in Mexico.[92] As Ana María Alonso writes of nineteenth- and early-twentieth-century "traditional" gender roles in frontier Mexico:

Just as women's bodies were closed off, women's lives are enclosed in the *casa* (home, domestic domain). Their passages into the public domain are restricted and contingent on the permission of patriarchal authorities. Fathers, brothers, and husbands oversee the entrances and exits of the *casa* as a zealously as they guard over the orifices of the female body. Women who violate the norms that prescribe bodily closure and domestic enclosure become construed as *mujeres prostituidas* or *putas* (whores).[93]

The community organizations of school and work all acted as gatekeepers for the female residents of the community and revived the role of the traditional woman in the face of the revolution.

While life in María Auxiliadora reflected the attempt to create a conservative and religious society, that conservatism was not synonymous with subservience to the whims and will of the local clergy or the Roman Catholic Bishop's Council of Mexico. If Abascal sought to create a traditional Catholic village, he also perpetuated the long tradition in Mexican Catholicism of the villagers' resistance to the excesses of clerical authority. Abascal's complaints against the local clergy begin by saying that María Auxiliadora needed its own priest (instead of sharing one with neighboring pueblos), and that the local priest, Father Zavala, had abandoned them (*nos abandonaba*) while the colony still paid 608 pesos monthly for his services.[94] In another instance, Abascal discovered an unmarried couple (with two children) passing themselves off as married while the "wife" was still married in the Catholic Church to another man. To Abascal's dismay, the priest suggested the man simply sleep in another room in the house they shared. Scandalized, Abascal sent the common-law "husband" to La Paz to watch over sick colonists in the hospital, circumventing Zavala. The trusting Father Zavala, however, was welcome in the community compared to Father Campos, a replacement who arrived in December 1942.

Abascal's wife, Guadalupe, referred to Father Campos as a "puritana" who, as she remembers the priest, had everyone so offended and frightened they refused to confess.[95] For example, the priest was so focused on rejecting material comfort that he condemned the farmers for snacking on *jitomates* between meals (gluttony) and he attacked Abascal for wearing gloves on a cold day.[96] Finally, when Abascal lent him ten men to build a new church and a school, the priest used them to dig yet another well in the area—for which they had neither a pump nor even a need. Fed up with the interference of the priest, Abascal requested his removal, but to no avail. Finally, when Abascal sought baptism for his new infant, the priest refused to accept a stand-in as a proxy godfather for an uncle who could not travel to María Auxiliadora for the ceremony. Father Campos then gave Abascal an ultimatum: Choose godparents from the colony or he would not baptize the baby. Terrified of having an unbaptized child, the Abascals gave in and chose godparents from their immediate neighbors, leaving Guadalupe Abascal "inconsolable." After telling the story he makes a short note: "Se fue el Padre definitivamente"—the priest left for good.[97] Abascal's point of view is further clarified in an exchange he reports with future president of Mexico Miguel Alemán. The interior secretary pointedly told Abascal that "the [Catholic] Church will never return to hold power in Mexico," to which Abascal replied that he and Alemán agreed.[98] If at one point Abascal sounds like a Franciscan utopianist, the tone of his program was that of the early colonial *encomendero* who hired priests to evangelize "their" Indians. For Abascal, the priest exists to *aid* in local order not to set it.[99]

While the ideal community of religious devotion, gender separation, and increased lay participation in religion was supposed to bring the community together, the village was not without conflict—much of which seems to be attributed to the presence of Abascal himself. The former UNS leader reports in the April 30, 1942, edition of *El Sinarquista* that he was doing his best to stamp out "murmuring and gossip" rampant in the community. The same article also refers to deserters from the colony, though several families quickly took their place.[100] What these murmurings were about, however, are difficult to ascertain, although *El Sinarquista* felt compelled to run several articles stating that Abascal was not making a fortune on the colony.[101]

While the conflict with the colonists died down between spring of 1943 and spring of 1944, when the colony lost no members, it continued to suffer severe setbacks, equipment failure, and a slowing flow of funds from the UNS leadership in Mexico City, the latter of which seems connected with UNS politics in the capital. As Abascal paints the picture, the UNS leadership in Mexico City refused to send funds despite the colony's desperate pleas for medicine, food, money, and equipment as long as the former leader remained in charge of the colony. He made an extended visit to Mexico City to try to extract donations from wealthy *sinarquistas* and the leadership of the UNS, but his weeks of fundraising went almost entirely unrewarded.[102] The autumn of 1943 found Abascal in open conflict with the leadership of the UNS over his allegations that they withheld funds, and as he made his return trip to María Auxiliadora, he conspired with other *sinarquistas* to oust those leaders during a late 1944 leadership meeting.[103] Unfortunately for Abascal, the UNS leadership struck first.

In the December 23, 1943, issue of *El Sinarquista*, the UNS published a letter of support for President Ávila Camacho, backing his centrist approach to governing and supporting his expressed desire to unify Mexicans. They end by voicing their support for the "conversion into reality" of all of his plans for the last three years of his presidential term. Salvador Abascal was livid. Firing off letters of condemnation, he declared that the UNS leadership had not only betrayed Mexico, but Catholicism as well. Why? Because part of the "unity" that Ávila Camacho supported was the alliance with the United States that arose during World War II. For Abascal, this represented an alliance with Anglo values and industrial capitalism—the enemies of Hispanic, social Catholicism.[104]

Such declarations were too much for both the leadership of the UNS and the Roman Catholic Church in Mexico. Abascal's vocal condemnation of the Ávila Camacho administration threatened to stir up Catholics against the state, clearly violating the delicate peace that had been arranged between the ruling party and the Catholic leadership in Mexico after 1929 and the cessation of the most violent conflict between Catholics and the revolutionary state. By March 1944, a delegation of Catholic clergy and UNS leaders was deployed to María Auxiliadora to ask that Abascal withdraw from the colony and, by extension, from the UNS. Specifically, the clerical representative was Father Miguel Madrigal, his former seminary instructor from the years when Abascal had considered the priesthood. While Abascal at first argued that Madrigal and Luis María Martínez y Rodríguez (the archbishop of Mexico who had sent the priest) had no business in meddling with "civic business," he finally yielded to Madrigal as the representative of the *madre iglesia* and agreed to withdraw from María Auxiliadora. The archbishop, however, would later deny he had any involvement in Abascal's removal, though he did confirm with Abascal's father that he had saved Salvador from assassination—presumably meaning that had the former UNS leader not been forced from the organization he would have been removed from power by more nefarious means, though by whom the priest did not say.[105]

On March 31, 1944, Father Madrigal called all the colonists to María Auxiliadora's small chapel, and there he declared that Abascal was withdrawing from the community and surprised Abascal by producing a written oath that he would never again participate in affairs in María Auxiliadora. Abascal signed the document and left the colony five days later, taking three other families with him. On April 2, 1944, Abascal drafted a letter to his mother, informing her that he was leaving the colony and that she should know that "he would never again belong to the organization [the UNS]."[106] For their part, the UNS began circulating rumors that Abascal had gone insane in the desert, and that he was associating with Masons, as well as stating that he left voluntarily, no better than a common deserter.[107]

From summer 1944 forward, the slow death of the colony seems readily apparent in the pages of *El Sinarquista*. By monitoring the flow of donations to the colony from 1941 to the demise of *El Sinarquista* in 1944, one can see the high of donations at almost two thousand pesos a week to just two or three hundred a week to support all four of the colonies founded by the UNS. In 1944, *El Sinarquista* finally quit running the once frequent reports from the colonies, and readers could only have been left wondering at the fate of the once highly touted experiment.

The slow de-emphasis of the colony experiment paralleled a shift in the tone of *El Sinarquista*. By January of 1943, the once tacit support of Ávila Camacho was now explicit, and even pro-Roosevelt and pro-U.S. stories begin appearing.[108] It appears that the leadership of the UNS and its backer, La Base, were far more concerned with recognition from Mexico City than in the support of its radical base and the colonies they had once backed so enthusiastically. Even as the UNS scrambled for mainstream recognition, its membership began to decline, and the headline of *El Sinarquista* regarding the colonies from February 1942 proved prophetic: "We Triumph or Die."[109] As the colony experiments failed one by one through the 1940s, and as the UNS slowly crumbled in the 1950s, Abascal closes his memoirs stating that the failure of *sinarquismo* to stay "faithful to its ideals" had only played into the hands of the "Yankee embassy" who, he argues, surely had masterminded the divisions in the UNS. Mexico, he declared, was growing soft and corrupt on foreign "filthy diseases" and was only committing suicide.[110] A telling line from his memoirs, tucked into a footnote on his youth, may reflect how Abascal saw himself as his insistence on standing his ground cost him both leadership and the community that he worked so hard to build. Says Abascal: "My own father helped me to understand that a Marshall Pétain is far more valuable than a William II, because the first represents the Catholic spirit that fights, at great cost to his honor and life, for eternal values, while the second represents only force and his own aggrandizement. My father understood that a just judge in the middle of his people, like St. Louis IX of France, was worth more than a victorious conqueror."[111] No one could accuse Abascal of anything like victory by the end of 1944, and the leaders of the UNS and the ruling party would be perfectly happy to remember him as a figure akin to France's Marshal Pétain.

Conclusion

While the visions of Salvador Abascal differed from those of Mexican leftists like Lázaro Cárdenas or Francisco Mújica, who argued for land distribution and communal land projects, all three saw Mexico's future in a planned and ordered rural society. Indeed, while Abascal was in central Mexico for his own wedding in March 1942, both Cárdenas and Mújica passed through María Auxiliadora on a tour of Baja California. The duo—experienced, anticlerical revolutionaries that had engaged in repressing both the secret society of the "U" as well as the UNS—stayed in the village for two hours and expressed their approbation of the colonization project. Abascal wrote of the reports he received of the meeting: "General Mújica is a cordial and noble man. General Cárdenas is generous of heart: he recognized, without reservations, the merit of the colonization, and he said that we should all forget past bad feelings and work together for Mexico."[112] While each represented different aspects of the revolution—Abascal the opposition, Mújica the radical agrarian left, and Cárdenas a pragmatic governing center—they came together under the banner of probably the only undisputed winner of the revolution: the Mexican nationalism that bound them together across their oppositional histories.

While Mújica and Cárdenas ended their lives as well-remembered heroes of the Mexican Revolution, Abascal found himself on the fringe of Mexican history, perhaps appropriately thought of as a lone voice crying in the wilderness against a modernizing Mexico. The former UNS leader ended his days publishing defenses of his term in office, countering claims of academics like Jean Meyer, and trying to inspire a new generation of young Catholic thinkers by condemning liberalism in Mexico. Salvador

Abascal died just five months before the National Action Party (PAN) candidate, Vicente Fox, defeated the ruling PRI party in 2000. And although Abascal himself never embraced the PAN, that party's toppling of the PRI came as an extension of his own efforts—with his own son, Carlos Abascal Carranza, serving as the Fox administration's labor secretary.

Mexico did indeed pass through a social revolution, one in which factions on both the right and the left, as well as the poor, middle class, and rich, did battle for Mexican identity. The victorious *constitucionalistas* set the end of that struggle over identity in 1920, arguing that a grand period of reconstruction was underway, and then attempted to rule by politics and corporate sectors. That reconstruction era, however, ran counter to other groups who had also viewed the regimes of Porfirio Díaz and Huerta with as much suspicion and distrust as the constitutionalist movement. While 1920 to 1940 signified consolidation to the victors, it gave others more motivation to struggle for the right to define Mexico outside of the terms set by the official revolution. Salvador Abascal and the UNS represented a significant portion of the Mexican population yearning to build a different society from that of Porfirio Díaz, and when those hopes remained elusive after 1920, they struggled on physically and ideologically to create a new Mexico guided by religious principles but centered in the local community.

CHAPTER FOUR

Community, Law, and Religion

❧

☩ I HAVE EXAMINED THREE EXPRESSIONS OF intentional religious community initiated by Mexicans, for Mexicans, in the wake of the 1910 Revolution. In particular, I examined the intersection of revolution, religion, and community and how the urban and rural poor of Mexico used religion and community-building projects to interpret the revolution after the cessation of the armed conflict, particularly during Mexico's cultural golden age and the period known as the Economic Miracle, from 1940 to 1964. This has led me into three, intertwined main topics: local interpretations of revolutionary laws and culture; the absence of the rule of law and its relationship to religious human rights in Mexico; and the continued struggle to reconcile informal, religious, corporate identity with formal, secular identities. While the gaze of many Mexicans shifted to consumerism, urbanization, and a tacit acceptance of the ruling Institutional Revolutionary Party's definition of Mexican civic engagement and culture, some local movements interpreted the growth and success of the nation in their own local and religious terms.

Local Interpretations of the Revolution

Any discussion after the 1990s of local interpretations of the Mexican Revolution naturally evokes the historiography of hegemony. From historian Florencia Mallon's comparative study, including nineteenth-century Puebla, to Nicolina Montessino Montessori's twenty-first-century analysis of the battle for hegemony in the *zapatista* revolution of 1994, hegemony has dominated the discussion of "the people" versus "the state." Likewise, for every mention of hegemony and Antonio Gramsci, there seems to be a new way to read the author and define the concept so associated with him. As historian Derek Sayer quipped, regarding the essays on hegemony in the landmark *Everyday Forms of State Formation*, "I thought it might be helpful to go through the contributions and look at how many different definitions of hegemony I could find, but at some point I gave up."[1] As Sayer goes on to point out, the "Mexican diversities" found in *Everyday Forms of State Formation*, or for that matter, in Mexican historiography in general, make it difficult to "put" a single, narrowly defined theory on each case study "like a hat."[2] Thus, as historian Mary Kay Vaughn argues of her investigation of education in Mexico, between 1930 and 1940, of "two states and four rural societies," it is similarly both difficult and "risky to draw national conclusions" based on my own study of three religions movements in three Mexican states.[3] However, like Vaughn, I hope to encourage further investigation (in this case, of religion) in the interpretation of the Mexican Revolution during the decades that followed the most radical years of conflict and reform from 1910 to 1940.

Clearly, the groups cited in this book's case studies engaged in a discussion with local authorities (and in the case of the *sinarquistas*, the central state) on the origins and meaning of the revolution and, consequently, the best way to live out the idea of the revolution as a religious community. However, the goals of the "state" are fragmented at multiple points—even on basic applications of law: the same "state" attacked *sinarquistas* in one region and touted them as heroic colonizers in another; the same "state" raided LDM meetings and simultaneously warned them of the impending attacks; the same "state" jailed Margarito Bautista for having more than one wife and then publicly declared his religious right to do so. To deal with what might be seen as contradictions within "the state," we must do as sociologist Philip Abrams argued and get beyond "the reification [of the state] which in itself seriously obstructs the effective study of a number of problems."[4] For Abrams, that problem was political power. For this study, that problem is the question of religion's interpretation of the idea of the Mexican Revolution and how best to live a life that reflected both the saving grace of God and the revolution.

I argue that even though varying "official" definitions of revolution did emanate from Mexico City, the local and religious ability to negotiate those claims was made possible because the "state," as Sayer says, following Abrams, is nothing more than an attempt "to give unity, coherence, structure, and intentionality to what are in practice frequently disunited, fragmented, attempts at domination."[5] In short, if we move past the myth of the state, we can focus on the actions and beliefs of the parties involved, and by doing so we are able to find the limitations of their power, as well as the variations that exist within what might erroneously be conceived as an abstract leviathan of power, that is, the state. As historian Alan Knight has ably argued of the consolidation of the revolution, the power of ruling parties and Sonoran generals certainly had limits, and on the edges of those limits, we see an area of dynamic innovation.[6] Thus, my aim here has been to discuss, as Florencia Mallon describes it, the "processes, constant and ongoing, through which power relations are contested, legitimated, and redefined at all levels of society," by focusing on the local level of that conversation, as well as on (what might at first be considered unexpected) alliances.[7] By doing so, I hope to draw attention to the limitless and creative ways in which Mexicans defined their nation and the great social movements that affected them.

Consequently, I have engaged the category of religion, especially intentional communities, as a special subset for which I can develop a comparative analysis. As historian Arthur Schmidt points out, "Religion constitutes another neglected area in the history of contemporary Mexico where popular cultural creativity intertwines complex domestic and global networks of unequal power."[8] How was religion used as a device to interpret the revolution on the local level during the golden age of Mexican culture and the modernization of the Mexican Economic Miracle? How can religion help us read the desires and efforts of Mexicans that, for the most part, belonged to a class of people that seldom left their own first-hand accounts?

For the Luz del Mundo church, the Mexican Revolution served as a jumping-off point for the creation of their belief system. While the group rejects the violence of war and the earthly struggles of power, its members take great pains to point out the service of their leader, Aarón Joaquín, in the revolution. And while his official biographer could have chosen to portray his participation as something for which he was repentant, he instead shows it as an act of participating "fully in the social movement of the age, with the necessary determination to fight for just causes, and thus, not to teach letters but defend ideas, not to teach reading but to fight for a world that requires peace and justice as bases of human development."[9] While for Luz del Mundo the loss of human life was regrettable, the results were well worth the fight, making it possible for the new church to perpetuate its own message of peace, justice, and the restoration of the same Christianity as practiced by Christ and his apostles in a land LDM saw sorely in need of all three.

For the Iglesia del Reino de Dios en su Plenitud and Margarito Bautista, the Mexican Revolution was far more than just fortuitous, it was part of God's grand plan for the world. According to Bautista, by creating a liberal republic that was increasingly hostile to Catholicism, God was paving the way for the expansion of the restored gospel of Christ and the renewal of his covenants with Israel, that is, with the indigenous of Mexico. Like popular conceptions of Judas Maccabaeus throwing off Greek domination over Israel, the heroes of the revolution—such as Obregón and Calles— were men of God chosen to usher in an epoch of religious freedom: at least as far as the community of Colonia Industrial wanted to see it.

Similarly, both groups accepted the idea of performing Mexican nationalism, and, in particular, the kind of folk culture celebrated by many Mexicans after the revolution as well as celebrations of nineteenth-century Mexican liberalism. For example, Santa Cena celebrations in Hermosa Provincia with a parade of delegates dressed in "folkloric" costumes from around Mexico look very much like Mexican cinema or the famous Ballet Folklorico of Mexico City. In the Colonia Industrial, the Independence Day parade and Grito is a large production, accompanied during the days of Margarito Bautista by theo-nationalist pageants linking the Book of Mormon and Mexican nationalism. Children dressed as Book of Mormon figures while marching to celebrate the rise of the republic and its liberal constitution of 1857. In fact, the colony was officially incorporated on Independence Day, at which time they promptly held a dedicatory prayer to God and then formed a parade celebrating Mexican Independence.

These two performances stand in stark contrast to the style of independence celebrated by the *sinarquistas* of María Auxiliadora. While still celebrating independence, the colonists in Baja centered their celebrations on the Mexican emperor, Agustín de Iturbide, the hero of Mexican conservatives for his attempt to preserve monarchy in Mexico as well as Catholicism as a state-sponsored institution. Iturbide was Mexico's liberator, but for ideological reasons denied his glory in the pantheon of heroes by later liberal and revolutionary regimes. The *sinarquistas* also spent much time lauding the "tricolor flag," another inheritance of Iturbide, who called the flag that of the Three Guarantees: independence, purity of religion (Catholicism), and union (of Spaniards and Mexicans).

Such conservative oblations were hardly a part of the Luz del Mundo or the Reino de Dios en su Plenitud, whose supreme icon was Benito Juárez, foe of Catholicism and icon of secularism—and the president associated with Protestantism in Mexico for his support and enforcement of the 1857 Constitution that opened Mexico legally to all religions. Margarito Bautista's book makes wide mention of Juárez, and similarly, one of the first civic actions of Luz del Mundo was to dedicate a monument of Juárez at the entrance to the colony. It is no surprise that Juárez was also a special icon of the PRI, who used his image to portray themselves as the torch bearers of the *juarista* liberal legacy.[10] While Luz del Mundo and the Iglesia del Reino de Dios en su Plenitud appreciated the use of Juárez's legacy against the Catholics, they never understood the use of the liberal president after 1940: Juárez's declaration that the respect of others' rights brings peace (*el respeto al derecho ajeno es la paz*) was used by the government to justify its failure to enforce laws against religions, particularly the Catholic Church.[11]

On the other hand, a strategy that all three groups seemed to embrace was the use of *indigenismo* in their legitimizing efforts. For Luz del Mundo, that their prophet had *tez moreno*, or dark skin, explained partially why God would talk to him and instruct him to restore the gospel of Jesus Christ on the earth. Implicit in this statement is a humility and receptiveness to divine communication not as open to European members of Mexican society. Margarito Bautista, as well, was deeply involved in this approach to the role of the Indian in the national and religious scene. To be indigenous for Bautista meant to be under special covenant with God, as the indigenous were members of the tribe of Israel. With Indians involved in the reconstruction of Mexico, it brought a blessing from God: the revolution restored the power of the indigenous and the indigenous in turn gave divine power to the revolution. Even the *sinarquistas* got in on the action. When President Manuel Ávila Camacho referred to the UNS as an "exotic" movement based in Spanish fascism, Salvador Abascal argued to the contrary, using the number of indigenous members in their organization to prove that they were the "most Mexican" social movement of the time and that they fought the "racial, economic, and social" problems of the era.[12]

These attitudes fit comfortably with the revolutionary use of indigenous and colonial pasts. One need only consider the murals of Diego Rivera in the National Palace with their demon-faced, whip-wielding Spaniards to understand how Mexicans were intended to interpret the colonial past and their indigenous heritage. The Spaniards were invaders, conquerors, usurpers, and corruptors. By contrast, being able to tie into a pre-Hispanic past legitimized notions of who had, in truly essentialist terms, been here the longest and had a more truly authentic claim to Mexico. Indigenous art—from the most basic pot to complex weavings— were supposed to be the great artistic symbols of Mexicans of all racial backgrounds and classes, though many white elite did not necessarily buy into this celebration. For Mexicans, the indigenous became the *muy nuestro*, or "integral part of us all."[13]

A focus on *indigenismo* did not mean a rejection of Western education, however. When the revolution of guns turned into a revolution of chalkboards and books, Luz del Mundo fully embraced the literacy campaigns of the 1940s and 1950s that were continuations of the secular education projects of the 1920s and '30s (though to a less radical extent). The first *colonia* in Guadalajara to declare itself free of illiteracy, Luz del Mundo sought to promote literacy for more than just Bible reading. While Aarón Joaquín was content to let older generations work as day laborers or odd-job men, the colony put great effort into promoting higher education and the resultant better employment for its younger generations.[14] It is no coincidence that one of the most powerful wings of the Mexican Revolution was the Secretaría Educación Pública (SEP), or Ministry of Public Education.[15] Nevertheless, as Luz del Mundo members congregated about a central colony, their students dominated the local school (often taught by nonmembers) and mitigated the influence of exposure to the "worldly" influences of outsiders.

The Iglesia del Reino de Dios en su Plenitud and the UNS embraced education as well. Abascal's notion of education was based on traditional Catholic schooling, and he felt that his ideal community would be in the depths of despair without both a priest and a schoolteacher.[16] If the Porfirian society had neglected education, the *sinarquistas* would be part of the battle to better Mexico through the extension of education to all members of the community. This quest, however, was not to be left in the hands of the "atheist" revolutionary family (as Abascal still saw state-sponsored education after 1940), and only through their own traditional, Catholic efforts could the needs of Mexico's children be met. For Margarito Bautista, education was one of the great innovations of the revolution brought by Álvaro Obregón and furthered by both Calles and Cárdenas. The children of the Colonia Industrial attended the local public schools with their municipal peers, and their church duties required them to read not only scripture but the myriad of pamphlets generated by Bautista to defend the faith. As in the Progressive Era in the United States, literacy marked the truly dedicated and informed citizen of both the republic and the Kingdom of God.

Finally, when it came to the economic policy of the ruling party, Luz del Mundo embraced the idea of productivity as a benefit to the state. However, by first working as mobile salespeople and later in their own salsa bottling factory, members of Luz del Mundo were able to avoid joining the left-leaning unions that the state had co-opted. In addition, though they championed the state that saw consumerism as a mark of Mexican identity, it was their own moderate consumption and aid to the poor that provided them with a collective, social safety net needed to survive in the increasingly international market affecting Guadalajara. Similarly, productivity and access to traditional markets were the reasons Margarito Bautista and his followers retired to Ozumba from Puebla, convinced that economic and religious prosperity went hand-in-hand. However, against fluctuations in the national economy there existed the community's Law of Consecration (the ownership of all goods in common) and the assignment of property according to need, not market competitiveness. While Bautista embraced nationalist economics, stronger unions, and moderate consumer culture, ultimately the community would serve as the protection of personal temporal welfare, not the state. Thus, while an expanding welfare state offered benefits for the poor and unemployed, members of the Colonia Industrial de la Nueva Jerusalén continued to pool their assets and redistribute them according to need.

The *sinarquistas* of María Auxiliadora also placed great emphasis on hard work, but not as a means to accumulate wealth or "better" their position in life. The language of Abascal in *El Sinarquista* and in his memoir focuses on bettering society through the steady rhythms of work and the pace of the agricultural seasons. Cinema, radio, television—all of these luxuries of the new consumerist state were drugs, destined to rot a mind and keep the pocketbook in slavery.[17] Only the exaltation of village life and the dedication of income to the Church and charitable causes—such as *sinarquismo*—merited the sweat and labor it took to generate cash.

Importantly, one of the patterns perpetuated by the revolution was the elevation of the central patriarchal figure. Central figures of power were certainly not new to Mexico: Santa Anna, Benito Juárez, Porfirio Díaz— there is a long history of patriarchal figures who dominated Mexican society and power.[18] In addition, a myriad of caciques and caudillos dominated Mexico from the start of the independence movement. And while many in the Mexican Revolution may have had it in mind to use the revolution to do away with centralized personal power, they concluded that only centralized personal power was effective in keeping Mexico from slipping back into an abyss of chaos. All three of the case studies in this work examine movements that sought to avoid social "chaos" and, by extension, chose to adhere to communities with strong, long-lasting, patriarchal figures.

That a tradition of patriarchy influences people in the community they choose to join is not surprising. Sociologist Max Weber argues that the very roots of patriarchal orders are based on the idea of tradition, and that such traditions create a far more personal connection to the leader.[19] When one considers the loving cries of "tata" (father) directed at president Lázaro Cárdenas or the mountains of individual personal requests for aid from citizens to presidents of Mexico after his tenure, the concept of a patriarchal system in Mexican politics and society seems perfectly in line with Weber's theoretical approach. In addition, Weber posits that leaders who are not elected but are appointed by tradition or circumstance serve an important emotional function. Calling it *charisma*, these spiritual and motivational powers demand followers to obey, and in most cases seek to be above worldly cares and appetites.[20] Thus, one of the most common challenges to the central state is the charge of corruption, and in all three cases under study here, charges of association with "filthy lucre" were the basis for complaint or schism by members of the community. As with the revolution, while these communities sought worldly security, the appearance of the patriarch to move past what were considered "reasonable" limitations of enrichment was cause for cries of betrayal. Thus, patriarchal domination by charismatic leaders was present, but due to the nature of charisma, checks of tradition and perception were also at work on the leader.[21]

For instance, Salvador Abascal is referred to by almost all scholars of *sinarquismo* with the label given him by his opponents in the institutional revolution: caudillo. A talented speaker with an inexhaustible drive to excel, Abascal rallied hundreds of thousands of Mexicans to the cause of Catholic social doctrine and nationalist renewal under the banner of the Union Nacional Sinarquista. Not surprisingly, central to the concept of caudillo is the idea that a personal loyalty exists between the caudillo and the men that follow him. While in María Auxiliadora, Abascal dominated all facets of life, dictating work crews, sleep schedules, living quarters, and attendance at mass. Democracy was no replacement for the order of patriarchy.[22] It was only when Abascal was accused of enriching himself with donations to the colony (though not substantiated by evidence) that his charismatic, patriarchal power began to erode.

In the Hermosa Provincia, life centered around *apóstol* Aarón. Anthropologist Renée de la Torre categorizes life there as a totalizing institution, dominating all aspects of its adherents' lives.[23] This seems an apt description for a community with three main daily worship services, work crews, tithing, missionary work, and religious celebrations centered on the life of the apostle. And just like golden-age critiques of government and of Salvador Abascal, dissidents from Luz del Mundo always seemed to include self-glorification, enrichment, or sexual misconduct in their critique of the apostle. In response—especially during the 1943 schism—enrichment was the charge leveled by Luz del Mundo against those who broke away from their movement. In a movement like LDM, where followers seek to "restore" a belief system from what they perceive to be a fallen world, charges of "corruption" are particularly damaging.

In Colonia Industrial, as well, patriarchy and centralized power was the norm. Though to a lesser extent than Hermosa Provincia, Colonia Industrial also controlled individual schedules with multiple weekly activities and worship services. To a greater extent than LDM, however, the Reino de Dios en su Plenitud completely dominated the economic resources of the community. As seen in the examples of Felipe Burgos or Melessio Hernández, straying from the economic controls of the community, or even trying to live outside of the community, was cause for excommunication from the church. Also evident in the criminal charges brought against Margarito Bautista were charges from Hernández and Burgos that he had mishandled funds, violating the consecrated goods of the community of God—corruption.

Associated with desires for traditional, incorruptible, and personal power is the idea of divine authority, or priesthood, to officiate in religious ceremonies and regulate access to the sacred as dominated by men. One might be tempted to see a parallel between such an approach and the one taken by the ruling party. Almost entirely dominated by male power brokers, women would not get the right to vote in national elections until 1954 in Mexico. In addition, historian Ilene O'Malley has made much of the connection between the mythical and mystical control by the party of access to the state as being very much akin to a sacerdotal control of access to the sacred.[24] While the state may have delayed suffrage because women were perceived as more religious than men, that religiosity made them more susceptible to the orders of the male clergy. In addition, while the Mexican Catholic emphasis on the female divine (i.e., the Virgin of Guadalupe or other Marian expressions) assigns great power to female figures, the Virgin still maintains a second tier of power below the Trinity and Christ the King. For example, a Catholic can approach Mary to make intercession with the Trinity while the Trinity is too holy to be approached directly. Such patterns of male domination in the three communities under study are obvious.

The Catholic Church, of course, has a long history and continuing practice of limiting membership in the priesthood and top administrative positions to men. And though the María Auxiliadora was nothing more than a small village, great effort was taken to limit the contact between men and women. The ordered and traditional world that Abascal strove for would little endure departure from old Iberian traditions of confining "decent" women to indoor spaces away from the prying eyes of men. In Luz del Mundo, unlike many other Pentecostal movements in Mexico (and elsewhere in the world) that empower women, the highest levels of the ministry were limited to men. Although women led Bible studies and participated in proselytizing, the consolidated hierarchy of LDM after the 1943 schism was entirely in the hands of men. A simple glance at photos from the 1940s reveals that even the space inside chapels was divided into female and male sides. In accordance with the New Testament injunctions of Paul to Christians in Corinth, Luz del Mundo women covered their heads with veils during meetings, and, when men were present, females were not allowed to preach (1 Corinthians 11:1–16; 14:34). In addition, starting in its early years and continuing to the present, Luz del Mundo women are distinguished from the rest of Mexican society through their dresses that cover them from ankle to neck. No such clothing restrictions exist for men, except that they be neat and clean.

Finally, for the Iglesia del Reino de Dios en su Plenitud, men also dominated the religion, though with some checks on that authority. Priesthood authority was passed from male to male alone and allowed members of the order to run the administration of the organization. Women were allowed to serve only in auxiliaries of adult women (the Sociedad de Soccorro, or Relief Society), adolescent girls, children under twelve, or Sunday school positions, though all these were supervised by men. Although this picture of domination appears total, there were some balances in Colonia Industrial, especially in a least-expected place—marriage. Bautista's first wife left him (though the reason is not indicated), returning to the United States with their children to live.[25] In fact, of Bautista's eleven wives, six had affairs or chose to leave Bautista for men in or out of the community.[26] In one case, it appears that his tenth wife, Raquel Domínguez, kept Bautista from removing her brother from the community for allegedly trying to rape (or perhaps it was an interrupted consensual liaison) Bautista's fourth wife.[27] Just as the communities picked and chose from the results of the Mexican Revolution, it appears that members of the Colonia Industrial might pick and choose from community rules. In addition, with the admonition to the community from the municipal president to keep their extra wives in other communities, women took charge of their own households while men were still charged with the duty of providing for the material welfare of those wives and their children, even if he were absent.[28] In marriage, as in Mexico as a whole, the patriarch could never hope for total domination.

On a final note about the willingness of each group to enter into non-spiritual projects, each can be understood by their adherence and interpretation of past marriages of community and religion. Most notably, all had varying degrees of interest in association with the Christian interpretation of the Israel of the Old Testament as a marriage of both the political and spiritual Kingdom of God.[29] The willingness of the poor immigrants from Los Altos de Jalisco (a rural region known for its white, Catholic population), from which many of the LDM converts came, to believe themselves part of Israel may have come in part as a reaction to a long tradition in Los Altos linking the white settlers of the area to not only "French Spanish" but also Jewish converts to Catholicism.[30] For those poor mestizo and Indian immigrants leaving Los Altos and the bad treatment they received from whites there, joining LDM and other such "Israel"-centered movements could make them the "real" members of Israel.

As discussed in chapter 2, members of Luz del Mundo see themselves as a restoration of God's promises with the "chosen" people of Israel. And such is the enthusiasm for Israel in LDM that the Hermosa Provincia fairly drips with the iconography of Judaism, especially those that match well with Christian interpretations: lions (Judah and Jesus), grapes (sacred fruit of Israel and blood of Christ), olives (sacred fruit and Christ in the Garden of Gethsemane), standard menorahs (temple of Jerusalem and fire of the spirit and the restoration of the temple for Christ's second coming), and so on. Such visual links constantly before the congregation take the poorest peasants from the meanest conditions and reminds them that no matter their standing in "the world," within Luz del Mundo they are part of a grand unfolding plan of God. And, with the Old Testament tales of Israelite nationalism combined with Luz del Mundo emphasis on citizenship, that grand plan of God naturally includes the betterment of Mexico as a means of perpetuating the Kingdom of God.

Symbols of Judaism such as Stars of David, grapes, Lions of Judah, and so on decorate even the most mundane of items in Hermosa Provincia and signal to members that they are buying from a member of the church. August 14, 2007.
PHOTO COURTESY OF DAVID AGREN.

Margarito Bautista and the Colonia Industrial have as vocal a con-nection to Israel as Luz del Mundo, if not more so. Bautista's claim to be a literal descendant of the tribes of Israel and the colony's acceptance of Mormonism also connects them to the same great drama that Luz del Mundo claimed. In fact, both use many of the same scriptures in both the Old and New Testaments to lay claim to the title of "restorers" of a lost "true" religion that existed from the creation of the world until the death of Jesus' apostles. However, Bautista's reward would be no eternal singing and praising of God, but instead eternal power:

> Those mortal Israelites who are faithful in all things, who obey the full law of the Gospel, will continue on as members of the house of Israel in a future eternity, there ruling as kings and priests forever in the patriarchal chain.[31]

And how could such a glorious ending come about? Only by the freedom of religious choice instigated by the reforms of Benito Juárez, which limited the power of the Catholic Church, and the later Mexican Revolution, which reinforced religious diversity in Mexico, could the "blood" descendants of Israel (Lamanites/Indians) have the opportunity to hear the "restored" Gospel. Like ancient Israel, Mexico became a politi-cal space made safe for the practice of the "true" religion and an engine for redeeming all of the Israelites within its borders.

Finally, the Sinarquistas provide an interesting foil for this discussion of Israel. Although they made the fewest overt associations with the idea of the Old Testament of Israel, in the end they held the least "modern" views of the role of the state in religion and community. As discussed in chapter 3, the Sinarquistas certainly made allusions to going into the desert to colonize like Israel entering the promised land of Canaan. However, at no point did they feel they needed to invoke a direct line from Israel or even (perish the very anti-Castillian thought) of having direct blood ties to Israel and Judaism. Nevertheless, of all the three groups, the Sinarquistas had the highest hopes for a Mexico dedicated to a marriage between church and state. For the María Auxiliadora, independence celebrations included homage to Agustín de Iturbide—the liberator of Mexico who became the Emperor of Mexico after independence and the advocate of guaranteeing Mexico as the exclusive domain of the Roman Catholic Church. In fact, Abascal always refers to Iturbide with the respectful "don," and made it his mission to explain that the Liberator (as he calls Iturbide) stood for the "purity of the Catholic religion" in Mexico.[32] The conservative view as explained in chapter 1 remained Abascal's goals, a century after Benito Juárez had swept the merger of Church and state aside. While Aarón Joaquín and Margarito Bautista could operate within a separate Mexican state while they waited for Jesus to come again and reign as king on the earth, Abascal wanted to let Christ be the king now, and rule through the Catholic Church's marriage to what they hoped could be the exclusively Catholic state of Mexico.

Religious Rights and the Rule of Law

In historian Robert M. Buffington's *Criminal and Citizen in Modern Mexico*, he declares that "elite constructions of crime" intersected with "health, race, class, gender, and sexuality" to define citizenship, or "who belonged and who did not."[33] However, one of the great dramas of Mexican society linked to the question of being an "authentic" Mexican is missing from Buffington's list—religion. With certain beliefs and practices criminalized in the liberal state, religious Mexicans could turn to local elites with notions of citizenship more akin to their own and receive acceptance and praise (in the case of Luz del Mundo or even the *sinarquistas*) or at least tacit legal protection (in the case of the Iglesia del Reino de Dios en su Plenitud). This flexibility in the law is typically portrayed as a product of corruption rather than what could be a potentially fruitful avenue of research—different conceptions of justice at different levels of the nation's state-making project.[34]

While formal law from the center—the "claim" of those who rule—codified who belonged and who did not, when that formal law was inconvenient or distasteful to all participants on the periphery, local rulers adapted the formal and informal and made their own definitions about who belonged. For example, the police chief in Guadalajara and the municipal president of Ozumba each had different notions of freedoms of religion, speech, and marriage, prompting them to provide legal flexibility for Aarón Joaquín and Margarito Bautista, respectively. Little research has been done on judges and other law enforcement officers in modern Latin America, and a logical corollary to this work is research on who these legal officials are and why they behaved the way they did.[35] This stands in contrast to colonial historians who have certainly paid attention to such questions, especially since the crown tried to limit the ties of royal officials to the influence of local interests. As this work demonstrates, in the modern period, the lumping of all levels of government agents into the simple "state" category is insufficient for understanding the nature of law, legal culture, and popular culture in Mexico.

In the absence of the rule of law, the question of citizen security naturally arises. I have suggested that when faced with uncertainty or persecution, the subjects of my study formed closed religious communities as a refuge and chose to support an authoritarian local system with no, or only token, democracy present. The absence of the rule of law in Mexico created a circular situation for these groups. Failure by the state to stop persecution of religious minorities drove these same communities to seek protection in illegal or semilegal community projects. The colonies then garnered informal protection from local authorities because these new communities promoted state principles fostered in the closed community setting, such as by education or entrepreneurial business. Thus, the absence of the rule of law perpetuated local relationships instead of basing protections on constitutional or legal principles. In addition, those that adhered to the plan of the community patriarchs were welcome within the closed society, but those that failed to comply were considered schismatic, or apostate. When the punishment of those apostates violated the rights of citizens under Mexican law, local officials only reluctantly stepped in to mediate the dispute—reinforcing the dedication of the community (and the persecutors) to the state. These case studies seem to support the theory in political science that the lack of citizen security will lead community members to support strong community bonds ruled by hierarchies with little participatory discourse—in this case, closed, patriarchal, intentional religious communities.[36]

However, the absence of the rule of law clearly had a mixed effect on freedoms of worship for the communities in this study. On a regional and local level, religious people formed unexpected alliances and relied on various personal relationships for the protection they needed to express their religious inclinations. At times this came in the form of local officials who offered their own versions of religious freedom and justice for their neighbors. At other times it meant simply looking the other way as a result of well-established ties of patronage. While the absence of a Mexico-wide rule of law opened up these minority groups to persecution, it also allowed them the freedom of religious practice that would never have been possible under a strict enforcement of the law as written. Not everybody in

Mexico's "anonymous, urban, and highly mobile society" of the 1940s, '50s, and '60s demanded the rule of law.[37] On one hand, Mexico's inability to enforce the radical secularizing tenets of its anticlerical constitution could be seen as a failure: a failure to consolidate power and a failure of the revolution to be revolutionary. On the other hand, Mexico's informal position on enforcing laws regulating religion could be seen as a pragmatic move to follow established patterns from the past and preserve not only the state but the rights—whether intentional or not—of its citizens. In other words, the absence of the rule of law allowed for more religious toleration than would have been possible otherwise.

Such an approach is a new way of thinking about Mexico and the postrevolutionary years, or even Mexico after the reform of the 1850s—namely, that Mexico has served as a bastion for dissident religious traditions in the Western Hemisphere in a way that is usually associated only with the United States and Canada. Consider that, in 1921, it was to Mexico that many Mennonites fled—seeking refuge from the authoritarian, anti-German policies of the Canadian Federation—not to the United States, which they judged too interested in assimilating immigrants. Though Mormon colonists fled antipolygamy laws in the United States for both Canada and Mexico, it was only in Mexico that an explicit olive branch was extended to those colonists and an implicit legal ambiance that allowed them to practice their religion as they saw fit. Similarly, it is unlikely that the Olarte brothers of Colonia Industrial would have received good-natured counsel to "have as many women as you want" in the United States. And in the United States and Canada, *apóstol* Aarón may well have ended up in jail for civil disobedience and trespassing for his aggressive missionary style. Similarly, in the antifascism and fear of World War II, Salvador Abascal would have spent very little time outside of a jail cell, let alone been allowed to march through the streets with tens of thousands of antigovernment supporters or start his own colony by the sea. Very rarely is Mexico portrayed (or portrays itself) as a place of promise and opportunity, as it was considered by some.

As Mexico seeks, in the late twentieth century and early twenty-first, to establish the rule of law, it may need to look at the tradition of its own revolutionary heritage and recognize that making justice work equally for its citizens does not always mean flat application of laws to individuals—a thought important for both religious and indigenous informal, corporate bodies.

Establishing Law and Consolidating Power: Corporate Community in Mexico and Constitutional Reforms

I have argued that an affinity existed between the ruling Institutional Revolutionary Party (PRI)—and its antecedents—and patriarchal religious communities. In fact, I have argued that the Mexican Revolution—including the state projects that followed the shooting war—influenced the very community orientation of the three religious groups under study in this work, creating a society where construction and informal, corporate community formation was not only acceptable, but part of being accepted. Liberal ideals of patriotism, thrift, education, and industriousness married corporate values, turning those ideals into tools to help the community, not just the individual.

The informal corporate formations that supported the state most, but relied on it least, survived into the present (Luz del Mundo, El Reino de Dios en su Plenitud), while the group that tried hardest to play by the rules of the new state, the colonists of María Auxiliadora, were crushed under the sun of Baja California in just a few short years. Like a loosely crafted empire, Mexico required only the token tribute of political submission, according to the unwritten rules of the PRI, to trump all other aspects of the law, while those who adhered to the laws of Mexico on paper could be eliminated for their recalcitrance in obeying the party. Or, to play off a phrase from Alan Knight, cited in the introduction, a corporate body that tossed Leviathan a fish could get it to paddle to the other end of the pond—a corporate body that swam with Leviathan could only get devoured.[38]

Although the *sinarquistas* developed a plan far more nationalist and culturally part of *lo mexicano*, they failed in their project, mostly due to their distance from the political embrace of the ruling party. While LDM played the least overtly nationalist role, it embraced the party structure wholeheartedly. And finally, while Colonia Industrial de la Nueva Jerusalén also took a highly nationalist stand and embraced the party (though to a far lesser extent), their success depended more fully on their failure—their failure to grow beyond a few hundred followers and thereby attract undue attention to their questionable behavior. However, as Mexico has placed more emphasis on the rule of law, this raises the question about whether even small groups can continue to escape detection for evasion of that law. As historian Pamela Voekel has argued, Mexico has undergone a transition in which "elite liberalism" has attacked the informal corporatism of the local community and seeks "to eliminate corporate *fueros* [legal exemptions] and enshrine its notion of the rational individual as the country's fundamental constituent."[39]

In 1982, Mexico began to experience a political shift as old-time party rulers, known as "dinosaurs," gave way before a new generation of young, less charismatic, U.S.-educated party leaders, known as "technocrats." Perhaps the paramount example of that shift was the election of Carlos Salinas de Gortari in 1988, a Harvard graduate whose election saw the lowest voter turnout, highest abstention rate, and highest ever opposition vote against the Partido Revolucionario Institucional (PRI) in decades.[40] The election was also loudly criticized for its widely perceived corruption, perhaps the most widespread in PRI history.[41] As the PRI began to crumble after the electoral fraud of 1988, Salinas continued with unilateral moves toward neoliberal economic reforms—a move that would come in direct conflict with the corporate bodies antithetical to individualism and free markets that formed a base for the PRI. Unions, rural political bosses, and even state-run welfare programs were all revamped by Salinas in his rush to modernize Mexico.

In all of these reforms relating to Mexico's prosperity and future, what had happened to the longstanding debate regarding religion and the informal relationships that the state had cultivated with religious groups that either supported or denigrated the PRI? Even when it came to religion, Mexico's technocrats argued that as long as a gap existed between law and enforcement, their nation could never join the developed world and meet international standards of respect for religion as a human right. President Carlos Salinas de Gortari later said of this situation that "domestic changes allowed us to promote initiatives in favor of change . . . related to one of the fundamental human rights, the freedom of religious belief. A country could not be truly democratic without full recognition of that liberty."[42]

By the beginning of 1989, the assistant to President Salinas, José Córdoba Montoya, busily engaged in modifying the 1917 constitution, using the French, Polish, and U.S. constitutions as models. Such constitutions served Córdoba Montoya's intent to find a balance of religious separation that still allowed participation in politics (or at least voting) by individual clerics.[43] The only way that Salinas saw to ensure such human and civic rights issues was to eliminate the informal ties that linked both the religious and antireligious under the banner of the ruling Institutional Revolutionary Party. "Things in Mexico are going to change," Salinas told newsmagazine *Tiempo* in June of 1990. "We will confront new threats to human rights regardless of where they come from. Society and the state both demand the rule of law."[44]

However, even this decision to pursue the topic of religious human rights was not devoid of a free-market motivation. "Salinas de Gortari has stressed that national modernization will only be achieved according to law because 'it is the law that warrants change in our political and economic life.' Thus, the president has assumed the commitment to reaffirm the rule of law by means of strict constitutional principles."[45] Enforcing laws would inspire foreign investor confidence, and where laws failed to meet "the new reality of Mexico," the rule of law demanded there be modifications of both law and society.[46] In the case of the approval of the North American Free Trade Agreement (NAFTA) by the U.S. Congress, the connection between the worthiness of Mexico to enter into a trade pact with the United States and Canada and its ability to enforce the rule of law at home was open and explicit. United States Trade Representative Mickey Kantor directly addressed the Senate Finance Committee concerns about the lack of the rule of law in Mexico by pointing to President Salinas and his constitutional reforms as proof that the Mexican president "recognized the need" to reconcile law with enforcement.[47] Indeed, Mexican NAFTA lobbyist Herman Von Bertrab states that the most difficult obstacle to overcome in lobbying the U.S. Congress was the "image" of Mexico as lawless.[48]

In his November 1991 address to the nation, President Salinas de Gortari stated:

> Based on experience, the Mexican people do not want their clergy taking part in politics or amassing material wealth. The people, however, do not want to live a pretense or misguided complicity. The idea is not to return to the existence of privilege, but to reconcile the definite secularization of our society with effective freedom of beliefs, something that constitutes one of the most important human rights.[49]

Using the language of human rights, Salinas de Gortari was doing away with the unofficial system of compromise and *fueros* that existed for religious communities in a low key war of reform of his own. Though it was greeted by many religious groups with open arms, a group of conservative Catholics appears to have understood fully what this meant for their position in society. In 1992, the Conference of Religious Institutes of Mexico (CIRM) issued a statement condemning the changes to the Mexican Constitution and the establishment of the rule of law regarding church-state relations. The group—dominated by Jesuits, Franciscans, Dominicans, Benedictines, and Salesians—stated that the Catholic hierarchy and the state had not honestly assessed whether the changes "would benefit the people." The CIRM saw the normalization of the relationship as a way to depoliticize the church and shift the focus of the clergy and laity away from workers, peasants, and the poor (a process they call "reprivatization" of the Church). "The [Catholic] Church thus reprivatized engages in even less social confrontation than a Church that, despite the lack of juridical recognition, enjoyed an exceptional and privileged freedom in a de facto sense."[50] They also feared that such a move to provide religious human rights would give legitimacy to neoliberal economic reforms opposed by the Catholic Church.[51] And what of the more closed, right-wing communities, such as the UNS? In the age of neoliberalism and individualism, what became of the men and the movements examined in this work?

Conclusion: Brief Reflections on Religious Community in the Twenty-First Century

When Salvador Abascal withdrew from the *sinarquista* movement in 1944, he simply disappeared from the pages of *El Sinarquista*, and not long after Abascal vanished, so too did the newspaper, for lack of funds—just one of the signs that the movement was in decline. As for Abascal, he retreated to the world of editing and publishing where he wrote his own books for the ultraconservative Catholic press Editorial Tradición and translated literature for Editorial Jus, another conservative, religious press. His own works included a series on the Mexican Revolution, such as *Lázaro Cárdenas: Presidente communista* and *La constitución de 1917: Destructora de la nación Mexicana*, designed to unmask the "moral catastrophe" of the Mexican Revolution as a "Protestant, liberal, and Marxist" disaster. In addition, he continued his fight against modern society, giving his children "a medieval education because it is better. Neither cinema, television, or even radio have a part in our lives." However, he did admit to allowing his children to play soccer, "the only concession, albeit compulsory, to the actual age."[52] To the very end, Abascal saw the future of Mexico by looking to the past.

While the *sinarquistas* went into a steep decline by 1950, the movement continues to exist across Mexico, especially in the Bajío zone (Mexico's "breadbasket" zone north of Mexico City) where most of María Auxiliadora's colonists came from. Living members of the *sinarquista* movement still boast that several descendants of families of Querétaro hang on in the small village of María Auxiliadora—"one more footprint of *sinarquismo*, and of Querétaro, in Mexico."[53] Of its "Four Causes for Which We Fight: Freedom of Expression, Freedom of Worship, Freedom from Fear, and Freedom from Poverty," it counts freedom of worship as an accomplished goal after the 1991 constitutional reforms.[54] In addition, the UNS continues to implement local improvement programs, including a number of agricultural cooperatives such as for nut and fruit trees, as well as improving dairy production.[55] For the modern UNS—the most overtly political of the groups in this study—the reforms of Salinas de Gortari legitimized their struggle.

What about those groups who spoke so highly of the revolution and the state that institutionalized it, such as the Luz del Mundo and the Reino de Dios en su Plenitud? How have they fared in the increasingly global age and under the constitutional reforms of 1991? As I discussed in the introduction, the bulk of scholarship on Luz del Mundo has followed the path of the organization after the death of the group's founder, the apostle Aarón. Immediately after his death his son, Samuel, became the group's apostle and took charge of the organization. By 1974, the membership was just under eighty thousand, and by 1986 LDM counted one and a half million. As of 2006, membership had surpassed five million. Retention and participation numbers, however, have not been studied by sociologists, though if Luz del Mundo retention comes anywhere close to that of other Protestant organizations, they may lose as many members to general inactivity in the religion as well as to the charismatic Catholic movements that are flourishing across Latin America.[56]

Nevertheless, Samuel meticulously defined the organizational structure of the hierarchy, consolidated his position in leadership, and then expanded the evangelizing work, including the improvement and expansion of Hermosa Provincia communities around Mexico and in Central and South America.[57] Owing to the "development," "unity," "liberty," and "security" that members found in the original colony, "it is not just a colony located in Guadalajara in the Republic of Mexico. It is a colony of the children of God that goes beyond borders, crosses oceans, and has established itself in the heart of the members of the church located in more than thirty-five nations as an icon of faith, unity, and love."[58]

As LDM grows, especially in Latin America, it has adopted an image that aims to transcend its Mexican roots, with some rhetoric referring to their founder as a "Simón Bolívar" destined to bring unity. Within Guadalajara they have almost totally occupied several neighborhoods to the east of the original Hermosa Provincia, including one named after their founder (Colonia Maestro Joaquín). In a twist of irony, one of the neighborhoods they nearly dominate is the neighborhood of San Joaquín—founded near Hermosa Provincia by Catholics in direct opposition to Aarón Joaquín and named after the Catholic saint. The communities in Guadalajara are no longer strictly closed, however, as members of many faiths own homes in those neighborhoods, even in the original Hermosa Provincia.

The group's political power and influence in Mexico increased with the rise of Samuel Joaquín in 1964, but fell off rapidly after the administration and reforms of Carlos Salinas. In 1979, the church obtained ejidal land on which to construct another community—land that had recently been invaded by the Socialist Workers Party under the influence of liberationist priests in the Catholic base community of Santa Cecilia. Such a deal had the effect of stamping out popular efforts to redistribute land in Guadalajara and provide LDM with land and another victory over Catholicism—further deepening the divide between LDM and its neighbors.[59]

After 1992, however, the political influence of Luz del Mundo in Jalisco State went into decline as its patron, the PRI, lost power. As a series of ten devastating gas explosions rocked central Guadalajara, killing two hundred, leaving twenty thousand homeless, doing US$300 million in damage, and ripping up twenty-six blocks of the city, the writing was on the wall for the PRI. Attempts by the party to cover up the state-owned oil company's hand in destroying acres of Guadalajara were easily seen through by both the press and the populace, and no amount of trucked-in supporters could make up for the stunning series of electoral losses that first removed the PRI from city government in Guadalajara and then from the state of Jalisco.[60] In addition, the constitutional reforms of 1991 had eliminated the Luz del Mundo's real power by reducing them to the same political status as every other church and eliminating their disproportion-ate power in relationship to Catholics.

This decline, however, may be short lived. In states where opposi-tion parties took power, such as Michoacán, Luz del Mundo members vote increasingly for the state's new ruling party of the Partido de la Revolución Democrática (PRD).[61] In addition, in the 2006 presidential election, the victory hinged on little more than two hundred thousand votes—making a corporate body like LDM a potentially important inter-est group. Indeed, even the openly Catholic President Vicente Fox of the National Action Party attempted to woo Luz del Mundo members to his party after his 2000 electoral victory, sending a message to the group's Santa Cena celebrations announcing his dedication to "government for all the churches of Mexico."[62]

Importantly, while protection from officials was key to the group's initial growth, recent political shifts appear to have had little impact on the growth of the organization that has seen a 30 percent growth rate since 1986. A visit to Guadalajara during the month of August and the Santa Cena celebration is evidence enough of the continued success of Luz del Mundo throughout Mexico and Latin America. By the first week of August, all transportation is marked in the city by its proximity to the Hermosa Provincia, with buses and *peseros* (minibuses) painting a large "HP," "Hermosa Provincia," or "Provincia" on their windshields to alert potential riders to their destination. The hundreds of thousands of "dele-gates" who throng the area, packed around their central temple with arms extended in the air, remind one of pictures of pilgrims making the hajj to Mecca, or thronging Vatican City during Holy Week. Women, heads covered with lace scarves, and men in suits and ties, weep, pray, or speak in tongues as they experience "manifestations of the spirit." Eventually, in celebrating the Holy Supper or "Santa Cena" of Christ's last meal with his apostles, millions of pieces of unleavened bread baked by ministers who also work as bakers are distributed, along with thousands of liters of hand-squeezed nonalcoholic grape juice.[63] Providing the body and blood of Christ for three hundred thousand visitors is no small task.

As for the tiny Iglesia del Reino de Dios en su Plenitud in Colonia Industrial de la Nueva Jerusalén, there has been some change since the death of Margarito Bautista in 1961, but not much. As in years past, divi-sions continue within the community: Both the director of the archive at the Museo de Mormonismo en México and U.S. anthropologist Thomas

Murphy warned me that in making inquiries in the colony I would be steered away from some families and toward others to suit their own internal feuds. The original line of thatch huts for eighty people first built by the colonists has long since disappeared. What has replaced them is a modern neighborhood for nearly eight hundred people with wide, clean, paved streets, sidewalks, brick homes with picket fences, and large front yards filled with fruit trees. All of this surrounds a new meeting house next to a large white temple—the most sacred worship space for the community. In fact, while no signs indicate when you enter the colony, it is apparent by the appearance of a well-constructed sidewalk and quality road paving. Much of this quality infrastructure—including an impressive junior high school—is due to the efforts of contributed labor from the community using municipal resources.[64] In addition, the acceptance of the community in Ozumba seems apparent. While some members of the surrounding neighborhood joked about the *colonia* being "all cousins," the municipal secretary was a member of the faith, and the members of the church have a strong presence in the biweekly market, or *tianguis*. Also, "many members of the community work outside the community as lawyers, doctors, and accountants. One person is even pursuing a PhD in mathematics in England."[65]

The members of the community still practice the Law of Consecration and plural marriage, and as relations with the state have been regularized, the church's association has legal measures in place to prevent the sale of land to non-Mormons. As a leader of the congregation said, the colony is "100 percent Mormon," "100 percent Mexican," and "stronger than ever."[66] Anthropologist Murphy reports a second congregation affiliated with the Reino de Dios en su Plenitud living in Puebla. In addition, one Lorenzo Cuatli, an associate of Bautista who also rejected the invitation to return with his congregation back to the LDS Church, has an independent congregation of his own in San Gabriel Ometoxtla, Puebla. Murphy makes a pertinent observation of the Colonia Industrial de la Nueva Jerusalén group in the modern context:

> When compared in terms of numbers to the LDS church [one million LDS in Mexico as of 2005], these two small indigenous remnants of the Third Convention appear rather insignificant. But to deny or minimize their existence is to overlook the impressive diversity spawned . . . during its [Mormonism's] first decades

in the central valley of Mexico. Bautista's followers did not disappear, they endured immense persecution from Latter-day Saints and Catholics alike, to create an impressive communal society that is thriving in the midst of greater Mexico's embrace of neoliberal economics in a world market.[67]

And finally, what of Felipe Burgos, the centenarian and outcast who provided so much information on the colony? Burgos died in 2005 at age 102. Ever seeking access to the sacred, Don Felipe died firmly in his most recent faith: La Iglesia Cristiana Apostólica Pentecostes (the Apostolic Pentecostal Christian Church).[68] Indigenous, Catholic, Baptist, LDS, El Reino de Dios en su Plenitud, Pentecostal—and faithfully entrenched in the PRI—Don Felipe traveled many of Mexico's spiritual roads, ever seeking salvation, both temporal and spiritual.

NOTES

Introduction

1. For example, the Oneida or Shaker communities of the nineteenth-century United States are intentional religious communities. See Susan Love Brown's *Intentional Community: An Anthropological Perspective*.

2. Brown, *Intentional Community*, 153. For example, Brown highlights the Koinonian movement of the early 1940s U.S. South. The community was founded by two Baptist preachers for whites and blacks alike in reaction to the racial hatred that existed in the region. She also points to the early nineteenth-century New Harmony project that reacted to the growing power of the capitalist market in the United States and served as a "critique of capitalism and social and material inequality" (pp. 155–57).

3. Wallace, "Revitalization," 265.

4. Wallace, "Revitalization," 267. By "mazeway," Wallace refers to a personal or societal view of every aspect of their self-image and surroundings. "It includes perceptions of both the maze of physical objects of the environment (internal and external, human and nonhuman) and also of the ways in which this maze can be manipulated by the self and others in order to minimize stress."

5. Wallace, "Revitalization," 265.

6.   The first to investigate the Luz del Mundo, Alisa Lancyner Reisel and Araceli Ibarra Bellon both admit that many of their interviews were obtained with hidden tape recorders and by pretending to be interested in conversion to the group. Wherever possible, I include the few oral histories I was allowed to use—available in the case of Luz del Mundo only because the sources were members designated to speak with "outsiders" and therefore whose comments are open to public record.

7.   A. T. Vaughn, Review of *The Unredeemed Captive*, 197–98.

8.   The idea that religious affiliation is akin to a societal critique is not unique in the study of religion in Latin America. The work on Protestantism by scholars such as Jean Pierre Bastian, Virginia Garrard-Burnett, and Elizabeth Brusco, and on Catholics by Roger Lancaster and Julio Moreno, have all been influential in my conception of the interaction of communities with greater societal issues. For examples, see Jean Pierre Bastian, *Protestantismos y modernidad*; Virginia Garrard-Burnett, *Protestantism in Guatemala*; Elizabeth Brusco, *The Reformation of Machismo*; Roger N. Lancaster, *Thanks to God and the Revolution*; Julio Moreno, *Yankee Don't Go Home!*; and Jennie Purnell, *Popular Movements and State Formation in Revolutionary Mexico*. Each of these scholars explores how religious affiliation or participation in a religious community is also a way to critique the cultural, economic, or political direction of the nation in which they reside, as well as what they hope to "get out" of such an affiliation.

9.   Etzioni, *Rights and the Common Good*, iv.

10.   Simmons and Wilson, *Competing Visions*, 28.

11.   Bellah et al., *Habits of the Heart*, 295.

12.   Wiebe, *Search for Order*, 12, 132.

13.   In addition, though at various times throughout this work I refer to an inclination by the three groups to form close, tight-knit local religious communities and exalt the local village, this should not entirely be equated with "local religion," especially as defined by historian Adrian Bantjes. Bantjes limits local religion to Catholicism and uses the term interchangeably with "folk" Catholicism, especially as defined by anthropologist John Ingham as a "syncretic fusion of Mesoamerican and Catholic beliefs" (Bantjes, "Saints, Sinners, and State Formation," 146–47). While the groups examined in this work see the salvation of Mexico in the salvation of the individual and the local community, they are bitterly opposed to the kind of "local" religion described by Bantjes. The *sinarquistas* found "folk" practices particularly opposed to their notions of "pure" Catholicism, while the Pentecostal Luz del Mundo and the Mormon Iglesia del Reino de Dios en su Plenitud found in folk Catholicism the very reason Christianity needed to be "restored."

14.   Hammergren, "Corporatism," 446.

15.   Butler, "Revolution," 8.

16. Irene O'Malley's influential and rich analysis of the creation of national heroes and hero myths (*The Myth of the Revolution*) to consolidate power in the hands of the central state has been invaluably influential to my interpretation of Mexico after 1920. Likewise, Thomas Benjamin's *La Revolución: Mexico's Great Revolution as Memory, Myth, and History* examines how the battle to define the history of the Mexican Revolution in the 1920s led to the creation of an accepted manner or set of protocols by which to perform allegiance to that revolution in subsequent years.

17. Saragoza, "Selling of Mexico," 92.

18. Moreno, *Yankee*, 1–3, 130.

19. Krauze, *Biography of Power*, 529.

20. Joseph et al., "Assembling the Fragments," 10–11.

21. M. K. Vaughn, *Cultural Politics*, 20.

22. Knight, *Mexican Revolution*, vol. 2, *Counter-revolution and Reconstruction*, 2:335.

23. Knight, *Mexican Revolution*, vol. 2, *Counter-revolution and Reconstruction*, 2:518.

24. Schmidt, "Making it Real," 52.

25. Gregory, *Salvation at Stake*, 2.

26. O'Donnell, "Polyarchies," 307–8.

27. Hay, "Law and Society"; see also Ricardo Salvatore and Carlos Aguirre in the introduction to the same volume, *Crime and Punishment in Latin America*.

28. Thompson, *Essential E. P. Thompson*, 438.

29. Thompson, *Essential E. P. Thompson*, 438. Similar to Thompson in work on Latin America has been Sarah C. Chambers, who argues that the language of rights instituted by republics served to empower Creole elite in Peru, but also to provide a powerful weapon for legal defense for peasants. See Chambers, "Crime and Citizen," 30–32.

30. Fernández-Armesto, *Americas*, 17.

31. For more on Mennonites in Mexico, see Sawatzky, *They Sought a Country*. For Mormon colonization in Mexico, see Tullis, *Mormons in Mexico*.

32. For examples of actions against Protestants, see AGN-DGG 547.4/299, 547.1/161, 547.4/289, 547.5/22, 547.5/12, 547.4/331, 547.4/145, 547.1/8; AGN-MAC 547.1/12. For letters from Masonic lodges citing harassment of Protestants, see AGN-MAC 547.1/13, 547.1/4, 547.1/1.

33. AGN-DGG 547.4/51; AGN-MAC 547/6.

34. Garma Navarro, *Protestantismo*, 82.

35. Moreno, *Yankee*, 205–28.

36. Bowen, *Evangelism*, 44. Take, for example, the application of the Templo Espiritual del Divino Maestro Luz del Mundo, which applied to the state to function as a church instead of the standard neighborhood association, costing them approval as the state refused to recognize churches. The state in practice, of course, recognized churches as part of society by 1942, but the language necessary to unlock that recognition still had to be used. AGN-GOB 2/340 (11) 21159.

37. Cisneros Sosa, *La ciudad*, 117.

38. Krauze, *Biography of Power*, 545–46.

39. Cisneros Sosa, *La ciudad*, 124.

40. Medin, *Sexenio alemanista*, 124.

41. M. T. de la Peña, "Problemas demográficos," 282.

42. Torres Ramírez, *Utopia industrial*, 68–69.

43. M. T. de la Peña, "Problemas demográficos," 290.

44. M. T. de la Peña, "Problemas demográficos," 278.

45. Simmons and Wilson, *Competing Visions*, 20–21.

46. Van Young, *Other Rebellion*, 512.

47. Vanderwood, *Power of God*.

48. Lomnitz, "Mexico's Cultural Revolution," 335.

49. Most work on Luz del Mundo has been carried out by anthropologists more interested in the recent role of this large Mexican community as a global organization than its roots in Mexican history. For example, the only scholarly book-length treatment of the group by Mexican anthropologist Renée de La Torre covers seventy years of history in sixteen pages with only one archival reference. Similarly, article-length treatments by de la Torre or anthropologist Patricia Fortuny Loret de Mola deal in great depth with the sociological and anthropological theory involved in the current movement but spend little time with the group's founder or the context of Mexican history in which he and his group function. Finally, chapter 2 of this book will also deal with Luz del Mundo in a comparative perspective. While a similar approach was taken by Guillermo de la Peña and Renée de la Torre, the comparisons, again, were limited to contemporary manifestations of Luz del Mundo and had a limited reach into the foundational years of the group. See de la Torre, *Hijos*; Fortuny, "Origins,"and also *Creyentes*; de la Peña and de la Torre, "Religión y política."

50. See McConkie, *Mormon Doctrine*, 813, 158, 151. See Arrington et al., *City of God*.

51. The health code mentioned earlier (known as the Word of Wisdom) says that the code was given by God to protect people from the "consequence of evils

and designs, which do and will exist in the hearts of conspiring men." Joseph Smith, *Doctrine and Covenants*, 89:4. See also *Doctrine and Covenants*, 78:14.

52. Banner, "Christianity in Civil Society," 120–21.

Chapter One

1. Humberto Musacchio, "Luz del Mundo: Con raíces en la tierra," *Enfoque*, August 25, 2002; Pozos Bravo, "Análisis," 144. The number of five million members was still being publicized as total membership on the church's official Web page (www.lldm.org) in December 2009. The 2000 census simply addressed religion by giving respondents the choice of Catholic, Nothing, or Other. Due to the multitude of ways religious people might describe their belief, there is no accurate count on the 2000 census of religion in Mexico.

2. Though founded in 1926, the church failed to gain much attention with the majority of Mexicans until the late 1950s and early 1960s with its intentional communities, large chapels, and explosive growth in both rural and urban Mexico.

3. The most refined foundational works on LDM come from anthropologists Reneé de la Torre and Patricia Fortuny Loret de Mola. For de la Torre, see *Los hijos de la luz*; and *"Religión y política,"* with Guillermo de la Peña; also, "La construción de una identidad." For Fortuny Loret de Mola, see "Origins, Development, and Perspectives of the Luz del Mundo Church"; also *Creyentes y creencias en Guadalajara*. De la Torre and Fortuny Loret de Mola collaborated on "Mujer, participación, representación, simbólica y vida cotidiana en la Luz del Mundo." A secondary study by Rodolfo Morán Quiroz relies heavily on the studies of de la Torre and Fortuny. See *Alternativa religiosa en Guadalajara*. Several key masters' theses exist on the study. De la Torre and Fortuny Loret de Mola both cite as foundational the 1972 Universidad de Guadalajara master's thesis by Araceli Ibarra Bellon and Alisa Lancyner Reisel, "La Hermosa Provincia: Nacimiento y vida de una secta cristiana en Guadalajara." Responses to the work of de la Torre, Fortuny Loret de Mola, Morán, Ibarra, and Lancyner include the well-balanced 2001 University of Guadalajara master's thesis on state-church relations by Sara S. Pozos Bravo cited in note 1 above. In the interest of transparency regarding the thesis, as of September 2005, Pozos Bravo is also the assistant director of international affairs for LDM. Historian Israel Pineda (a vocal member of LDM) has also made an important if openly pro-LDM contribution to the study of urbanization and the foundation of the Hermosa Provincia in response to de la Torre and Fortuny Loret de Mola. See the February 13, 2003, conference in Guadalajara, *Guadalajara y una de sus colonias: Hermosa Provincia*, "Historia de la Hermosa Provincia y su fundador." Pineda did

not share the text of his presentation, but conceded me an interview on September 24, 2005, regarding his presentation.

4. Interview with members of LDM, Guadalajara, Jalisco, September 5, 2005. Though interviewees agreed to speak with me without audio recording in their capacity as greeters for the public at the LDM chapel in Hermosa Provincia, I have made the unilateral decision to list the interviewees as anonymous to avoid even the slightest negative response from other members of the community.

5. Interview with Sara Pozos Bravo, September 14, 2005; Pozos Bravo, "Análisis," 65. Pozos Bravo was my official, assigned, representative to LDM, and informed me I would not be allowed access to the official archive (she herself was not allowed access during her own research on LDM).

6. Fortuny, "Origins," 148. De la Torre, *Hijos*, 133–36. Interview with Sarah S. Pozos Bravo, September 14, 2005. Pozos Bravo gave "*tez moreno*" as one of her answers to the question "Why was Eusebio called by God?"

7. *Excélsior*, September 22, 1987. My translation.

8. Rentería, *Luz del Mundo*, 35–36. My translation.

9. Rentería, *Luz del Mundo*, 35–36. De la Torre (*Hijos*, 70) puts the date as 1913 when Eusebio joins the "constitutionalist forces."

10. Interview with Sara S. Pozos Bravo, September 14, 2005. The church cites Romans 13:1–6, Matthew 22:21, and 1 Timothy 2:1–3 as the rationale for the support of governments "puesto por Dios." See also *Excélsior*, September 22, 1987, for a political proclamation of LDM.

11. Rentería, *Luz del Mundo*, 37.

12. Rentería, *Luz del Mundo*, 37.

13. Fortuny, "Origins," 149.

14. *Los Angeles Daily Times*, April 18, 1906.

15. Morán Quiroz, *Alternativa*, 75–83. See also Gaxiola, *La serpiente y la paloma*; Jean Pierre Bastian, *Protestantismo y sociedad*.

16. Rentería, *Luz del Mundo*, 41–43.

17. Morán Quiroz, *Alternativa*, 85.

18. Rentería, *Luz del Mundo*, 49–53.

19. Rentería, *Luz del Mundo*, 56.

20. Ibarra and Lancyner, "La Hermosa," 9.

21. Rentería, *Luz del Mundo*, 136. Rentería reports that Eusebio called on his military connections to save him from hanging by a mob in the Altos of Jalisco. Pozos Bravo claims his military relationships got him out of jail five times when he was arrested for preaching in rural villages. Pozos Bravo, "Análisis," 47.

22. Interview with Pozos Bravo, September 14, 2005. In Pozos Bravo's own thesis, she reports that of modern members of LDM sampled by her research (an unscientific sampling of LDM members residing in Hermosa Provincia in 2000), 53 percent believe laws should be obeyed, even if they are unjust.

23. *Excélsior*, September 22, 1987. My translation.

24. Rentería, *Luz del Mundo*, 59–60.

25. Rentería, *Luz del Mundo*, 69.

26. 1 Samuel 3:1–10.

27. 1 Samuel 4. The importance of the story of Samuel is perhaps reflected in Eusebio's naming his son and consequent successor Samuel.

28. Rentería claims that Eusebio had never heard the name of Aarón before (*Luz del Mundo*, 71). Eusebio's biblical knowledge is somewhat contradictory at this point. Rentería claims Eusebio had been using the Bible to contradict the sexual peccadilloes of the preacher Silas, which caused Silas to burn Aarón's Bible. On the other hand, Rentería makes constant reference to Eusebio's knowledge of the Bible for the start of his missionary journey, where he knew he should go "without purse or scrip." He also observes that Elisa still had her Bible. He also points out that when Saulo tried to force him to return to the congregation, he confounded him with biblical passages. It is difficult to believe that Eusebio lost all biblical contact or that he had never heard the story of Aarón, brother of Moses and an integral player in the biblical story of Israel and the Ten Commandments.

29. Rentería, *Luz del Mundo*, 91.

30. Rentería, *Luz del Mundo*, 113.

31. Rentería, *Luz del Mundo*, 118.

32. AGN, OC 428-7-13, no. 28. The collection also contains letters of support for Zuno from the public.

33. AHEJ, G-4-927 ZAP/3423.

34. Morán Quiroz, *Alternativa*, 30.

35. As practitioners of adult baptism, the baptismal font itself would be several feet across and several feet deep, probably with steps leading down into the font and a covering for the top when not in use.

36. Rentería, *Luz del Mundo*, 14.

37. De la Torre, *Hijos*, 74.

38. Research in the Archívo General de la Nación and the Archívo Histórico del Estado de Jalisco shows no evidence of any direct investment in Aarón's ministry.

39. AMG, Iglesias no Católicas; Sacerdotes no Católicas; AGN-OC 514.1/1–28. Iglesias no Católicas and Sacerdotes no Católicas are both collections housed in the Archívo Municipal de Guadalajara.

40. Pozos Bravo, "Análisis," 39–40.

41. Rentería, *Luz del Mundo*, 162, 170.

42. Rentería, *Luz del Mundo*, 161.

43. AMG, Iglesias no Católicas, exp. [folder] 5. The letter is dated October 18, 1934—before the official approval of the church but after the submission of papers to the state.

44. AMG, Correspondencia 1933, 14/2; 5–44.

45. AMG, Correspondencia 1937, 1–02–118.

46. AHEJ, G-4–938 TOA/3680.

47. AHEJ, IP-1–935 AT-3083, 3091.

48. AMG, Iglesias no Católicas.

49. Butler, "Revolution," 10–12.

50. AMG, Iglesias no Católicas, exp. 8.

51. AMG, Correspondencia 1939, 1–08–7; Iglesias no Católicas, exp. 8.

52. AMG, Iglesias no Católicas, exp. 22; Iglesia Recinto Espiritual Templo de la Infancia de Maria y Tiempo de Maestro.

53. Rentería, *Luz del Mundo*, 138.

54. Brusco, *Reformation of Machismo*.

55. Rentería, *Luz del Mundo*, 138.

56. Rentería, *Luz del Mundo*, 134.

57. Fortuny, "Origins," 152–53.

58. Interview with Sara Pozos Bravo, September 14, 2005.

59. Rentería, *Luz del Mundo*, 203.

60. Butler, "Revolution," 4.

61. Pozos Bravo, "Análisis," 46.

62. Rentería, *Luz del Mundo*, 141–42.

63. AMG, Templos Otros Credos, exp. Iglesia Pentecostes Independiente.

64. AMG, Correspondencia 1938, 1–02–160.

65. Fortuny and de la Torre, "Mujer," 125–50.

66. Rentería, *Luz del Mundo*, 168. Rentería's book is notably lacking in exact dates in most instances. This first naming of the pastor appears to be in the early 1930s.

67. Rentería, *Luz del Mundo*, 186.

68. Interview with members of LDM, Guadalajara, Jalisco, September 5, 2005.

69. Rentería, *Luz del Mundo*, 156–58.

70. Rentería, *Luz del Mundo*, 158–59.

71. De la Peña and de la Torre, "Religión," 574–76; de la Peña, "Microhistoria," 119. Between 1900 and 1920, the population grew from 100,000 to 147,000. This makes an influx during the shooting portion of the revolution of some 30,000. By 1930, the population reached 185,000—at least 50,000 can be attributed to the Cristero War. The major growth in the city, however, appears to take place in the '40s and '50s, growing to 250,000 by 1940, and 378,000 by 1950. The urban explosion came in connection not with Mexico's most major crises but with its "golden years" of success.

72. AHEJ, ES-4-932 375 F, 123 f; AMG, Correspondencia 1-00-471. Aarón, working as a *zapatero* (shoe sales) may have made just over a peso a day, and many of the converts that worked as bread bakers could expect the same wage. The daily cost of living in Jalisco was listed as 1 peso 72 centavos.

73. AHEJ, ES-4-932/123 f.

74. De la Torre, *Hijos*, 60.

75. Rentería, *Luz del Mundo*, 175.

76. A list of signatures on a petition in 1935 reveals a small concentration of members in the area, but many still appear spread out in nearby neighborhoods. AMG, Iglesias no Católicas, exp. 5.

77. AMG, Iglesias no Católicas, exp. 5.

78. AGN, Gobernación, May 2, 1935; AMG, Iglesias no Católicas, exp. 5.

79. AMG, Iglesias no Católicas, exp. 5.

80. AMG, Iglesias no Católicas, exp. 5. See also AMG, Sacerdotes no Católicas, exp. Iglesia Espiritual Cristiana. Also Oficio 2/52, November 12, 1954. Copy in possession of the author.

81. AMG, Iglesias no Católicas, exp. 5.

82. Torres Sánchez, *Revolución*, 89–90.

83. AMG, Correspondencia 1952, I-4-35-92.

84. *Excelsior*, February 4, 1937; AMG, Correspondencia 1955, 1–08–13; 1950, 4-35-26, 4-35-35.

85. AHEJ, Mapoteca, Fotos Areas E XI S.L. 1949 and DXIII S.R. 1948. Unfortunately, the urban planners of Guadalajara only took photos of *manzanas* 320 and 345 and not *manzanas* 237 and 242—the blocks with the temple and the homes of Eusebio's closest followers. Today much of the property remains in the hands of Aarón's daughter, Ana María Joaquín de Chic (Catastro del Estado de Jalisco, 15931 #2).

86. AMG, Iglesias no Católicas, exp. 5.

87. AMG, Iglesias no Católicas, exp. 5; *Hermosa Provincia*.

88. Rentería, *Luz del Mundo*, 206.

89. AMG, Correspondencia 1957, I-4-30-8.

90. AMG, Iglesias no Católicas, exp. 5; AHEJ, Mapoteca, Fotos Areas E XI S.L. 1949 and DXIII S.R. 1948. The membership list is characteristic of LDM beliefs that men and women should be separated, and two lists exist for men and women. By creating an alphabetical database of street addresses, I was able to complete the households in a single list. The task of matching the two sources was made difficult by the lack of urban development in the area, meaning that only a provisional numbering of *manzanas* and lots was assigned, if any such process was carried out at all.

91. AMG, Iglesias no Católicas, exp. 5; AGN, DGG 2/340/(11)1 (7:25). The group also requested a copy of the approval of the church so that they could present the letter to "Hacienda y Crédito Pública [Department of Finance and Credit]," but do not give the reason.

92. De la Torre, *Hijos*, 80.

93. Rentería, *Luz del Mundo*, 214.

94. Ibarra and Lancyner, "La Hermosa," 45.

95. Rentería reports that 500 went to the new church called the Buen Pastor (*La Luz*, 225). De la Torre puts the number at 250 (*Hijos*, 80). The AGN shows that Lino Figueroa had applied to Gobernación (Department of the Interior) to open a church in Totoltepec in May of 1942 as part of the "evangelical movement Luz del Mundo," but returned in September to say the church now belonged to the Buen Pastor church. Gobernación approved the transfer. AGN-GOB 2/343 (12) caja 12.

96. AMG, Iglesias no Católicas, exp. 5.

97. Rentería, *Luz del Mundo*, 235.

98. De la Torre, *Hijos*, 81.

99. Ibarra and Lancyner, "La Hermosa," 22.

100. Such is the connection felt between the People of Israel and LDM, that Fortuny was moved to view the religion as "syncretic" with Judaism ("Origins," 147). De la Torre claims that LDM requested that Eusebio/Aarón be buried in the Jewish cemetery in Guadalajara. The request was denied (*Hijos*, 85).

101. Ibarra and Lancyner, "La Hermosa," 2–3; Rentería, *Luz del Mundo*, 185.

102. The tensions between LDM and the Catholic Church reached a boiling point in the late 1980s after increasing Catholic protest against the fraud perpetrated by the PRI in the Chihuahua governor's election. The LDM responded with attacks on the involvement of the Catholics in the matter as well as questioning the ability of a Mexican to be both Catholic and a good citizen. See de la Torre, *Hijos*, for a full account.

103. See O'Malley, *Myth*, 113.

104. See Camp, *Crossing Swords*.

105. AHEJ, IGJ/1943–1947, exp. 0020, Memoria del Poder Ejecutivo.

106. AMG, Iglesias no Católicos, Sacerdotes no Católicos; AGN-DGG 2/340 (11) 21159.

107. AMG, Actas de Cabildo (Notes of the Municipal Council), October 24, 1952, November 7, 1952, April 2, 1954, April 9, 1954; AGN-MAV 515/9152. Urbanization in Guadalajara had been relatively unplanned until 1940, but then only when imposed by the state. No city planning appeared until 1947 and continued to remain insufficient until the late 1950s. See Irma Beatriz García Rojas in *Vivir en Guadalajara*, 167.

108. AMG, Iglesias no Católicas, exp 5. On June 18, 1951, Julián Zamora requested copies of his registration as a preacher as he had been "robbed of all his documents" in the church.

109. Rentería, *Luz del Mundo*, 258.

110. Rentería, *Luz del Mundo*, 257.

111. AMG, Iglesias no Católicas, exp. 21. Twelve churches compared to fifty-four, however, marks a steady rate of growth from 1930, when Guadalajara had only two registered Protestants, and from 1935 with only three (LDM does not appear on the list of approved Protestant churches), and ten Protestant *templos* in the whole state of Jalisco. See AGN-DGG 2.340 (11)/10516; 2.340 (11)83.

112. AMG, Templos Otro Credos; Correspondencia 1953, 1–20–4. Two pastors of Cristal Numero 1 Israelita Espiritual, both employees of Gobernación (the interior department), sought to bring in municipal authorities in their battle to control their church.

113. García de la Mora, "50 años," 10.

114. AMG, Correspondencia 1955, I-4-31-147.

115. AGN-ARC 418.2/216; 418.2/533.

116. AMG, Actas de Cabildo, July 10, 1953; AHEJ, MP 5.4 1952 7. The Comisión de Planeación Estado de Jalisco de 1952 lists the area as a *zona ganadera*, or agricultural zone. See also AHEJ, PL 7.3 1953 231. Humberto García de la Mora places the distance as around four kilometers ("50 años," 10).

117. C. Castañeda, *Vivir en Guadalajara*, 162. The author describes it as a limitation of "horizontal" growth.

118. De la Mora, "50 años," 11.

119. Despite searches in the collections of Iglesias no Católicas, Sacerdotes no Católicas, Fraccionamientos (private housing projects), Actas de Cabildo, and Correspondencia, I was unable to find a copy in the municipal archive of the above-mentioned document. I obtained the following copy from LDM Assistant Director of International Relations Sara S. Pozos Bravo. Pozos Bravo says she did research in the municipal archive, though she does not

remember the provenance of this particular document. See note 145 in this chapter.

120. AMG, Correspondencia 1962, 3–20–13. The *Gaceta Municipal* of Guadalajara for December of 1962 mentions the dedication of the market but without the descriptive history of the area that other market dedications receive. In addition, President Adolfo López Mateos attended the dedication of the market in his spring 1962 trip to Guadalajara, but that also escapes more than a brief mention in the *Gaceta Municipal* and no mention in local newspapers. The market, as the land later dedicated for the gravesite, was listed under the name of Eusebio/Aarón's daughter and son-in-law, the Mozqueda family. All the land for the cemetery and market were registered officially in the 1961 antecedent land register under the Mozqueda name. Israel Pineda says that the son-in-law of Eusebio/Aarón acted as the land representative for the *colonia* so that the apostle could dedicate himself to the ministry. If this is the case, all the land in Hermosa Provincia may have been registered with the state under the single name of Mozqueda in 1961.

121. AMG, Correspondencia 1954, 1–06–46; 4–31–22; 4–31–307.

122. AMG, Correspondencia 1957, 4–32–51.

123. Lomelí Suárez, *Guadalajara*. See also the popular version (a cartoon) by Rodríguez Gurrola and Madragal, *Los barrios de Guadalajara*.

124. In 1957 (the centennial of the 1857 liberal constitution), LDM dedicated a monument to Benito Juárez at the entrance to Hermosa Provincia with attending municipal authorities, though the dedication of the monument was not mentioned in archival documents such as the *Gaceta Municipal*, Actas de Cabildo, or Correspondencia. Other monuments celebrating Juárez elsewhere in the city received detailed attention in all three sources, however. It wasn't only monuments that the *Gaceta Municipal* fails to list: Hermosa Provincia is also absent from a compilation of *fracciones* (private housing projects) that paid their municipal taxes. Either the colony was not paying taxes or they were deliberately left off the list. Indeed, even in 1959, after the establishment of a civil registry in the *colonia* and the submission of plans to municipal authorities for electricity, Hermosa Provincia still does not appear in a published list of *Fraccionamientos de Guadalajara* (private housing projects of Guadalajara) (AMG, Correspondencia 1959, 4–30–179). Plans and maps of the city vary in their recognition and planning of the neighborhood, demonstrating a lack of planning for the eastern portion of the city in general and of public knowledge of the new *colonia* in particular. A 1955 plan of the city of Guadalajara shows Hermosa Provincia, but maps from 1956 do not. There even seems to be confusion regarding street names. In 1955, the city plan lists the central west-east street in the *colonia* as Esteban Alatorre—an extension of the Guadalajara street that still, at this time, did not connect to the colony. However, a 1959 map shows the same street as Galilea—the name given the street by Aarón; but the street named Jerusalem is misspelled as

Versalem. Two 1960 maps by the University of Guadalajara and the public works department do not even agree on the name, and in 1964 the street appears as Alatorre, Eulogia Parra, and Galilea. Even maps by private parties, such as the bilingual tourist map by Editorial Flecha, get the location wrong, listing Hermosa Provincia in the wrong area of Sector Libertad. AMG, Correspondencia 1954 4–31–20; AHMG Planes Electorales, 1959; AHEJ, PL 7.3 1955 27; G 11.1 PL/1956; PL 7.3 1960 525; PL 7.3 1960 616; PL 7.3 1960 351; PL 2.1 1964 501.

125. AMG, Correspondencia 1954, 4–31–20.

126. De la Torre, *Hijos*, 82.

127. De la Mora, "50 años," 17.

128. AMG, Iglesias no Católicas, exp. 5; de la Mora, "50 años," 17; *Gaceta Municipal*, January 1960. The project was actually approved, however, as early as May or July of 1959. AMG, Correspondencia 1959, 4–33–29.

129. De la Torre, *Hijos*, 83.

130. De la Peña, "Microhistoria," 128–32.

131. AMG, Actas de Cabildo, July 3, 1953, July 9, 1954, May 31, 1954.

132. AMG, Correspondencia 1957, 4–32–150. Chavero Ocampo started as the director of public sanitation before working his way up to the state legislature. The Archívo del Congreso del Estado de Jalisco holds no record of the interaction between Chavero Ocampo and LDM. All correspondence between representatives and constituents remains in the possession of the representative. See also López, *Guadalajara*. AMG, Correspondencia 1959, 1–01–2.

133. AMG, Correspondencia 1959, 4–30–184.

134. "Beautiful Situation" in the King James Version; "Well Situated" in the Septuagint.

135. Psalms 48:2, "Beautiful for situation, the joy of the whole earth, is Mount Zion, on the sides of the north, the city of the great King" (KJV translation).

136. 1 Kings 8:1, 2 Samuel 5:6–7.

137. Such a comparison, again, allows for a symbolic and real replacement of the "foreign" Roman Church.

138. "For, lo, the kings were assembled, they passed by together. They saw it, and so they marveled; they were troubled, and hasted away" (KJV translation).

139. Interview with Pozos Bravo, September 14, 2005.

140. Rentería, *Luz del Mundo*, 265.

141. Rentería, *Luz del Mundo*, 262–64.

142. De la Peña and de la Torre, "Religión y Política," 589.

143. Interview with members of LDM, Guadalajara, Jalisco, September 5, 2005. One member reports that this is where he began his training for a prosperous business.

144. Interview with members of LDM, Guadalajara, Jalisco, September 12, 2005.

145. Pozos Bravo, de la Mora, and Rentería all recognize the absence of any formal charitable networks or associations until after the death of Aarón and his replacement by his son, Samuel. This sort of insular behavior—both moral and economic—has led to some charges that LDM erected a "great wall" around the colony (de la Torre, *Hijos*, 71; and Fortuny, *Religion*). Members of LDM deny ever having erected a wall around the colony and the report seems to be based on the passing observation by Lancyner and Ibarra that they observed the "ruins" of a wall around the colony in 1971–72. Israel Pineda contends that what they saw was the remains of the former wall that kept traffic from the road to Colimillo out of the fields of the Hacienda Rancho Blanco. Photos of the colony published in *Hermosa Provincia* seem to support the argument that no wall was built around the community. Anthropologists seeking to explain the transition from the church use the "disappearance" of the physical wall as a symbol of the disappearance of the social wall between LDM and the rest of Guadalajara.

146. AMG, *Gaceta Municipal*, January 1959; Correspondencia 1959 1–06–57, 1–06–23; 1960 1–06–23; 1961 1–06–14; 1962 1–06–10; 1963 1–06–18; 1964 1–06–17.

147. De la Mora, "50 años," 17.

148. AHEJ, IGJ/1943–1947, exp. 0020—*Memoria del Poder Ejecutivo.*

149. De la Peña and de la Torre, "Religión y política," 589n27.

150. When I contacted de la Torre about the absence of the letters, she claims that a member of LDM took the papers for copying. She claims to have made photocopies of the documents, which she gave to the architect and scholar of Guadalajara urbanization David Vázquez, who died in 2004. Vázquez's former secretary claims that all of the architect's papers, unfortunately, were turned over to his family who, she claims, are "hicks that don't care about such items." She was unable to provide the contact information for the family of Vázquez.

151. Pozos Bravo, "Análisis," 70.

152. Pessar, *From Fanatics to Folk*, 136–37.

153. While the ability of the PRI to return large votes in its favor was constructed of efforts in individual communities, such as Hermosa Provincia, considering the long and well-documented history of fraud and vote control, one is forced to ask the question an elections officer in Chalco put to me when I requested elections data from the 1950s, "What does it matter? Who else would they vote for, and would that even have value?"

154. See Lieuwin, *Mexican Militarism.*

155. De la Peña and de la Torre, "Religión y política," 577. Interviews with urban immigrants to religious colonies—both Catholic and LDM—show very low participation in union activity.

156. AMG, Correspondencia 1950, 4–30–86; 1952 1–09–14; 1959 1–09–37; 1960 1–09–07; 1962 1–00–73. Membership in the FOPJ may even have helped in such mundane tasks as getting an LDM truck out of the municipal impound yard when it was towed for not having plates (1960 2–12–2).

157. De la Peña and de la Torre, "Religión y política," 573.

158. AMG, Correspondencia 1959, 1–00–0.

159. Rentería, *Luz del Mundo,* 253; Ibarra and Lancyner, "La Hermosa," 63.

160. AMG, Correspondencia 1960, 4–31–58.

161. AMG, Correspondencia 1960, 1–08–35. In 1960, a cantina was built at the eastern edge of Hermosa Provincia, and members of LDM, through the FOPJ, helped get it shut down.

162. AMG, Correspondencia 1935, 1–0–253; 1941 1–0–63; 1942 1–08–1; 1961 1–00–0.

163. Rentería, *Luz del Mundo,* 298.

164. Rentería, *Luz del Mundo,* 299.

165. AMG, Actas de Cabildo, June 12, 1964; Ramo Fraccionamientos, exp. Hermosa Provincia.

166. AMG, Correspondencia 1954, 4–37–38. The American Society of Guadalajara also made a similar request in 1952, though I found no mention of approval.

167. AMG, Ramo Fraccionamientos, exp. Hermosa Provincia, carpeta [folder] 8.

168. AMG, Ramo Fraccionamientos, exp. Hermosa Provincia, carpeta 8.

169. *Time Magazine,* August 13, 1990.

170. As anthropologist Reneé de la Torre explores in her work, *Hijos de la Luz,* the real influence of LDM would not truly be realized until the heir of Aarón—his son Samuel—leveraged the growing number of converts across Mexico into contacts within the PRI during the 1970s and 1980s.

171. Guillermo de la Peña argues that opposition from the Catholic left has been far more abundant and consistent than from the right. See de la Peña and de la Torre, "Religión y política," 572.

172. De la Torre, *Hijos,* 153.

173. *Excélsior,* September 22, 1987. My translation.

Chapter Two

1. El Museo de Historia del Mormonismo en México (hereafter MHMM), *Margarito Bautista Valencia*, 1, and MHMM, *Diario de Ammon M. Tenney*, 25–26. See also Margarito Bautista, "Faith Promoting Experience," 23. The LDS practice of "administering" or giving "blessings for healing" is a form of "laying on of hands" for healing.

2. Murphy, "Guatemalan Hot/Cold Medicine," 297. Murphy's work on Mormons in Guatemala serves as a corrective to Martin's assumption that Mormonism equals acculturation to U.S. American culture.

3. I will refer to Margarito Bautista Valencia as simply Margarito Bautista, or Bautista, as he frequently signs as "Margarito Bautista" without the use of Valencia.

4. MHMM, *Margarito*, 4.

5. Hereafter referred to as the LDS Church. Members of the LDS Church are also known as Mormons. However, groups that have separated themselves from the Church of Jesus Christ of Latter-day Saints also often refer to themselves as Mormons. While it is not strictly appropriate to refer to those who leave the LDS Church as Mormons—such as Margarito Bautista—I will do so in this work in deference to what he and his followers chose to call themselves.

6. MHMM, *Margarito*, 4. Also Bautista, "Faith Promoting Experience," 23.

7. MHMM, *Diario*, 126, 129, 162, 202. The term *elder* is not age-associated in the LDS Church. It is an office in the Melchizedek priesthood—the divine authority or permission Mormons claim in order to carry out ordinances and to preach. There are several "preparatory" steps before this authority is given, so Bautista's rapid progression is notable, though perhaps not so rare for the mission field. That Bautista went on a "pequeña gira misional" may also mean that he received this authority directly after baptism. On sermons: Mormons believe in a lay clergy and generally the only thing needed for men and women to deliver a sermon is membership and good standing in the church.

8. Joseph Smith, *Doctrine and Covenants*, 88:68.

9. The LDS Church claims that Jesus' three chief apostles, Peter, James, and John, visited Joseph Smith Jr., in resurrected form, laying their hands on his head and bestowing upon him the same permission, or authority (called priesthood), to carry out ordinances in the name of Jesus Christ and give them validity. Without that authority, they argue, no Christian ordinance has validity in the eyes of God. See Joseph Fielding Smith, *Doctrines of Salvation*, 1:173–74.

10. Joseph Fielding Smith, *Teachings of the Prophet*, 334. Joseph Smith, *Doctrine and Covenants*, 131:2–3, 76: 52, 58–60.

11. MHMM, *Margarito*, 5.

12. Traditionally the term *polygamy* has been used to describe the marriage of one man to multiple women, but it means in fact that women, too, can have multiple husbands. I use the term *polygyny*, which specifically denotes the male to multiple-female arrangement found among Mormons, as women were not allowed to participate in polyandry—the female to multiple-male polygamous relationship. Despite legal restrictions, polygyny continues to be practiced in both the United States and Mexico by those excommunicated by the LDS Church, as well as other religious traditions, such as practitioners of Islam, and those who practice forms of polygamy without any religious predilections.

13. Shipps, *Mormonism*, 61–63.

14. Tullis, *Mormons in Mexico*, 57–58.

15. Alexander, *Mormonism in Transition*, 60–63, 72.

16. Alexander, *Mormonism in Transition*, 74.

17. Joseph F. Smith, "The Truth About Mormonism," 242.

18. Joseph F. Smith, *Deseret Weekly*, August 19, 1893, 283.

19. Alexander, *Mormonism in Transition*, 76. Alexander points out that economic studies of Utah at the time reveal that four-fifths of "the best residential property," four-fifths of department stores, and almost all downtown Salt Lake City businesses were in the hands of Republican "gentiles," or non-Mormons.

20. Foster, "Between Two Worlds," 75.

21. Tullis, *Mormons in Mexico*, 58. See also Hart, *Empire and Revolution*, 238–46, 389. On the evangelical Protestant leanings of Pascual Orozco, see Baldwin, *Protestants and the Mexican Revolution*. Baldwin lays out the longstanding connection of New England evangelical Protestant groups to Mexico, such as the Congregationalist group to which Orozco belonged. I suggest that because such groups were actively "anti-Mormon" through this period, perhaps Orozco's animosity was not only nationalist but possibly religious as well.

22. MHMM, *Margarito*, 5–6. See also Ventura, *History of the Mexican Branch*.

23. Bautista, "Faith Promoting Experience," 23.

24. Iber, *Hispanics*, 28.

25. Obregón, *Pensamiento político*, 155. One of the president's definitions of the sort of "men of capital" he wished to come to Mexico can be seen in a speech delivered one month later to a group of businessmen from San Francisco: "The government that I represent and the people of Mexico gladly open our arms to the businessmen of the United States that seek just advantages in the exploitation of our natural resources while respecting our law."

26. Obregón, *El problema agrícola*, 4. In an interesting side note, the English translation generated in 1924, by the minister of international relations, replaces the reference to "Comrade" with "The Honorable."

27. Bautista, *La evolución*, 85, 123. My translation.

28. *Excelsior* (Mexico City), February 2, 1923.

29. *Excelsior* (Mexico City), February 2, 1923. Obregón stated on multiple occasions that he saw his efforts as "Christian." See Walling, *Mexican Question*, 42.

30. Among Domench's long résumé of accomplishments is serving as chaplain to the Hapsburg emperor, Maximilian, and writing several works on the history of Mexico and his travels in Texas.

31. Ivins, *Right Relation*.

32. Ivins, *Right Relation*.

33. Bautista, *La Evolución*, 63. Bautista spends much time talking about the evolution of society, but he simultaneously dedicates much space to attacking the social Darwinism of the Porfirian positivists (p. 136).

34. Bautista, *La evolución*, 85, 123.

35. Bautista, *La evolución*, 121.

36. Bautista, *La evolución*, 79.

37. *The Evolution of Mexico, Its Real Progenitors and Origin: The Destiny of America and Europe.*

38. Bautista, *La evolución*, 50.

39. Bautista, *La evolución*, 55, 61.

40. Bautista, *La evolución*, 73.

41. Bautista, *La evolución*, 72.

42. Bautista, *La evolución*, 72.

43. Joseph Smith, *The Book of Mormon*, 1 Nephi 13:34.

44. Joseph Fielding Smith, *Teachings*, 85.

45. Bautista, "Faith Promoting Experience," 23.

46. Bautista, *La evolución*, 25.

47. MHMM, *Margarito*, 7.

48. Joseph Smith, *The Book of Mormon*, 2 Nephi 30:4.

49. Talmage, *Great Apostasy*.

50. Joseph Smith, *The Book of Mormon*, 1 Nephi 13:14.

51. Bautista, *La evolución*, 43.

52. Bautista, *La evolución*, 43; Joseph Smith, *The Book of Mormon*, 1 Nephi 13:34–40.

NOTES TO PAGES 74–76

53. Murphy, "Racist Stereotype," 453, 469.

54. This is not a unique position. Consider the 1794 speech by Fray Servando Teresa de Mier who declared that the natives of Mexico had been taught by the apostle St. Thomas and that the Virgin of Guadalupe had appeared in the Americas long before the arrival of the Spanish in Mexico. In effect, the Dominican theologian declared Mexico spiritually independent of Spain, negating the claims of legitimacy for the Spanish empire, that of the bringers of Christianity. In an age of revolutions, Servando Teresa de Mier was escorted from the rostrum and hustled off across the Atlantic for confinement in a Dominican priory in Spain. Brading, *First America*, 583–87.

55. Shipps, *Mormonism*, 51.

56. Bautista, *La evolución*, 21, 48, 54–55, 65–67.

57. Bautista, *La evolución*, 397, 502.

58. Bautista, *La evolución*, 134–35. Though he claims primogeniture over the "Old World" Israelites, Bautista is also careful not to use anti-Semitic language. For example, he takes great pains to lay the crucifixion of Christ squarely at the feet of political leaders (Roman and Jewish), and not "the Jews" in general (p. 140).

59. For more on the postrevolutionary use of liberalism, see Reyes Heroles, *El liberalismo mexicano*. Bautista's position on Juárez is strikingly similar to that of the central state. Bautista calls Juárez a "Moses" for bringing law to Mexico, but goes on to say that Juárez was even better than Moses, because he brought the gift of freedom to choose your religion. *La evolución*, 54–55.

60. Bautista, *La evolución*, 63.

61. Bautista, *La evolución*, 41.

62. For example, see Knight, *Mexican Revolution*, 2:350–52.

63. Gómez, *Darkness into Light*, 28.

64. MHMM, *Margarito*, 7. Murphy, "Christianizing Quetzalcoatl."

65. MHMM, *Margarito*, 7. The MHMM cites Bautista's personal journal of 1935 as the source. Tullis states that Bautista arrived in Mexico in 1934, not 1935.

66. Olga Arzate Cuellar, *Apolonio B. Arzate, 1893–1965*, unpublished biography, MHMM. Arzate Cuellar is the daughter of Dr. Arzate and states that meetings with top government officials occurred in the family residence at 185 Dr. Balmis, Mexico City.

67. Tullis, *Mormons*, 122–24.

68. Tullis, *Mormons*, 123. Tullis cites Pratt's journal as the source.

69. According to early LDS organization, an area with minimal membership fell under the supervision of a "mission president," under which existed districts headed by presidents of their own. Within those districts existed wards (large congregations headed by bishops) and branches (small congregations

headed by branch presidents). In central Mexico, the district president was Isaías Juárez, a Mexican of *raza y sangre* (race and blood) and cofounder of the National Campesino's Confederation (CNC). All bishops and branch presidents outside of the Mormon colonies in Chihuahua were Mexicans of *raza y sangre*.

70. Tullis, *Mormons*, 139. The director of the MHMM argues that the Third Convention was *not* a nationalist move, but an attempt to stabilize the LDS Church in Mexico after the disruptions of the revolution. He ignores, however, cries of the convention for Mexicans of *raza y sangre*, and their rejection of Mexican citizens of Anglo descent. Gómez, *Darkness into Light*, 42–47.

71. Tullis, *Mormons*, 142–43.

72. President George Albert Smith traveled to Mexico where he not only arranged the reconciliation with the Convention, but he also met with President Manuel Ávila Camacho, who lauded the Mormon colonies' contribution to the Mexican economy and said of Smith, "the Mexican people have a friend in him." *Deseret News*, May 27, 1946.

73. The Third Convention movement never changed the name of the church but kept the official name of the mainline organization as their own.

74. Joseph Smith, *The Book of Mormon*, 3 Nephi 20:16–17.

75. Bautista, *La evolución*, 209.

76. Tullis, *Mormons*, 147.

77. AGN, LCR, 111/2097.

78. I was unable to locate the complete plans for the community on two separate trips to the AGN in 2003 and 2005.

79. Cisneros Sosa, *Ciudad que construimos*, 70–73.

80. MHMM, Margarito Bautista's 1937 diary, 257–300.

81. The practice was most prevalent before the death of Brigham Young, but remained active in pockets of Utah, Arizona, and Northern Mexico until the turn of the century.

82. McKonkie, *Mormon Doctrine*, 157.

83. Bautista, *La evolución*, 77.

84. Concerning the supposition of Bautista's intent to replace all things Anglo LDS, we can reference his 1951 pamphlet, *¿Es Una Disciplina Una Ley?* where he creates his own Mexican First Presidency—the top-most ruling body of the LDS church made up of four men.

85. Bautista, *La evolución*, 48, 91.

86. Bautista, *La evolución*, 538.

87. Tenochtitlan was the Aztec capital—today known as Mexico City. MHMM, Margarito Bautista's 1937 diary. My translation.

88. Bautista, *Dedicado a la época histórica*. The pamphlet is a condemnation of the 1946 return of *convencionistas*.

89. In his 1940 pamphlet, *La verdad que ellos me enseñaron*, Bautista refers to LDS members outside of his persuasion as "anti-convencionista."

90. Bautista is much given to the use of uppercase letters in his writing. Bautista, *La verdad que ellos me enseñaron*, 136.

91. Bautista, *Dedicado a la época histórica*, 69. My translation. Bautista uses the phrase "El Blanco."

92. Bautista may not have been the model of Mormonism he styled himself to be for his followers. MHMM director Fernando Gómez alleges that Bautista may have been excommunicated while living in Salt Lake City over some problem in the Spanish congregation in that city. He was unsure of the nature of the offense, as LDS Church courts leading to excommunication are confidential. Felipe Burgos alleges the excommunication was for adultery and expressed disillusion at finding out about past misconduct by Bautista. Gómez cites the diary of Harold W. Pratt in his allegations of misconduct by Bautista. Writes Pratt: "Had a long talk with Margarito about his plans to publish his writings, also about his former difficulties, and requested him to avoid making trouble this time. Demonstrated a good spirit he is capable of doing much good if he will just stay in line." Gómez, *Darkness into Light*, 30n90.

93. The 1920 Spanish version of the Book of Mormon carries a footnote reference to "un profeta Lamanita" or "Indian Prophet" in the English. The footnote was a debated point in LDS theology found in reference to 2 Nephi 3:24, which says that a powerful prophet would arise in the last days. Sergio Pagaza of the MHMM speculates that Bautista was influenced by the footnote as a prophetic reference to himself, though there is little documentation of the point in Bautista's writing.

94. AGN-OC 408-M-27; 241-G-0–11; 408-M-27.

95. Bojorges Oliva, *Ozumba*, 91.

96. Revelation 21:2.

97. *Bible Dictionary* (Salt Lake City: Church of Jesus Christ of Latter-day Saints, 1991). The group associates Zion with another city with little scriptural illumination, the City of Enoch, said to have been taken up to heaven for the purity in heart of the inhabitants. See Joseph Smith, *Doctrine and Covenants*, 42, 45, and 84.

98. For corruption in Mexico during this era, see Niblo, *Mexico in the 1940s*, 253. Niblo argues that corruption was a lively part of the public discourse from 1940 forward.

99. Bautista, *La evolución*, 41.

100. Bautista, *La evolución*, 229. Bautista often painted himself as a modern-day Joseph, denied the birthright but truly the son most beloved by Israel. MHMM, Analco, *Historia de La Colonia Industrial Mexicana, Ozumba, Estado de México* (unpublished manuscript, August 2, 1989), 45. My translation.

101. Phelan, *Millennial Kingdom*, 72–73.

102. Phelan, *Millennial Kingdom*, 69, 104. Not surprisingly, these millennial visions not only took hold in New Spain, but also in Spain's other prized holding, Peru. Fray Gonzalo Tenorio (1602–82) reflected on the New World in comparison to Europe and decided that the chosen people of the New Testament—Catholic Europeans—were in danger of losing their position through sin and corruption. His answer was that the Indies represented a new stage of divine interaction with humanity and that Christ channeled this power through the Virgin to the Indies. Phelan, *Millennial Kingdom*, 123.

103. Van Young, *Other Rebellion*, 457.

104. Bautista, *¿Restituirás . . . el Reino?*

105. Bautista, *La evolución*, 41, 48, 191.

106. Olarte, *Historia*, 43–44.

107. Olarte, *Historia*, 10–11.

108. AGN-MAV 2/340 (29)/42.

109. Eventually Bautista formed a loose association with another Anglo organization headed by Rulon C. Allred that still operates within the Rocky Mountain West of the United States from Montana to Arizona and known as the Apostolic United Brethren.

110. Bautista, *¿Es Una Disciplina Una Ley?*, 14. My translation.

111. Matthew 13:33.

112. Hall, "From 'Religion and Society' to Practices."

113. Olarte, *Historia*, 1.

114. Olarte, *Historia*, 1. The namesake of Olarte, Nefi, is a primary character in the Book of Mormon, as is Alma.

115. The ordinance of "blessing" infants in the LDS Church is a promissory blessing administered generally by fathers to infants at birth in front of the congregation. The process inscribes the infant in the records of the church but does not make them a "member" of the congregation. Alma is a common male LDS name, and with the naming of Olarte's brother, Nefi, we see a pattern of naming children after Book of Mormon prophets. It is possible that Olarte was born *after* the conversion of his parents but was still baptized as an infant in the Catholic Church, a possibility if his parents were not initially active in the movement or divided in membership. It is also likely

his parents changed his name at his blessing ceremony. Either way, we see a certain amount of doctrinal flexibility.

116. Olarte, *Historia*, 2.

117. Olarte, *Historia*, 2.

118. AGN-LCR 111/2897. The telegram originated from General Plata 29 Col. Observatorio in Mexico City.

119. An examination of the Ávila Camacho collection at the AGN did not turn up such a request. Neither did I find a request for chapel construction in the papers of Gobernación (Department of the Interior) for that year.

120. Olarte, *Historia*, 3; Bautista, *La evolución*, appendix 1.

121. Again we see another parallel rivalry—April is the time for the annual General Conference of the LDS Church.

122. Clawson, "Religious Allegiance," 506.

123. AGN-MAV 547.4/167. The letter from San Gabriel Ometoxtla complains of the "existence in this place of houses of prayer pertaining to the Church of the Mormons which function at the margins of our laws and as their members disrespect the national symbols, among those the image of the Virgin of Guadalupe, they provoke serious incidents." A second telegram requests the nationalization of said chapels.

124. Olarte, *Historia*, 3–4.

125. Olarte, *Historia*, 3. "Regarding spiritual things I say frankly that I did not like to study the scriptures and though I attended services in Tecalco, I did not take it seriously."

126. Olarte, *Historia*, 59.

127. Olarte, *Historia*, 18. Considering later tensions about Burgos's contributions to the colony and its impoverished condition, the colonists were probably as damaged by the loss of his carpentry skills as his ecclesiastical service.

128. Interview with Felipe Burgos, July 21 and 22, 2003, in Colonia Alzate, Ozumba, Mexico. In July 2003, José Felipe Antonio de Jesús Burgos González (called Don Felipe by his neighbors) was 100 years old and living in Colonia Alzate, Ozumba—about a quarter-mile and across a small arroyo from Colonia Industrial Mexicana de la Nueva Jerusalén. On a 2003 research trip to Ozumba, I met Don Felipe by accident when a local photographer and historian referred me to him as one who was *muy sabio* when it came to Ozumba and its *colonias* in the 1940s. Though his interests lay in his current community's struggles for access to potable water and schools, he did agree to discuss Colonia Industrial as the background to his current position in Ozumba.

129. Nutini, "Polygyny."

130. Nutini, *San Bernardino Contla*, 304. Nutini explicitly points out that the polygyny that he describes in San Bernardino Contla is *not* the phenomenon of the *casa chica* or "the practice of keeping a separate household for a concubine—but a well-organized, socially sanctioned practice in the social structure of the *municipio*." Nutini does state that the immediate surrounding *municipios* appear not to have practiced similar polygynous marriages. Nutini, writing forty years after Bautista began arguing for plural marriage, states that polygyny in Mesoamerican Indian communities is a "rather uncommon feature of Mesoamerican Indian society today [1968]." Nutini, "Polygyny," 305.

131. Acceptance has not always been the case. Nutini notes that the presence of polygyny in Contla is found in colonial documents leveled against Indians in the Contla area through the end of the eighteenth century. Nutini, "Polygyny," 312n6.

132. Olarte, *Historia*, 18.

133. Archívo Municipal Histórico de Ozumba (AMHO), Presidencia, 1951, fj. 2. Though I give rough organizational guides for the AMHO, the collection is not described and was in the process of preservation by the municipal historian in 2003.

134. I have chosen the rather arbitrary age of twelve in 1921 as a cut-off point for placement in military service by 1920.

135. If Felipe Burgos is any indication, however, they may have owned tools just as Felipe owned his own tools.

136. AMHO, Presidencia, 1953, Censo Colonia Industrial.

137. The decline may not have been as pronounced as the numbers show. As Olarte points out, at any one time members of the community might be selling flowers in Mexico City or visiting relatives in Puebla or the surrounding area.

138. While fertility maximization can be one reason to accept polygyny, most anthropologists argue that notions of male desire for multiple sexual partners are simplistic at best. Nutini, *San Bernardino Contla*, 312. White and Burton, "Causes of Polygyny," 871. For more on wealth and the productive contribution of women, see White and Burton, "Rethinking Polygyny," 529–72; and Mulder, "Polygyny," 178–80.

139. In an interesting twist, neither lived totally severed from the mainstream LDS Church. Alma de Olarte Analco gave his diary and unpublished history to the MHMM, which, though not affiliated with the LDS Church, is headed by "orthodox" Mormons associated with the church based out of Salt Lake City. As for Burgos, he has signed photos of Arwell Pierce, the LDS mission president who facilitated the return of the Third Convention. He also spoke of welcomed visits by local members of Ozumba's several LDS congregations.

140. Olarte, *Historia*, 6.

141. Olarte, *Historia*, 17.

142. Olarte, *Historia*, 10. AHMO, Presidencia, 1953.

143. AHMO, Presidencia, 1953. How the community knew about this is not indicated.

144. O'Malley, *Myth*, 6, 8, 114–32.

145. On land distribution in Mexico, see Niblo, *Mexico in the 1940s*, 4. Niblo cites de Navarrete, *Bienestar campesino*.

146. Knight, "Cardenismo," 76–78, 92–93.

147. Rubin, "Popular Mobilization," 247–49.

148. AHMO, Presidencia, 1951.

149. Joseph Smith, *Doctrine and Covenants*, 135:1.

150. Olarte, *Historia*, 20, 71. Interestingly, there is no record of this occurrence in the AHMO, as the 1951 box is missing from the Justicia collection and neither preceding or following years yielded any evidence.

151. Olarte, *Historia*, 21.

152. Olarte, *Historia*, 22.

153. Olarte, *Historia*, 22. Searches in the municipal archive of Chalco uncovered no mention of the case, nor of Bautista as a prisoner in the jail in that city, either in 1951 or the years before or after. During a visit to the district justice ministry, I discovered that records prior to 1968 were removed to the state justice archive in the state capital of Toluca, where I was denied permission to search the archives of that collection.

154. Olarte, *Historia*, 46.

155. Olarte, *Historia*, 49–50.

156. AMHO, Presidencia, 1953.

157. Lockridge, *New England Town*, 79–90.

158. Thelma Gómez Durán, "Los otros mormones," *Milenio*, July 23, 2001.

Chapter Three

1. Abascal, *Mis Recuerdos*, 1. My translation.

2. Abascal, *Mis Recuerdos*, 1–2.

3. Abascal, *Mis Recuerdos*, 6.

4. Abascal, *Mis Recuerdos*, 38.

5. Abascal, *Mis Recuerdos*, 44.

6. Abascal, *Mis Recuerdos*, 47.

7. Abascal, *Mis Recuerdos*, 110.

8. Abascal, *Mis Recuerdos*, 69.

9. Abascal, *Mis Recuerdos*, 122.

10. Three of the most prolific and astute scholars on the foundation and later political activity of the UNS are Jean Meyer, Pablo Serrano Álvarez, and Lorenzo Covarrubias. For Meyer's perspective as a historian, see *El Sinarquismo ¿Un Fascismo Mexicano?* For Serrano Álvarez, see *La batalla del espíritu: El movimiento sinarquista en el Bajío (1932–1951)*. For Covarrubias, see his doctoral dissertation, "Ideology, Brokers, Political Action, and the State: The Strategies and Historical Transformation of a Counterrevolutionary Urban and Peasant Movement in Mexico." Also by Covarrubias, "Intercambio social, gestoría política y sinarquismo en (Querétaro) México," 55.

11. Skillen and McCarthy, *Political Order*, 161.

12. Skillen and McCarthy, *Political Order*, 163.

13. Wiarda, *Transition to Democracy*, 27.

14. Wiarda, *Transition to Democracy*, 27.

15. For UNS support of *Rerum Novarum* and *Quadragesimo Anno*, see *El Sinarquista*, May 15, 1941.

16. Meyer, *El sinarquismo*, 34.

17. While some *sinarquistas* saw democracy as a natural extension of Catholic social doctrine, others found it chaotic and wanted to rely on local leadership based on experience, piety, status, and charisma.

18. BFXC-AUNS, caja [box] 2, exp. [folder] 49.

19. Abascal, *Mis Recuerdos*, 236.

20. Covarrubias, "Ideology," 107.

21. Brunk, *Emiliano Zapata*, 21.

22. Knight, "Peculiarities of Mexican History," 115n75.

23. Burns, *Poverty of Progress*, 81–83.

24. BFXC-AUNS, caja 1, 26, 34.

25. BFXC-AUNS, caja 1, 23.

26. Covarrubias, "Ideology," 59.

27. Abascal, *Mis Recuerdos*, 102.

28. Serrano Álvarez, *Batalla*, 47.

29. Serrano Álvarez, *Batalla*, 44.

30. Abascal, *Mis Recuerdos*, 236.

31. Abascal, *Mis Recuerdos*, 47–48.

32. Abascal, *Mis Recuerdos*, 240.

33. Abascal, *Mis Recuerdos*, 242.

34. Abascal, *Mis Recuerdos*, 236.

35. BFXC-AUNS, caja 2, 44. The UNS used a red banner with a map of Mexico in the center, but the tricolor flag of Mexico was also present at rallies.

36. BFXC-AUNS, caja 1, 37. I should note, however, as historian Daniela Spenser has persuasively demonstrated, there was very little influential connection between Moscow and Mexico City. See Spenser's *Impossible Triangle*.

37. AGN-MAC, 544.61/39. Telegram dated September 2, 1941. Abascal also says they are based in a doctrine of Christ as laid out by Popes Leo XIII, Pius XI, and Pius XII. For the UNS, Catholic social doctrine was not considered an imported idea. See also *Mis Recuerdos*, 334.

38. *El Sinarquista*, July 1, 1943.

39. Abascal, *Mis Recuerdos*, 153, 334.

40. Serrano Álvarez, *Batalla*, 34.

41. Abascal, *Mis Recuerdos*, 183.

42. Abascal, *Mis Recuerdos*, 339.

43. *El Sinarquista*, June 12, June 26, July 3, July 17, July 24, 1941.

44. Abascal, *Mis Recuerdos*, 291.

45. *Historia gráfica del sinarquismo*, 212.

46. Abascal, *Mis Recuerdos*, 334, 339–43.

47. *El Sinarquista*, September 11, 1941.

48. AGN-MAC 544.61/39.

49. *El Sinarquista*, September 25, 1941.

50. Weekly donation statistics appear in *El Sinarquista* from December 1941 until early 1944.

51. Shields, "Sinarchists Organize."

52. *Historia gráfica*, 209.

53. AGN-MAC 544.61/39.

54. Abascal, *Mis Recuerdos*, 413, 431.

55. AGN-MAC 544.61/39.

56. Abascal, *Mis Recuerdos*, 430–35.

57. *El Sinarquista*, December 18, 1941.

58. AMG, Correspondencia 1941. This is official State of Jalisco, Executive Power, letterhead in use during 1941.

59. AGN-LCR 503.11/212. AGN-MAC 503.11/185. Projects include the Cárdenas era approval of revolutionary veterans living in Los Angeles, California, as well as other military colonies approved by Ávila Camacho.

60. AGN-MAC 544.61/39.

61. AGN-MAC 544.61/39.

62. In *El Sinarquista*, December 18, 1941, the paper reports that Mex$28,886.49 had been donated by UNS members for colonization. Almost all of that money was gone by the end of December for transportation costs to Baja as well as the new Sonora enterprise. The January 29 issue of the newspaper puts the price of transportation to Baja as Mex$39,000.

63. *El Sinarquista*, January 1, 1942.

64. Meyer, *El sinarquismo*, 80.

65. *El Sinarquista*, February 5, 1942.

66. Meyer, *El sinarquismo*, 196–97.

67. Abascal, *Mis Recuerdos*, 451.

68. Abascal, *Mis Recuerdos*, 460.

69. Abascal, *Mis Recuerdos*, 460.

70. Meyer, *El sinarquismo*, 82. Those twenty-one deaths occurred between April and August of 1942. No mention of them is made by *El Sinarquista*.

71. *El Sinarquista*, January 8, 1942. The paper did make the statement, however, that "Sinarquistas don't work miracles—we need money."

72. Abascal, *Mis Recuerdos*, 449–50.

73. Abascal, *Mis Recuerdos*, 452.

74. Abascal, *Mis Recuerdos*, 452.

75. "Sinarquistas of Mexico Seek New Life in Desert," *Palm Beach Post*, November 15, 1942, 4.

76. Abascal, *Mis Recuerdos*, 450.

77. Abascal, *Mis Recuerdos*, 454.

78. Abascal, *Mis Recuerdos*, 454.

79. Wallace, "Revitalization Movements," 275.

80. Mann, "Annunciation Chapel," 120.

81. Frederick Holweck, "Feast of Our Lady, Help of Christians," in *The Catholic Encyclopedia*, vol. 11 (New York: Robert Appleton Company, 1911), http://www.newadvent.org/cathen/11360c.htm (accessed March 15, 2010).

82. *El Sinarquista*, February 12, 1942.

83. BFXC-AUNS, caja 2, exp. 42, 51.

84. *El Sinarquista*, April 30, 1942.

85. AGN-MAC 544.61/39.

86. BFXC-AUNS, caja 2, exp. 42. Abascal describes the need for teachers and priests as "truly urgent."

87. Abascal, *Mis Recuerdos*, 656.

88. Abascal, *Mis Recuerdos*, 467.

89. Abascal, *Mis Recuerdos*, 680.

90. BFXC-AUNS, caja 1 and caja 2, both contain significant collections of material on women in the UNS movement.

91. Abascal, *Mis Recuerdos*, 507.

92. Rubenstein, "War on '*Las Pelonas*,'"65.

93. Alonso, *Thread of Blood*, 86–87.

94. Abascal, *Mis Recuerdos*, 506.

95. Abascal married in March 1942.

96. Abascal, *Mis Recuerdos*, 746.

97. Abascal, *Mis Recuerdos*, 610.

98. Abascal, *Mis Recuerdos*, 343–44.

99. W. Eugene Shields, a U.S. American Catholic and Jesuit, applauded the *sinarquista* position that "laymen, and not the clergy, are the ones to marshal the multitude in political and social movements" (see his 1942 article in *America: A Catholic Review of the Week*, "Sinarchists Organize"). For examples of tension regarding secular authority in New Spain, see also Inga Clendinnen, *Ambivalent Conquests*; William B. Taylor, *Magistrates of the Sacred*; and Nancy Farriss, *Crown and Clergy*.

100. *El Sinarquista*, April 30, 1941; May 7, 1942.

101. *El Sinarquista*, October 22 and 29, 1942.

102. Abascal, *Mis Recuerdos*, 625–28.

103. Abascal, *Mis Recuerdos*, 629.

104. Abascal, *Mis Recuerdos*, 653–56.

105. Abascal, *Mis Recuerdos*, 691–93, 697.

106. Abascal, *Mis Recuerdos*, 679–85.

107. Abascal, *Mis Recuerdos*, 686, 690.

108. *El Sinarquista* March 18, 1943, and April 22 and 29, 1943. This shift lends credence to Abascal's allegations that La Base and Manuel Torres Bueno were looking to mainstream themselves within the government. As early as June of 1942, Torres Bueno had pledged full support to the war effort, despite previous UNS declarations that the war was a product of Big Capital, international Jewry, and a Roosevelt-Stalin communist alliance. AGN-MAC 704/28.

109. *El Sinarquista*, February 12, 1942.

110. Abascal, *Mis Recuerdos*, 718.

111. Abascal, *Mis Recuerdos*, 6n1.

112. Abascal, *Mis Recuerdos*, 493.

Chapter Four

1. Sayer, "Everyday Forms," 367.

2. Sayer, "Everyday Forms," 368.

3. Vaughn, *Cultural Politics*, 20.

4. Abrams, "Notes," 63.

5. Sayer, "Everyday Forms," 371.

6. Knight, *Mexican Revolution*, 2:518.

7. Mallon, "Reflections," 70.

8. Schmidt, "Making it Real," 52.

9. Rentería Solís, *Luz del Mundo*, 36.

10. Jimenez, "Making the City Their Own."

11. Benito Juárez first made this statement on July 15, 1867, before the Mexican Congress in celebration of the republic's victory over the Emperor Maximilian and his conservative and foreign supporters.

12. AGN-MAC, 544.61/39. Telegram dated September 2, 1941.

13. Rick López, "Noche Mexicana," 33.

14. Interview with members of LDM, Guadalajara, Jalisco, September 5, 2005.

15. Vaughn, *Cultural Politics*.

16. BFXC-AUNS, caja [box] 2, exp. [folder] 42. Abascal describes the need for teachers and priests as "truly urgent."

17. Abascal, *Mis Recuerdos*, 102.

18. Krauze, *Mexico*, 552.

19. Weber, *Economy*, 2:1006.

20. Weber, *Economy*, 2:1111–13.

21. Weber, *Economy*, 2:1113.

22. Abascal, *Mis Recuerdos*, 47–48.

23. De la Torre, *Hijos*, 187.

24. O'Malley, *Myth*, 130–32.

25. MHMM, de Olarte Analco, *Historia de la Colonia Industrial Mexicana*, 113–14.

26. MHMM, de Olarte Analco, *Historia*, 47.

27. MHMM, de Olarte Analco, *Historia*, 49.

28. MHMM, de Olarte Analco, *Historia*, 47, 114.

29. For example, LDM was not the only group that readily identified with, or as, Israel after the revolution. In just one Guadalajara example, Jesús Héctor Godínez Hernández led the Iglesia Israelita/Casa de Dios in the poor Sector Libertad area of town. AMG, Iglesias no Católicas, Iglesia Israelita.

30. Cardaillac, "Profetismo y mesianismo."

31. McKonkie, *Mormon Doctrine*, 389.

32. Abascal, *Mis Recuerdos*, 347–48.

33. Buffington, *Criminal and Citizen*, 8.

34. For an example of the corruption focus, see Picatto, *City of Suspects*, 185–87.

35. Aguirre and Salvatorre, "Writing the History of Law," 19–25.

36. See Fruhling, Tulchin, and Golding, eds., *Crime and Violence in Latin America*. See especially the recommendations made by Tulchin and Golding in the conclusion, 259–65.

37. Vaughn, *Cultural Politics*, 24.

38. Knight, *Mexican Revolution*, 2:518.

39. Voekel, *Alone Before God*, 225–26.

40. Centeno, *Democracy Within Reason*, 57.

41. *Washington Post*, September 11, 1988, A30.

42. Salinas de Gortari, *Mexico*, 257.

43. Chac and Pastor Escobar, *Ha vuelto Dios a México*, 90.

44. *Tiempo* (Mexico City), June 6, 1990.

45. *Carlos Salinas de Gortari—A Portrait*, 22.

46. Carlos Salinas de Gortari, Toma de Posesión (Inaugural Address). Mexico City, December 1, 1988.

47. U.S. Congress, Senate, Committee on Finance, "U.S. Trade Policy and NAFTA."

48. Von Bertrab, *Negotiating NAFTA*, 123–25. See also Jorge Castañeda, *Mexican Shock*, 6.

49. Grayson, *Church in Contemporary Mexico*, 83.

50. Grayson, *Church in Contemporary Mexico*, 84.

51. Grayson, *Church in Contemporary Mexico*, 84.

52. Wilkie and Monzón de Wilkie, *Frente a la Revolución Mexicana*, 76.

53. Covarrubias, "Sentimientos Queretanos."

54. Union Nacional Sinarquista, *Guión de capacitación*.

55. The UNS appears to have undergone a split in the mid-1990s, creating two organizations with the same name. The UNS group I refer to is the one recognized by the Mexican government as an official APN, or National Political Association, and studied by political scientist Lorenzo Covarrubias. The other UNS feels the officially recognized group has acted as a traitor by holding democratic elections within the group and accepting money from the Mexican Federal Electoral Institute. See *Falange Hoy*, June 27, 2002.

56. Garrard-Burnett and Stoll, *Rethinking Protestantism*, 9–10. Cleary, "The Catholic Church Faces Its Future."

57. De la Torre, *Hijos*, 87.

58. Morales Robles, "Hermosa Provincia," 40–41.

59. De la Peña and de la Torre, "Religión y política," 586, 592.

60. Hughes, *Newsrooms in Conflict*, 3. The explosion registered as a 7.1 on the Richter scale in Mexico City—two hundred miles to the east.

61. De la Torre, *Hijos*, 142.

62. *Mural* (Guadalajara), August 10, 2000.

63. *Mural* (Guadalajara), August 14, 2000.

64. Interview with Laura Elena Alvarez Espinoza, July 22, 2003. Alvarez would only speak on record about questions restricted to municipal improvements of infrastructure.

65. Murphy, "'Stronger Than Ever,'" 10–11.

66. Murphy, "'Stronger Than Ever,'" 10–11.

67. Murphy, "'Stronger Than Ever,'" 10–11.

68. Felipe Burgos, *Testimony and Observations on the Millennium as a Member of the Iglesia Cristiana Apostólica Pentecostes*, handwritten testament in the possession of the author. My translation.

BIBLIOGRAPHY

Archives

Archívo General de la Nación (AGN)

- Obregón/Calles (OC)
- Lázaro Cárdenas del Río (LCR)
- Colección Lázaro Cárdenas (CLC)
- Manuel Ávila Camacho (MAC)
- Miguel Alemán Valdés (MAV)
- Dirección General de Gobernación (DGG)

Archívo del Congreso del Estado de Jalisco (ACEJ)

Archívo Histórico del Estado de Jalisco (AHEJ)

Archívo Municipal de Guadalajara (AMG)

Archívo Municipal Histórico de Ozumba (AMHO)

Archívo Municipal de Tala (AMT)

Biblioteca Francisco Xavier Clavijero (BFXC)

- Archívo Unión Nacional Sinarquista (AUNS)
- *El Sinarquista*

El Museo de Historia del Mormonismo en México (MHMM)

- Arzate Cuellar, Olga, *Apolonio B. Arzate, 1893–1965*
- *Margarito Valencia Bautista,* 2002
- Alma de Olarte Analco, *Historia de La Colonia Industrial Mexicana, Ozumba, Estado de Mexico,* August 2, 1989
- *Diario de Ammon M. Tenney,* Spanish translation

Interviews (Chronological)

Felipe Burgos, July 21–22, 2003, Colonia Alzate, Ozumba, Mexico

Laura Elena Alvarez Espinoza, July 22, 2003, Colonia Industrial, Ozumba, Mexico

Members of Luz del Mundo and residents of Hermosa Provincia, September 5, 2005, Hermosa Provincia, Guadalajara, Mexico

Sara Pozos Bravo, September 14, 2005, Hermosa Provincia, Guadalajara, Mexico

Israel Piñeda, September 24, 2005, Zapopan, Mexico

Newspapers and Magazines

Deseret Weekly   *Milenio*

Deseret News   *Mural*

El Universal   *New York Times*

Excélsior   *Palm Beach Post*

Falange Hoy   *Processo*

Los Angeles Times   *Tiempo*

Los Angeles Daily Times   *Washington Post*

Primary Sources

Abascal, Salvador. *Mis Recuerdos: Sinarquismo y Colonia María Auxiliadora.* Mexico City: Tradición, 1980.

Alemán Valdes, Miguel. *Remembreanzas y testimonios.* Mexico City: Editorial Grijalbo, 1987.

Ávila Camacho y su ideología: La revolución en marcha! Jira electoral. Mexico City: La Impresora, 1940.

Bautista, Margarito. "A Faith Promoting Experience." *Improvement Era* (September 1920).

———. *Apostasia Universal.* Ozumba, Mexico: Colonia Industrial Mexicana, 1957.

———. *El Reino de Dios en Los Ultimos Dias.* Colonia Agricola Industrial, Ozumba, Mexico: Imprenta La Nueva Jerusalem Mexicana, 1960.

———. *¿Es Una Disciplina Una Ley?* Colonia Industrial Mexicana, Mexico, 1951.

———. *Dedicado a la época histórica*. Mexico, 1946.

———. *Himnos de la dispensación Lamanita*. Colonia Agricola Industrial, Ozumba, Mexico: Imprenta La Nueva Jerusalem Mexicana, n.d.

———. *La evolución de México, sus verdaderos progenitores y su origen: El destino de América y Europa*. Mexico City: Apolono Alzate, 1936.

———. *La verdad que ellos me enseñaron*. Mexico, 1940.

———. *¿Restituirás . . . el Reino?* Ozumba, Mexico: Colonia Industrial Mexicana, 1950.

Bible Dictionary. Salt Lake City: The Church of Jesus Christ of Latter-day Saints, 1991.

Burgos, Felipe. *Testimony and Observations on the Millennium as a Member of the Iglesia Cristiana Apostólica Pentecostés*. Unpublished handwritten testimonial.

Cabrera, Luis. *Los problemas trascendentales de México*. Mexico City: Editorial Cultura, 1934.

Cárdenas del Rio, Lázaro. *Obras: Apuntes*. Vol. 1. Mexico City: UNAM, 1972.

Carlos Salinas de Gortari—A Portrait. Mexico City: Office of the Press Secretary to the President, 1991.

Cuevas, R. P. Mariano, S.J. *Historia de la iglesia en México*. El Paso, TX: Editorial Revista Católica, 1928.

de la Peña, Moises T. "Problemas demográficos y agrarios." In *Problemas agricolas e industriales de México*. Vol 2., nos. 3–4. Mexico City: Talleres Gráficos de la Nación, 1950.

Elías Calles, Plutarco. *Informe presidencial correspondiente a 1924–1925 presentado al H. congreso de la union*. Mexico City: Secretaría de Relaciones Exteriores, 1925.

———. *Informes*. Mexico City: Talleres Gráficos de la Nación, 1925.

Historia gráfica del sinarquismo. Mexico City: Comité Nacional de la U.N.S., n.d.

Ivins, Anthony W. *The Right Relation of Church and State*. Salt Lake City, Utah, 1926.

McKonkie, Bruce R. *Mormon Doctrine*. Salt Lake City, UT: Deseret Book Company, 1979.

Museo Nacional de Arte. *Arqueología del Régimen*. Mexico City: Banamex, CONACULTA, INBA, 2003.

Obregón, Álvaro. *El pensamiento político de Álvaro Obregón*, edited by Narcisso Bassols Batalla. Mexico City: Nuestro Tiempo, 1967.

———. *El problema agrícola y agrario: Conferencia dada en la Cámara Agricola Nacional Jalisciense el día 18 de noviembre de 1919*. Guadalajara, Mexico: J. M. Yguiniz, 1922.

Procaduria General de la República. *Boletin 422/00*, August 10, 2000.

Redondo, Regino Díaz. *El bienestar de los mexicanos ya no puede esperar*. Mexico City: Presidencia de la República—Direccion General de Comunicacíon Social, 1989.

Reyes Heroles, Jesus. *El liberalismo mexicano*. Mexico City: Universidad Nacional Autónoma de México, Facultad de Derecho, 1957–61.

Ruiz Cortines, Adolfo. *Discursos de Ruiz Cortines*. Mexico, 1952.

Salinas de Gortari, Carlos. *Mexico: The Policy and Politics of Modernization*. Barcelona, Spain: Plaza and Janés, 2002.

———. *Toma de Posesión* [Inaugural Address]. Mexico City, December 1, 1988.

Shields, W. Eugene. "Sinarchists organize for a New Order in Mexico." *America: A Catholic Review of the Week*, April 18, 1942.

Smith, Joseph, Jr. *El Libro de Mormon*. Salt Lake City, UT: The Church of Jesus Christ of Latter-day Saints, 1920.

———. *The Book of Mormon*. Salt Lake City, UT: The Church of Jesus Christ of Latter-day Saints, 1937.

———. *The Doctrine and Covenants*. Salt Lake City, UT: The Church of Jesus Christ of Latter-day Saints, 1937.

Smith, Joseph F. "The Truth About Mormonism." *Out West: A Magazine of the Old Pacific and the New* (September 1905).

Smith, Joseph Fielding. *Teachings of the Prophet Joseph Smith*. Salt Lake City, UT: Deseret Book Company, 1976.

———. *Doctrines of Salvation*. Salt Lake City, UT: Bookcraft, 1955.

Talmage, James E. *The Great Apostasy Considered in the Light of Scriptural and Secular History*. Salt Lake City, UT: Deseret Book Company, 1909.

Union Nacional Sinarquista. *Guión de capacitación sinarquista*. Mexico City: UNS Comité Nacional, 2001.

U.S. Congress. Senate. Committee on Finance. *U.S. Trade Policy and NAFTA: Hearing Before the Committee on Finance*. 103rd Cong., 1st sess., March 9, 1993.

Wilkie, James, and Edna Monzón de Wilkie. *Frente a la Revolución Mexicana: 17 protagonistas de la etapa constructiva, entrevistas de historia oral*. Vol. 3. Mexico City: UNAM, 2002.

Secondary Sources

Aboites, Luis. *Breve Historia de Chihuahua*. Mexico City: Fondo de Cultura Económica, 1994.

Abrams, Philip. "Notes on the Difficulty of Studying the State." *Journal of Historical Sociology* 1, no. 1 (March 1988).

Aguirre, Carlos, and Ricardo D. Salvatorre. "Writing the History of Law, Crime, and Punishment in Latin America." In *Crime and Punishment in Latin America*, edited by Ricardo Salvatore et al. Durham, NC: Duke University Press, 2001.

Alexander, Thomas G. *Mormonism in Transition: A History of the Latter-day Saints, 1890–1930*. Urbana: University of Illinois Press, 1996.

Alonso, Ana María. *Thread of Blood: Colonialism, Revolution, and Gender on Mexico's Northern Frontier*. Tucson: University of Arizona Press, 1995.

Altman, Ida, Sarah Cline, and Juan Javier Pescador. *The Early History of Greater Mexico*. Upper Saddle River, NJ: Prentice Hall, 2003.

Arrington, Leonard J., Feramorz Y. Fox, and Dean L. May. *Building the City of God: Community and Cooperation Among the Mormons*. Salt Lake City, UT: Deseret Book Company, 1976.

Bailey, David C. "Revisionism and the Recent Historiography of the Mexican Revolution." *Hispanic American Historical Review* 58, no. 1 (1978): 62.

Baldwin, Deborah J. *Protestants and the Mexican Revolution*. Urbana: University of Illinois Press, 1990.

Banner, Michael. "Christianity in Civil Society." In *Alternative Conceptions of Civil Society*, edited by Simone Chambers and Will Kymlicka. Princeton, NJ: Princeton University Press, 2001.

Bantjes, Adrian. *As If Jesus Walked on Earth: Cardenismo, Sonora, and the Mexican Revolution*. Wilmington, DE: SR Books, 1998.

———. "Religion and the Mexican Revolution: Towards a New Historiography." In *Religious Culture in Modern Mexico*, edited by Martin Nesvig. Lanham, MO: Rowman and Littlefield Publishers, 2007.

———, "Saints, Sinners, and State Formation." In *The Eagle and the Virgin: Nation and Cultural Revolution in Mexico, 1920–1940*, edited by Mary Kay Vaughn and Stephen Lewis. Durham, NC: Duke University Press, 2006.

———. Review of *Fragments of a Golden Age: The Politics of Culture in Mexico Since 1940*, edited by Gilbert Joseph, Anne Rubenstein, and Eric Zolov. *Hispanic American Historical Review* 82, no. 2 (May 2002): 381–83.

Bastian, Jean Pierre. *Protestantismos y modernidad latinoamericana: Historia de unas minorías religiosas activas en América Latina*. Mexico City: Fondo de Cultura Económica, 1994.

———. *Protestantismo y sociedad en México*. Mexico City: Casa Unida de Publicaciones, 1983.

Bellah, Robert N., Richard Madsen, William M. Sullivan, Ann Swidler, and Steven M. Tipton. *Habits of the Heart: Individualism and Commitment in American Life*. Berkeley: University of California Press, 1985.

Benjamin, Thomas. *La Revolución: Mexico's Great Revolution as Memory, Myth, and History*. Austin: University of Texas Press, 2000.

Benjamin, Thomas, and Mark Wasserman. *Provinces of the Revolution: Essays on Regional Mexican History, 1910–1929*. Albuquerque: University of New Mexico Press, 1990.

Betancourt, Francisco. "Brujería como un mal social en 1960 en San Luis Mextepec." In *Chamanismo, curanderismo, y brujeria en México*, edited by Gema Uriostegui Flores and Mauricio Garcia Sandoval. Toluca, Mexico: Universidad Autonoma del Estado de México, 2000.

Bojorges Oliva, Fernando. *Ozumba: Monografía Municipal*. Toluca, Mexico: Instituto Mexiquense Cultural, 1999.

Borah, Woodrow. *Justice by Insurance: The General Indian Court of Colonial Mexico and the Legal Aides of the Half-Real*. Berkeley: University of California Press, 1984.

Bowen, Kurt. *Evangelism and Apostasy*. Montreal, Canada: McGill-Queen's University Press, 1996.

Brading, D. A. *The First America: The Spanish Monarchy, Creole Patriots, and the Liberal State, 1492–1867*. Cambridge: Cambridge University Press, 1991.

Brenner, Anita. *The Wind That Swept Mexico*. Austin: University of Texas Press, 1943.

Brown, Susan Love. "Community as Cultural Critique." In *Intentional Community: An Anthropological Perspective*, edited by Susan Love Brown. Albany: State University of New York Press, 2002.

———, ed. *Intentional Community: An Anthropological Perspective*. Albany: State University of New York Press, 2002.

Brunk, Samuel. *Emiliano Zapata: Revolution and Betrayal in Mexico.* Albuquerque: University of New Mexico Press, 1995.

Brusco, Elizabeth. *The Reformation of Machismo: Evangelical Conversion and Gender in Colombia.* Austin: University of Texas Press, 1995.

Buffington, Robert M. *Criminal and Citizen in Modern Mexico.* Lincoln: University of Nebraska Press, 2000.

Burns, E. Bradford. *The Poverty of Progress.* Berkeley: University of California Press, 1980.

Butler, Matthew. "A Revolution in Spirit." In *Faith and Impiety in Revolutionary Mexico,* edited by Matthew Butler. New York: Palgrave Macmillan, 2007.

Camp, Roderic Ai. *Crossing Swords: Politics and Religion in Mexico.* Oxford: Oxford University Press, 1997.

———. *Politics in Mexico.* Oxford: Oxford University Press, 1993.

Cardaillac, Louis. "Profetismo y mesianismo en Jalisco." *Estudios Jaliscences* 60 (May 2005): 31–47.

Cárdenas Ayala, Elisa. "El Partido Catolico Nacional: Política, religión, estereotipos." *Estudios Jalisciences* 58 (November 2004): 6–22.

Castañeda, Carmen. *Vivir en Guadalajara.* Guadalajara, Mexico: Ayuntamiento de Guadalajara, 1992.

Castañeda, Jorge G. *Perpetuating Power.* New York: The New Press, 2000.

———. *The Mexican Shock.* New York: The New Press, 1995.

Centeno, Miguel. *Democracy Within Reason: Technocratic Revolution in Mexico.* University Park, PA: Penn State University Press, 1994.

Chac, Manuel, and Raquel Pastor Escobar. *Ha vuelto Dios a Mexico: La transformación de las relaciones iglesia estado.* Mexico City: UNAM, 1997.

Chambers, Sarah C. "Crime and Citizen: Judicial Practice in Arequipa, Peru, during the Transition from Colony to Republic." In *Reconstructing Criminality in Latin America,* edited by Carlos A. Aguirre and Robert Buffington. Wilmington, DE: SR Books, 2000.

Cisneros Sosa, Armando. *La ciudad que construimos: Registro de la expansión de la Ciudad de México, 1920–1976.* Mexico City: UAM-Ixtapalapa, 1993.

Clawson, David. "Religious Allegiance and Economic Development in Rural Latin America." *Journal of Interamerican Studies and World Affairs* 26, no. 4 (November 1984): 499–524.

Cleary, Edward. "The Catholic Church Faces Its Future: CELAM V." Presentation at the 2006 Latin American Studies Association Conference, San Juan, Puerto Rico.

Clendinnen, Inga. *Ambivalent Conquests: Maya and Spaniard in Yucatan, 1517–1570.* Cambridge: Cambridge University Press, 1987.

Connaughton, Brian F. *Clerical Ideology in a Revolutionary Age: The Guadalajara Church and the Idea of the Mexican Nation, 1788–1853.* Calgary, Canada: University of Calgary Press, 2003.

Covarrubias, Lorenzo. "Ideology, Brokers, Political Action, and the State: The Strategies and Historical Transformation of a Counterrevolutionary Urban and Peasant Movement in México." PhD diss., University of California, Santa Barbara, 1999.

———. "Intercambio social, gestoría política y sinarquismo en (Querétaro) México." *Auriga: Revista de Filosofía, Antropología, e Historia* 13 (Enero-Junio 1998): 55–71.

———. "Sentimientos Queretanos: El ideal *sinarquista* de los años 30s y 40s." *Debarrocorazón* 2 (Enero 1995): 19–22.

Curley, Robert. "Slouching Towards Bethlehem: Catholics and the Political Sphere in Revolutionary Mexico." PhD diss., University of Chicago, 2001.

de la Peña, Guillermo, and Renée de la Torre. "Religión y política en los barrios populares de Guadalajara." *Estudios Sociologicos* 24 (1990): 571–602.

de la Torre, Renée. 1991. "La construction de una identidad nacional el La Luz del Mundo." *Cristianismo y Sociedad* 29/3, no. 109 (1991).

———. 2000. *Los hijos de la luz: Discurso, identidad y poder en la Luz del Mundo.* Guadalajara, Mexico: CIESAS, 2000.

———. 2001. *La Ciudadanizacion de la politica en Jalisco.* Tlaquepaque: ITESO, 2001.

———. "Microhistoria de un barrio tapatío: Santa Teresita, 1930–1980." In *Vivir en Guadalajara*, edited by Carmen Castañeda. Guadalajara, Mexico: Ayuntamiento de Guadalajara, 1992.

de Navarrete, Ifegenia M. *Bienestar campesino y desarollo económio.* Mexico City: Fondo de Cultura Económica, 1971.

Dormady, Jason H. "Rights, Rule, and Religion: Old Colony Mennonites and Mexico's Transition to the Free Market, 1920–2000." In *Religious Culture in Modern Mexico*, edited by Martin Nesvig. Lanham, MO: Rowman and Littlefield, 2006.

Dulles, John W. F. *Yesterday in Mexico: A Chronicle of the Revolution, 1919–1936.* Austin: University of Texas Press, 1961.

Espinosa, David. "Jesuit Higher Education in Post-Revolutionary Mexico: The Iberoamerican University (1943–1971)." PhD diss., University of California, Santa Barbara, 1998.

Etzioni, Amitai. *Rights and the Common Good.* New York: St. Martin's Press, 1995.

Fallaw, Ben. *Cárdenas Compromised: The Failure of Reform in Post Revolutionary Mexico.* Durham, NC: Duke University Press, 2001.

Farriss, Nancy M. *Crown and Clergy in Colonial Mexico, 1759–1821.* London: Athlone Press, 1968.

Fein, Seth. "Myths of Cultural Imperialism and Nationalism in Golden Age Mexican Cinema." In *Fragments of a Golden Age: The Politics of Culture in Mexico Since 1940*, edited by Gilbert Joseph, Anne Rubenstein, and Eric Zolov. Durham, NC: Duke University Press, 2001.

Fernández-Armesto, Felipe. *The Americas: A Hemispheric History.* New York: Modern Library, 2005.

Florescano, Enrique. *Imágenes de la patria a través de los siglos.* Mexico City: Taurus, 2005.

Foran, John. "Reinventing the Mexican Revolution: The Competing Paradigms of John Mason Hart and Alan Knight." *Latin American Perspectives* 23, no. 4 (Autumn 1996): 115–31.

Fortuny Loret de Mola, Patricia. "Origins, Development, and Perspectives of the Luz del Mundo Church." *Religion* 25, no. 2 (1995): 147–62.

———. 1999. *Creyentes y creencias en Guadalajara*. Guadalajara, Mexico: CIESAS, 1999.

Fortuny Loret de Mola, Patricia, and Renée de la Torre. "Mujer, participación, representación, simbólica y vida cotidiana en la Luz del Mundo: Estudio de caso en la Hermosa Provincia." *Estudios sobre las culturas contemporáneas* (Universidad de Colima) 4, no. 12 (1991).

Foster, Lawrence. "Between Two Worlds: Community, Liminality, and the Development of Alternative Marriage Systems." In *Intentional Community: An Anthropological Perspective*, edited by Susan Love Brown. Albany: State University of New York, 2002.

Fruhling, Hugo, Joseph S. Tulchin, and Heather A. Golding, eds. *Crime and Violence in Latin America: Citizen Security, Democracy, and the State*. Baltimore, MD: Johns Hopkins University Press, 2003.

Ganster, Paul. "Churchmen." In *Cities and Society in Colonial Latin America*, edited by Louisa Schell Hoberman and Susan Migden Socolow. Albuquerque: University of New Mexico Press, 1986.

García de la Mora, Humberto. "50 años de ser el gozo de toda la tierra." In *Hermosa Provincia, 1954–2004*, edited by Humberto García de la Mora. Guadalajara, Mexico: Libreria Hermosa Provincia, 2004.

Garma Navarro, Carlos. *Protestantismo en una communidad totonaca*. Mexico City: Instituto Nacional Indigenista, 1988.

Garrard-Burnett, Virginia. *Protestantism in Guatemala : Living in the New Jerusalem*. Austin: University of Texas Press, 1998.

Garrard-Burnett, Virginia, and David Stoll. *Rethinking Protestantism in Latin America*. Philadelphia, PA: Temple University Press, 1993.

Gaxiola, Manuel. *La serpiente y la paloma*. Pasadena, CA: W. Carey Library, 1970.

Gilly, Adolfo. *El cardenismo: Una utopía mexicana*. Mexico City: Cal y Arena, 1994.

Gómez, Fernando. *From Darkness into Light*. Mexico City: MHMM, 2005.

Grayson, George W. *The Church in Contemporary Mexico*. Washington, DC: Center for Strategic and International Studies, 1992.

Gregory, Brad S. *Salvation at Stake: Christian Martyrdom in Early Modern Europe*. Cambridge, MA: Harvard University Press, 2001.

Guerra, François-Xavier. *México: Del antiguo régimen a la revolución*. Vol. 1. Mexico City: Fondo de Cultura Económica, 1985.

Hale, Charles A. "Jose María Luis Mora and the Structure of Mexican Liberalism." *Hispanic American Historical Review* 45, no. 2 (May 1965): 196–227.

———. *Mexican Liberalism in the Age of Mora, 1821–1853*. New Haven, CT: Yale University Press, 1968.

Hall, David. "From 'Religion and Society' to Practices." In *Possible Pasts: Becoming Colonial in Early American*, edited by Robert Blair St. George. Ithaca, NY: Cornell University Press, 2000.

Hammergren, Linn A. "Corporatism in Latin American Politics: A Reexamination of the 'Unique' Tradition." *Comparative Politics* 9, no. 4 (July 1977): 446.

Hamnet, Brian. *A Concise History of Mexico*. Cambridge: Cambridge University Press, 1999.

———. *Juárez*. London: Longman, 1994.

Hart, John Mason. *Empire and Revolution: The Americans in Mexico Since the Civil War.* Los Angeles: University of California Press, 2002.

Hay, Douglas. "Law and Society in Comparative Perspective." In *Crime and Punishment in Latin America*, edited by Ricardo Salvatorre et al. Durham, NC: Duke University Press, 2004.

Hughes, Sallie. *Newsrooms in Conflict: Journalism and the Democratization of Mexico.* Pittsburgh, PA: University of Pittsburgh Press, 2006.

Ibarra Bellon, Araceli, and Alisa Lancyner Reisel. "La Hermosa Provincia: Nacimiento y vida de una secta cristiana en Guadalajara." Master's thesis, Universidad de Guadalajara, 1972.

Iber, Jorge. *Hispanics in the Mormon Zion, 1912–1999.* College Station: Texas A&M Press, 2000.

Illades, Carlos. *Rhodakanaty y la formación del pensamiento socialista en México.* Barcelona, Spain: Anthropos, 2002.

Jiménez, Christina M. "Making the City Their Own: Popular Groups and Political Culture in Morelia, Mexico, 1880 to 1930." PhD diss., University of California, San Diego, 2001.

Jiménez, Jorge H. *La traza del poder: Historia de la política y los negocios urbanos en el Distrito Federal.* Mexico City: Dédalo, 1993.

Joseph, Gilbert M., Anne Rubenstein, and Eric Zolov. "Assembling the Fragments: Writing a Cultural History of Mexico Since 1940." In *Fragments of a Golden Age: The Politics of Culture in Mexico Since 1940*, edited by Gilbert Joseph, Anne Rubenstein, and Eric Zolov. Durham, NC: Duke University Press, 2001.

Juster, Susan. *Doomsayers: Anglo-American Prophecy in the Age of Revolution.* Philadelphia, PA: University of Pennsylvania Press, 2003.

Knight, Alan. *The Mexican Revolution.* 2 vols. Lincoln: University of Nebraska Press, 1986.

———. "Cardenismo: Juggernaut or Jalopy?" *Journal of Latin American Studies* 26, no. 1 (February 1994).

———. "The Peculiarities of Mexican History: Mexico Compared to Latin America, 1821–1992." *Journal of Latin American Studies* (Quincentenary Supplement) 24 (1992).

Knowlton, Robert. *Church Property and the Mexican Reform.* Dekalb: Northern Illinois University Press, 1976.

Krauze, Enrique. *Mexico: Biography of Power, A History of Modern Mexico 1810–1996.* New York: Harper Collins, 1997.

Lancaster, Roger N. *Thanks to God and the Revolution: Popular Religion and Class Consciousness in the New Nicaragua.* New York: Columbia University Press, 1988.

Latin American Studies Association. "Mexico and the 1940s: A Decade of Transformation." Workshop 157 // HIS042, March 15, 2006.

Lavrín, Asuncion. "Female Religious." In *Cities and Society in Colonial Latin America*, edited by Louisa Schell Hoberman and Susan Migden Socolow. Albuquerque: University of New Mexico Press, 1986.

Lear, John. *Workers, Neighbors, and Citizens: The Revolution in Mexico City.* Lincoln: University of Nebraska Press, 2001.

Lewis, Stephen E. "Education and the 'Indian Problem.'" In *The Eagle and the Virgin: Nation and Cultural Revolution in Mexico, 1920–1940*, edited by Mary Kay Vaughn and Stephen Lewis. Durham, NC: Duke University Press, 2006.

Lieuwin, Edwin. *Mexican Militarism: The Political Rise and Fall of the Revolutionary Army, 1910–1940*. Westport, CT: Greenwood Press, 1981.

Lockhart, James, and Stuart B. Schwartz. *Early Latin America: A History of Colonial Spanish America and Brazil*. Cambridge: Cambridge University Press, 1985.

Lockridge, Kenneth A. *A New England Town: The First Hundred Years*. New York: W. W. Norton, 1970.

Lomelí Suárez, Victor Hugo. *Guadalajara y sus barrios*. Guadalajara, Mexico: Ayuntamiento de Guadalajara, 1982.

Lomnitz, Claudio. "What Was Mexico's Cultural Revolution?" In *The Eagle and the Virgin: Nation and Cultural Revolution in Mexico, 1920–1940*, edited by Mary Kay Vaughn and Stephen Lewis. Durham, NC: Duke University Press, 2006.

López, Juan. *Guadalajara y sus madatarios, 1532 a 1986*. Guadalajara, Mexico: Gobierno del Estado de Jalisco, 1987.

López, Rick A. "The India Bonita Contest of 1921 and the Ethnicization of Mexican National Culture." *Hispanic American Historical Review* 82, no. 2 (May 2002): 291–328.

———. "The Noche Mexicana and Popular Arts." In *The Eagle and the Virgin: Nation and Cultural Revolution in Mexico, 1920–1940*, edited by Mary Kay Vaughn and Stephen Lewis. Durham, NC: Duke University Press, 2006.

Mallon, Florencia. "Reflections on the Ruins: Everyday Forms of State Formation in Nineteenth-Century Mexico." In *Everyday Forms of State Formation*, edited by Gilbert Joseph and Daniel Nugent. Durham, NC: Duke University Press, 1997.

Mann, Judith W. "The Annunciation Chapel in the Quirinal Palace, Rome: Paul V, Guido Reni, and the Virgin Mary." *Art Bulletin* 75, no. 1 (March 1993).

McCaa, Robert. "Missing Millions: The Human Cost of the Mexican Revolution." http://www.hist.umn.edu/~rmccaa/missmill/mxrev.htm. University of Minnesota Population Center [online database], 2001 (accessed April 19, 2005).

Medin, Tzvi. *El sexenio alemanista*. Mexico City: Ediciones Era, 1990.

Méndez, Juan D., et al. *The (Un)Rule of Law and the Underprivileged in Latin America*. Notre Dame, IN: University of Notre Dame Press, 1999.

Meyer, Jean. *The Cristero Rebellion: The Mexican People Between Church and State, 1926–1929*. Cambridge: Cambridge University Press, 1976.

———. *El sinarquismo ¿Un fascismo mexicano?* Mexico City: Editorial Joaquín Mortiz, 1978.

———. "Revolution and Reconstruction in the 1920s." In *Mexico Since Independence*, edited by Leslie Bethell. Cambridge: Cambridge University Press, 1991.

"Mexico: Context for a Renewable Energy Rural Electrification Program." World Bank reports on rural and renewable energy, sections 4.97–4.99, www.worldbank.org [online database] (accessed April, 2005).

Mexico, End of An Era, 1982–1988. Part 3 of 3. WGBH Boston, PBS, 1988.

Morales Robles, Bethzabé. "Hermosa Provincia: Un modelo que se ha extendido por el mundo." In *Hermosa Provincia, 1954–2004*, edited by Humberto García de la Mora.

Guadalajara, Mexico: Libreria Hermosa Provincia, 2004.

Morán Quiroz, Rodolfo. *Alternativa religiosa en Guadalajara.* Guadalajara, Mexico: Universidad de Guadalajara Press, 1990.

Moreno, Julio. *Yankee Don't Go Home! Mexican Nationalism, American Business Culture, and the Shaping of Modern Mexico, 1920–1950.* Chapel Hill: University of North Carolina Press, 2006.

Mulder, Monique Borgerhoff. "Polygyny and the Extent of Women's Contributions to Subsistence: A Reply to White." *American Anthropologist*, n.s., 91, no. 1 (March 1989): 178–80.

Muranaka, Therese Adams. *The Russian Molokan Colony at Guadalupe, Baja California: Continuity and Change in a Sectarian Community.* PhD diss., University of California, San Diego, 1992.

Murphy, Thomas W. "'Stronger Than Ever': Remnants of the Third Convention." *Journal of Latter-day Saint History* 10 (1988): 8–11.

———. "From Racist Stereotype to Ethnic Identity: Instrumental Uses of Mormon Racial Doctrine." *Ethnohistory* (Summer 1999): 451–80.

———. "Christianizing Quetzalcoatl. Mexicanizing Mormonism." Paper presented at the annual meeting of the Society for the Scientific Study of Religion, San Diego, California, 1997.

———. "Guatemalan Hot/Cold Medicine and Mormon Words of Wisdom: Intercultural Negotiation of Meaning." *Journal for the Scientific Study of Religion* 36, no. 2 (1997).

Musacchio, Humberto. "Luz del Mundo: Con raíces en la tierra." *Enfoque*, August 25, 2002.

Niblo, Stephan R. *Mexico in the 1940s: Modernity, Politics, and Corruption.* Wilmington, DE: Scholarly Resources Books, 2000.

Nutini, Hugo. "Polygyny in a Tlaxcalan Community." *Ethnology* 4, no. 2 (April 1965): 123–47.

———. *San Bernardino Contla: Marriage and Family Structure in a Tlaxcalan Municipio.* Pittsburgh, PA: University of Pittsburgh Press, 1968.

O'Donnell, Guillermo. "Polyarchies and the (Un)Rule of Law." In *The (Un)Rule of Law and the Underprivileged in Latin America*, edited by Juan D. Méndez et al. Notre Dame, IN: University of Notre Dame Press, 1999.

O'Malley, Ilene. *The Myth of the Revolution: Hero Cults and the Institutionalization of the Mexican State, 1920–1940.* Westport, CT: Greenwood Press, 1986.

Orozco, Monica I. "Protestant Missionaries, Mexican Liberals, Nationalism, and the Issue of Cultural Incorporation of Indigenous Peoples of Mexico, 1870–1900." PhD diss., University of California, Santa Barbara, 1999.

Pessar, Patricia R. *From Fanatics to Folk: Brazilian Millenarianism and Popular Culture.* Durham, NC: Duke University Press, 2007.

Phelan, John Leddy. *The Millennial Kingdom of the Franciscans in the New World.* Berkeley: University of California Press, 1970.

Picatto, Pablo. *City of Suspects: Crime in Mexico City, 1900–1931.* Durham, NC: Duke University Press, 2001.

Powell, T. G. "Priests and Peasants in Central Mexico: Social Conflict During 'La Reforma.'" *Hispanic American Historical Review* 57, no. 2 (May 1977): 296–313.

Pozos Bravo, Sara Susana. "Análisis de la cultura política en la Iglesia La Luz del Mundo." Master's thesis, University of Guadalajara, Mexico, 2001.

Purnell, Jennie. *Popular Movements and State Formation in Revolutionary Mexico: The Agraristas and Cristeros of Michoacán.* Durham, NC: Duke University Press, 1999.

Quinones, Sam. *True Tales from Another Mexico.* Albuquerque: University of New Mexico Press, 2001.

Redding, Andrew. "Mexico's Addiction to the Narcodollar." *Journal of Commerce*, November 7, 1997.

Reich, Peter. *Mexico's Hidden Revolution: The Catholic Church in Law and Politics Since 1929.* Notre Dame, IN: University of Notre Dame, 1995.

Rentería Solís, René. *La Luz del Mundo, historia de la iglesia cristiana, vida y obra del Apostol Aarón Joaquín.* Bogotá, Colombia: Panamerica Formas, 1997.

Rodríguez Gurrola, Chuy, and Pancho Madragal. *Los barrios de Guadalajara: Breve y compendiosa historia.* Guadalajara, Mexico: Ayuntamiento de Guadalajara, 1987.

Rubenstein, Anne. "The War on *'Las Pelonas,'* Modern Women and Their Enemies, Mexico City, 1924." In *Sex in the Revolution: Gender, Politics, and Power in Modern Mexico*, edited by Jovelyn Olcott et al. Durham, NC: Duke University Press, 2006.

Rubin, Jeffrey. "Popular Mobilization and the Myth of State Corporatism." In *Popular Movements and Political Change in Mexico*, edited by Joe Foweraker and Ann L. Craig. Boulder, CO: Lynne Rienner Publishers, 1990.

Russell, Philip L. *Mexico Under Salinas.* Austin, TX: Mexico Resource Center, 1994.

Rust, Val D. *Radical Origins: Early Mormon Converts and Their Colonial Ancestors.* Urbana: University of Illinois Press, 2004.

Saragoza, Alex. "The Selling of Mexico: Tourism and the State, 1929–1952." In *Fragments of a Golden Age: The Politics of Culture in Mexico Since 1940*, edited by Gilbert Joseph, Anne Rubenstein, and Eric Zolov. Durham, NC: Duke University Press, 2001.

Sawatzky, Harry Leonard. *They Sought a Country: Mennonite Colonization in Mexico.* Berkeley: University of California Press, 1971.

Sayer, Derek. "Everyday Forms of State Formation: Some Dissident Remarks on Hegemony." In *Everyday Forms of State Formation*, edited by Gilbert Joseph and Daniel Nugent. Durham, NC: Duke University Press, 1997.

Schmidt, Arthur. "Making It Real Compared to What? Reconceptualizing Mexican History Since 1940." In *Fragments of a Golden Age: The Politics of Culture in Mexico Since 1940*, edited by Gilbert Joseph, Anne Rubenstein, and Eric Zolov. Durham, NC: Duke University Press, 2001.

Schwaller, John F. "The Clergy." In *The Countryside in Colonial Latin America*, edited by Louisa Schell Hoberman and Susan Migden Socolow. Albuquerque: University of New Mexico Press, 1997.

Serrano Álvarez, Pablo. *La batalla del espíritu: El movimiento sinarquista en el Bajío (1932–1951).* Mexico City: Consejo Nacional para la Cultura y las Artes, 1992.

Shields, W. Eugene. "Sinarchists Organize for a New Order in Mexico." *America: A Catholic Review of the Week*, April 18, 1942.

Shipps, Jan. *Mormonism: The Story of a New Religious Tradition.* Chicago and Urbana: University of Illinois Press, 1985.

Simmons, John K., and Brian Wilson. *Competing Visions of Paradise: The California Experience of Nineteenth-Century American Sectarianism.* Santa Barbara, CA: Fithian Press, 1993.

Sinkin, Richard N. *The Mexican Reform, 1855–1876: A Study in Liberal Nation Building.* Austin: University of Texas Press, 1979.

Skillen, James, and Rockne M. McCarthy. *Political Order and the Plural Structure of Society.* Atlanta, GA: Emory University Press, 1991.

Spenser, Daniela. *The Impossible Triangle: Mexico, Soviet Russia, and the United States in the 1920s.* Durham, NC: Duke University Press, 1999.

Stern, Steven J. *Peru's Indian Peoples and the Challenge of Spanish Conquest: Huamanga to 1640.* Madison: University of Wisconsin Press, 1982.

Tangerman, Michael. *Mexico at the Crossroads: Politics, the Church, and the Poor.* Maryknoll, NY: Orbis Books, 1995.

Tardanico, Richard. "State, Dependency, and Nationalism: Revolutionary Mexico, 1924–1928." *Studies in Society and History* 24, no. 3 (July 1982): 400–423.

Taylor, William B. *Magistrates of the Sacred: Priests and Parishoners in Eighteenth-Century Mexico.* Stanford, CA: Stanford University Press, 1996.

Thompson, E. P. *The Essential E. P. Thompson*, edited by Dorothy Thompson. New York: The New Press, 2001.

Torres Ramírez, Blanca. *Hacia la utopia industrial, 1940–1952.* Mexico City: El Colegio de México, 1984.

Torres Sánchez, Rafael. *Revolución y la vida cotidiana: Guadalajara.* Culiacán, Mexico: Galileo Ediciones, 2001.

Tuck, Jim. *The Holy War in Los Altos.* Tucson: University of Arizona Press, 1982.

Tullis, F. LaMond. *Mormons in Mexico: The Dynamics of Faith and Culture.* Logan: Utah State University Press, 1987.

Van Young, Eric. *The Other Rebellion: Popular Violence, Ideology, and the Mexican Struggle for Independence, 1810–1821.* Stanford, CA: Stanford University Press, 2001.

Vanderwood, Paul. *The Power of God Against the Guns of Government: Religious Upheaval in Mexico at the Turn of the Nineteenth Century.* Stanford, CA: Stanford University Press, 1998.

Vaughn, Alden T. Review of *The Unredeemed Captive: A Family Story From Early America* by John Demos. *Journal of American History* 82, no. 1 (June 1995): 197–98.

Vaughn, Mary Kay. *Cultural Politics in Revolution: Teachers, Peasants, and Schools in Mexico, 1930–1940.* Tucson: University of Arizona Press, 1997.

Vasconcelos, José. *The Cosmic Race.* Baltimore, MD: Johns Hopkins University Press, 1997.

Ventura, Betty G. *The History of the Mexican Branch in Salt Lake, 1920–1960.* Salt Lake City, n.p., 1998.

Verástique, Bernardino. *Michoacán and Eden: Vasco de Quiroga and the Evangelization of Western Mexico.* Austin: University of Texas Press, 2000.

Voekel, Pamela. *Alone Before God: The Religious Origins of Modernity in Mexico*. Durham, NC: Duke University Press, 2002.

Von Bertrab, Herman. *Negotiating NAFTA*. Westport, CT: Praeger, 1997.

Wallace, Anthony F. C. "Revitalization Movements." *American Anthropologist* 58 (1956): 265.

Walling, William English. *The Mexican Question: Mexico and American-Mexican Relations Under Calles and Obregón*. New York: Robins Press, 1927.

Weber, Max. *Economy and Society*. 2 vols. Berkeley: University of California Press, 1978.

Weiner, Richard. "Trinidad Sánchez Santos: Voice of the Catholic Opposition in Porfirian Mexico." *Mexican Studies/Estudios Mexicanos* 17, no. 2 (Summer 2001): 321–49.

White, Douglas R., and Michael L. Burton. "Causes of Polygyny: Ecology, Economy, Kinship, and Warfare." *American Anthropologist*, n.s., 90, no. 4 (December 1988).

———. "Rethinking Polygyny: Co-Wives, Codes, and Cultural Systems." *Current Anthropology* 29, no. 4 (August–October 1988).

Wiarda, Howard. *The Transition to Democracy in Spain and Portugal*. Washington, DC: American Enterprise Institute for Public Research, 1989.

Wiebe, Robert H. *The Search for Order, 1877–1920*. New York: Hill and Wang, 1967.

Wilson, Brian. "The New World's Jerusalems: Franciscans, Puritans, and Sacred Space in the Colonial Americas, 1519–1820." PhD diss., University of California, Santa Barbara, 1996.

Wimbush, Vincent. "Excavating Darkness: African Americans, Scriptures, and the Quest for Social Memory." Presentation at the Michaelson Endowed Visiting Scholars Series at the University of California at Santa Barbara, November 30, 2004.

Womack, John. "The Mexican Revolution." In *Mexico Since Independence*, edited by Leslie Bethell. Cambridge: Cambridge University Press, 1991.

Wright Rios, Edward. "Piety and Progress: Vision, Shrine, and Society in Oaxaca, 1887–1934." PhD diss., University of California, San Diego, 2004.

Zolov, Eric. "Discovering a Land 'Mysterious and Obvious': The Renarrativizing of Postrevolutionary Mexico." In *Fragments of a Golden Age: The Politics of Culture in Mexico Since 1940*, edited by Gilbert Joseph, Anne Rubenstein, and Eric Zolov. Durham, NC: Duke University Press, 2001.

INDEX